TRANSNATIONAL CINEMA,
THE FILM READER

Transnational Cinema, the Film Reader provides an overview of the key concepts and debates within the developing field of transnational cinema.

Bringing together seminal essays from a wide range of sources, this volume engages with films that fashion their narrative and aesthetic dynamics in relation to more than one national or cultural community, and that reflect the impact of advanced capitalism and new media technologies in an increasingly interconnected world-system. The essays demonstrate that, in an era no longer marked by the sharp divisions between communist and capitalist nation states, or even "first" and "third" worlds, Europe and the U.S. must be factored into the increasingly hybrid notion of "world cinema."

The reader is divided into four sections:

- From national to transnational cinema
- Global cinema in the digital age
- Motion pictures: film, migration and diaspora
- Tourists and terrorists

When read in juxtaposition, these essays make clear that the significance of crossing borders varies according to the ethnic and/or gendered identity of the traveler, suggesting that the crossing of certain lines generates fundamental shifts in both the aesthetics and the ethics of cinema as a representational art.

Contributors: Homi K. Bhabha, Peter Bloom, Robert E. Davis, Jigna Desai, David Desser, Elizabeth Ezra, John Hess, Andrew Higson, David Murphy, Hamid Naficy, Diane Negra, John S. Nelson, Terry Rowden, Elana Shefrin, Ella Shohat, Ann Marie Stock, Patricia R. Zimmermann.

Elizabeth Ezra teaches in the School of Languages and Cultures at the University of Stirling. She is author of *The Colonial Unconscious* and *Georges Méliès: The Birth of the Auteur*, editor of *European Cinema*, and co-editor of *France in Focus*.

Terry Rowden teaches in the Department of English at the College of Wooster. His essays and reviews have appeared in *Southern Review, MELUS* and *College Literature*.

In Focus: Routledge Film Readers

Series Editors: Steven Cohan (Syracuse University) and Ina Rae Hark (University of South Carolina)

The In Focus series of readers is a comprehensive resource for students on film and cinema studies courses. The series explores the innovations of film studies while highlighting the vital connection of debates to other academic fields and to studies of other media. The readers bring together key articles on a major topic in film studies, from marketing to Hollywood comedy, identifying the central issues, exploring how and why scholars have approached it in specific ways, and tracing continuities of thought among scholars. Each reader opens with an introductory essay setting the debates in their academic context, explaining the topic's historical and theoretical importance, and surveying and critiquing its development in film studies.

TRANSNATIONAL CINEMA,
THE FILM READER

Edited by Elizabeth Ezra
and Terry Rowden

Routledge
Taylor & Francis Group

LONDON AND NEW YORK

First published 2006
by Routledge
2 Park Square, Milton Park, Abingdon, Oxon OX14 4RN

Simultaneously published in the USA and Canada
by Routledge
270 Madison Avenue, New York, NY 10016

Routledge is an imprint of the Taylor & Francis Group

Selection and editorial matter © 2006 Elizabeth Ezra and Terry Rowden
Individual chapters © 2006 the chapter authors

Designed and typeset in Novarese and Scala Sans by
Keystroke, Jacaranda Lodge, Wolverhampton
Printed and bound in Great Britain by
Antony Rowe Ltd, Chippenham, Wiltshire

British Library Cataloguing in Publication Data
A catalogue record for this book is available from the British Library

Library of Congress Cataloging in Publication Data
Transnational cinema: the film reader/edited by Elizabeth Ezra and Terry Rowden.
     p. cm. — (In focus—Routledge film readers)
   Includes bibliographical references and index.
   1. Motion pictures. I. Ezra, Elizabeth, 1965– II. Rowden, Terry. III. Series.
   PN1994.T685 2005
   791.43—dc22   2005016520

ISBN10: 0–415–37157–0   ISBN13: 9–78–0–415–37157–5 (hbk)
ISBN10: 0–415–37158–9   ISBN13: 9–78–0–415–37158–2 (pbk)

Contents

PART FOUR: TOURISTS AND TERRORISTS   **167**

Acknowledgments

1. Andrew Higson, "The Limiting Imagination of National Cinema" from *Cinema and Nation*, eds. Mette Hjort and Scott Mackenzie (London and New York: Routledge 2000), pp. 63–74. © 2000. Reproduced by permission of Routledge/Taylor and Francis Books, Inc.

2. David Murphy, "Africans Filming Africa: Questioning Theories of an Authentic African Cinema." *Journal of African Cultural Studies* 13, No. 2, December 2000, pp. 239–49. © 2000. Reprinted by permission of Taylor and Francis (http://www.tandf.co.uk).

3. Ella Shohat, "Post–Third-Worldist Culture: Gender, Nation, and the Cinema" from *Feminist Genealogies, Colonial Legacies, Democratic Futures*, eds. Jacqui Alexander and Chandra T. Mohanty (London and New York: Routledge 1996), pp. 183–209. © 1996. Reproduced by permission of Routledge/Taylor and Francis Books, Inc.

4. Jigna Desai, "Bombay Boys and Girls: The Gender and Sexual Politics of Transnationality in the New Indian Cinema in English" from *South Asian Popular Culture* 1, No. 1, April 2003, pp. 45–61. © 2003. Reprinted by permission of Taylor and Francis (http://www.tandf. co.uk).

5. Robert E. Davis, "The Instantaneous Worldwide Release: Coming Soon to Everyone, Everywhere" from *West Virginia University Philological Papers*, Vol. 49, 2002–2003; pp. 110–16. © 2003. Revised version published by permission of the author.

6. Elana Shefrin, "*Lord of the Rings, Star Wars*, and Participatory Fandom: Mapping New Congruencies Between the Internet and Media Entertainment Culture" from *Critical Studies in Media Communication* 21, No. 3, September 2004, pp. 261–81. © 2004. Reprinted by permission of Taylor and Francis (http://www.tandf.co.uk).

7. John Hess and Patricia R. Zimmermann, "Transnational Documentaries: A Manifesto" from an earlier version published in *Afterimage* 1997 (February): pp. 10–14. Reprinted by permission of the publisher and the authors.

8. Hamid Naficy, "Situating Accented Cinema" from *An Accented Cinema: Exilic and Diasporic Filmmaking*, Princeton University Press, 2001, pp. 10–39. © 2001 by Princeton University Press. Reprinted by permission of Princeton University Press.

9. Peter Bloom, "Beur Cinema and the Politics of Location: French Immigration Politics and the Naming of a Film Movement" from *Social Identities* 5, No. 4, December 1999, pp. 469–87. ©1999. Reprinted by permission of Taylor and Francis (http://www.tandf.co.uk).

10. David Desser, "Diaspora and National Identity: Exporting 'China' through the Hong Kong Cinema" from *Post Script: Essays in Film and the Humanities* 20, Nos. 2–3, Winter/Spring/Summer 2001, pp. 124–36. © 2001. Reprinted by permission of the general editor of *Post Script: Essays in Film and the Humanities* and Post Script, Inc.

11. Ann Marie Stock, "Migrancy and the Latin American Cinemascape: Towards a Post-National Critical Praxis" from *Revista Canadiense De Estudios Hispanicos* 20, No. 1, Fall 1995, pp. 19–30. Reprinted by permission of the author and the publisher.

12. Diane Negra, " Romance And/As Tourism: Heritage Whiteness and the (Inter)National Imaginary in the New Woman's Film" from *Keyframes: Popular Cinema and Cultural Studies*, Routledge, 2001, pp. 82–97. © 2001. Reprinted by permission of Taylor and Francis (http://www.tandf.co.uk).

13. John S. Nelson, "Four Forms for Terrorism: Horror, Dystopia, Thriller, and Noir" from *Poroi* 2, No. 1, August 2003. © 2003. Reprinted by permission of the author.

14. Homi K. Bhabha, "Terror and After . . ." from *Parallax* 8, No. 1, January–March 2002, pp. 3–4. © 2002. Reprinted by permission of Taylor and Francis (http://www.tandf.co.uk).

General Introduction:
What is Transnational Cinema?

ELIZABETH EZRA AND TERRY ROWDEN

In its deployment and extension of the idea of the transnational as a critical concept, this collection seeks to go beyond the primarily economic and sociopolitical origins of the term in order to reveal its value as a conceptual tool within the evolving field of film studies. In its simplest guise, the transnational can be understood as the global forces that link people or institutions across nations. Key to transnationalism is the recognition of the decline of national sovereignty as a regulatory force in global coexistence. The impossibility of assigning a fixed national identity to much cinema reflects the dissolution of any stable connection between a film's place of production and/or setting and the nationality of its makers and performers. This is not in itself a new phenomenon; what is new are the conditions of financing, production, distribution and reception of cinema today. The global circulation of money, commodities, information, and human beings is giving rise to films whose aesthetic and narrative dynamics, and even the modes of emotional identification they elicit, reflect the impact of advanced capitalism and new media technologies as components of an increasingly interconnected world-system. The transnational comprises both globalization—in cinematic terms, Hollywood's domination of world film markets—and the counterhegemonic responses of filmmakers from former colonial and Third World countries. The concept of transnationalism enables us to better understand the changing ways in which the contemporary world is being imagined by an increasing number of filmmakers across genres as a global system rather than as a collection of more or less autonomous nations.

Transnational Hollywood

There are a number of factors that have problematized the category of national cinema. One of these is the increasing permeability of national borders. This phenomenon is being generated by the acceleration of global flows of capital and a shifting geopolitical climate that includes, notably, the end of the Cold War and the creation of the European Union. Another factor is the vast increase in the circulation of films enabled by technologies such as video, DVD, and new digital media, and the heightened accessibility of such technologies for both filmmakers and spectators. However, equally important in the transformation of the global cinematic landscape is the changing shape of mainstream American cinema. Hollywood, which for many critics has become a synecdoche for popular film as such, has both influenced and been influenced by the flows of cultural exchange that are transforming the ways people the world over are making and watching films.

As Ella Shohat and Robert Stam have noted, in the critical discourse of transnational cinema "Hollywood" functions as a term meant "not to convey a kneejerk rejection of all commercial cinema, but rather as a kind of shorthand for a massively industrial, ideologically reactionary, and stylistically conservative form of 'dominant' cinema" (Shohat and Stam 1994: 7). Since its ascendancy around the time of the First World War, the American film industry has systematically dominated all other film cultures and modes of cinematic imagery, production, and reception. Hollywood has succeeded in maintaining its hegemonic influence in large part by imagining the global audience as a world of sensation-starved children. This vision has created a situation in which the U.S. film industry has perhaps irreversibly committed itself to the production of empty and costly cinematic spectacles that, in order to maintain their mainstream inoffensiveness, must be subjected to increasingly thorough forms of cultural and ideological cleansing before being released into the global cinemascape. This homogenizing dynamic can be seen to function even at the level of individual performers. In the careers of trans- (as opposed to inter-)national superstars such as the Australian Russell Crowe, the Irish Colin Farrell, the British Kate Winslet and Jude Law, the French Juliette Binoche, the Welsh Catherine Zeta-Jones, and the Spaniards Penelope Cruz and Antonio Banderas, national identity has been jettisoned as a marker of cultural specificity to an extent that goes beyond what might be necessary for the demands of a particular role. The performance of Americanness is increasingly becoming a "universal" or "universalizing" characteristic in world cinema.

But although mainstream Hollywood's key role in U.S. cultural imperialism cannot be ignored, it is also important to recognize the impossibility of maintaining a strict dichotomy between Hollywood cinema and its "others." Cinema has from its inception been transnational, circulating more or less freely across borders and utilizing international personnel. This practice has continued from the era of Chaplin, Hitchcock, and Fritz Lang up to contemporary directors like Ang Lee, Mira Nair, and Alfonso Cuarón. Euro-American coproductions go back at least as far as the Hollywood-on-the-Tiber, toga-and-sandals epics of the 1950s and 60s. Today, the transnationalization of cinema extends beyond European and Euro-American coproductions to include international production centers in, most notably, South and East Asia. In an increasingly interconnected world, these hybridizing tendencies have become predominant. One of the most significant aspects of transnational cinema as both a body of work and a critical category is the degree to which it factors Europe and the U.S. into the problematics of "world cinema." Without succumbing to the exoticizing representational practices of mainstream Hollywood films, transnational cinema—which by definition has its own globalizing imperatives—transcends the national as autonomous cultural particularity while respecting it as a powerful symbolic force. The category of the transnational allows us to recognize the hybridity of much new Hollywood cinema (witness, for example, the importance of Asian martial arts films to the work of Quentin Tarantino and the influence of European auteur cinema on the work of directors such as Martin Scorsese, Francis Coppola, and, with parodic self-consciousness, Woody Allen).

Conversely, this hybridity also problematizes the term "foreign film." In the U.S. and the U.K. this term has functioned primarily as a signifier for non-English language films. Practically it has served to relegate those films, and the force of their images of cultural alterity, to the so-called "art-house circuit" and to the select audiences that frequent them. As Jigna Desai has written, "[t]he phenomenon of the art house is based on positioning 'foreign' films as ethnographic documents of 'other' (national) cultures and therefore as representatives of national cinemas" (Desai 2004: 39). This phenomenon has served to reinforce the notion that U.S. cinema is the site of entertainment (i.e., a commodity that people are willing to pay for), while other cinemas are sites of instruction or edification (a non-commercial art form to which people submit, with varying degrees of reluctance, or, at best, a sense of cultural duty, in the classroom or the heavily subsidized specialist cinema). This traditional dichotomy has been complicated, first of all, by the fact that Hollywood has influenced cinematic traditions the world over, an influence reflected, for example, in the terms "Bollywood" and "Nollywood" (shorthand for the mass-market film industries of India and Nigeria, respectively), and in the fact that the majority of the world's film industries include American-style action films among their output. The rigid distinction between globally marketed American blockbusters and worthy-but-obscure "other" film traditions has also been challenged by the worldwide dissemination and box-office success of "non-western" films, particularly those from the Pacific Rim (such as Ang Lee's *Crouching Tiger, Hidden Dragon* (2000), Wong Kar-wai's *In the Mood for Love* (2000), Zhang Yimou's *Hero* [2002] and *House of Flying Daggers* [2004], and martial arts films starring Jackie Chan or Jet Li).

From National to Transnational Cinema

There is no doubt that nationalism has played a key role in the evolution and critical legitimation of film studies and to varying degrees, national elites have sought to use film to establish or solidify official cultural narratives. (For example, the notion of the "auteur" as representative and bearer of national and/or ethnic identity has been central to the international reception and reputations of filmmakers as varied as Jean Renoir, Satyajit Ray, Lena Wertmuller, Akira Kurosawa, and Spike Lee.) However, transnational cinema imagines its audiences as consisting of viewers who have expectations and types of cinematic literacy that go beyond the desire for and mindlessly appreciative consumption of national narratives that audiences can identify as their "own." Film is rapidly displacing literature (in particular the novel) as the textual emblematization of cosmopolitan knowing and identity. For instance, there are few contemporary novelists whose names have the international recognition across a range of disciplines and trend-setting communities as those of filmmakers such as Pedro Almódovar, Lars Von Trier, Wim Wenders, Ousmane Sembene, Agnès Varda, Krzysztof Kieslowski, Atom Agoyan, and Mira Nair. This global cine-literacy has been created and made necessary by the degree to which capitalism as the catalytic agent in the expansion of popular culture has undermined the viability of cultural or national insularity.

Central to the creation of this cine-literacy has been the proliferation of film festivals as an alternative means of film distribution and presentation. Although film festivals are usually instigated by the desire to represent certain types of distinctively ethnic, national, or identitarian communities in their cultural specificity, the increasing visibility of film festivals and their growing impact on international circuits of distribution often serve to generalize the manifestly particularizing narratives that might actually be presented in the films themselves. Cinema's function as what Peter Bloom calls "visual currency" (Bloom, chapter 9, p. 139) is being drastically reshaped by the possibilities for global and transcultural knowledge that accompany the movement into transnationalism and that underpin the film festival as a site for the fashioning of cosmopolitan citizenship. Although it can be argued that, as a spectatorial object, each film requires a particular epistemological and referential framework in order to be "fully" readable, increasingly these frameworks are losing the national and cultural particularity they once had. Because narrative film as a dramatic medium relies largely on emotional identification to do its work, the sense of familiarity with other cultures and with the natives of those cultures as people worthy of the two or three hours of intense emotional investment that a given cinematic text demands weakens the ability of cultural authorities to deploy the binarized us/them narratives upon which xenophobic nationalisms depend.

As a marker of cosmopolitanism, the transnational at once transcends the national and presupposes it. For transnationalism, its nationalist other is neither an armored enemy with whom it must engage in a grim battle to the death nor a verbose relic whose outdated postures can only be scorned. From a transnational perspective, nationalism is instead a canny dialogical partner whose voice often seems to be growing stronger at the very moment that its substance is fading away. Like postmodernism and poststructuralism, other discourses that have complicated the notion of unmediated representation, transnationalism factors heterogeneity into its basic semantic framework. This recognition of the essentially imaginary nature of any notion of cultural purity is not, however, unilateral and untroubled. The space of the transnational is not an anarchic free-for-all in which blissfully deracinated postnational subjects revel in ludically mystified states of ahistoricity. The continued force of nationalism, especially nationalism grounded in religious cultures, must be recognized as an emotionally charged component of the construction of the narratives of cultural identity that people at all levels of society use to maintain a stable sense of self.

Transnational cinema arises in the interstices between the local and the global. Because of the intimacy and communal dynamic in which films are usually experienced, cinema has a singular capacity to foster bonds of recognition between different groups, or what Vertovec and Cohen have called "trans-local understandings" (Vertovec and Cohen 1999: xvii). These bonds of recognition, however, must not be confused with the false unity imposed by discourses that lump all sites of local identity together in opposition to some nebulously deindividualizing global force. Transnational cinema as a category moves beyond the exceptionalizing discourses of "Third Worldism" and the related notion of Third Cinema, terms that have become increasingly problematic in a world no longer marked by the sharp divisions between Communism, Capitalism, and the rest. Third Cinema, initially a site of discursive resistance to cultural imperialism, soon came to be equated with all cinema made in the "Third World," though this conflation was quickly complicated by the presence of neocolonial forces within the postcolonial world, and by the fact that many "Third World" filmmakers were trained in the West. Because of the hybridized and cosmopolitan identities of so many contemporary filmmakers, it could be argued that binary oppositions and tertiary relations have lost even their heuristic value in the complexly interconnected world-system with which even the most marginalized of them must now contend.

A certain anxiety of authenticity underlies the notion of culturally "correct" filmmaking, which assumes a heightened representational access by ethnic and cultural insiders to a stable and culturally distinct reality. But because transnational cinema is most "at home" in the in-between spaces of culture, in other words, between the local and the global, it decisively problematizes the investment in cultural purity or separatism. The failure of Third Cinema as a sociocritical discourse to achieve its revolutionary objectives does not, however, nullify the liberating force that it had in grounding critical counternarratives to the Euro-American image of cinema that was being fashioned as film studies coalesced as a discipline. As Ella Shohat and Robert Stam have pointed out, "In relation to cinema, the term 'Third World' is empowering in that it calls attention to the collectively vast cinematic productions of Asia, Africa, and Latin America and of minoritarian cinema in the First World" (Shohat and Stam 1994: 27). However, it is important to recognize that the term is more relevant from a historical perspective than in the current global context.

The most critically significant attempt in recent years to recuperate the national as a site for positive self-fashioning has been the concept of the "postcolonial." Ato Quayson has proposed a working definition of postcolonialism as "a studied engagement with the experience of colonialism and its past and present effects, both at the local level of ex-colonial societies, as well as at the level of more general global developments thought to be the after-effects of empire" (Quayson 2000: 93–94). However, as with notions of a "Third World" and "Third Cinema," the concept of the transnational also problematizes "postcolonialism" as an attempt to maintain and legitimize conventional notions of cultural authenticity. Despite its still significant analytical force in a wide range of critical projects, the concept of postcolonialism across its many registers has not proven to be as flexible a tool as it initially seemed for charting the media cultures of advanced capitalism. The post in "postcolonialism" has foundered on the same terminological shoals as the "post" in postnational, which is not strictly or even primarily a temporal designation, since the postnational and the national can, and no doubt for decades if not centuries to come will, function side by side. Tied, despite the myriad attempts that have been made to broaden its descriptive range, to particular conditions of imperial oppression, postcolonialism loses its conceptual coherence when it is called upon to provide analytical grounding for situations that do not have or that have not been defined exclusively by the imperial or colonial pre-histories of which it has functioned as a deconstructive critique. Alternatively, transnationalism offers a more multivalenced approach to considering the impact of history on contemporary experience owing to the fact that the issues of immigration, exile, political asylum, tourism, terrorism, and technology with which it engages are all straightforwardly readable in "real world" terms. And increasingly, this real world is being defined not by its colonial past (or even its neocolonial present), but by its technological future, in which previously disenfranchized people will gain ever greater access to the means of global representation.

Global Cinema in the Digital Age

Ultimately, the conceptual force of a term like transnationalism is determined by a number of factors, ranging from the permeability of national borders (itself determined by local and global political and economic conditions) to the physical or virtual mobility of those who cross them. In a similar way, cinema is borderless to varying degrees, subject to the same uneven mobility as people. Although Hollywood cinema knows few boundaries, and films from Hong Kong, Korea, and India are finding ever larger global audiences, most films from the vast majority of the world's film-producing countries rarely find audiences (that is, audiences rarely find them) outside their own national borders. To a large extent, cinematic mobility, like human mobility, is determined by both geopolitical factors and financial pedigree. Because of their higher production values and access to more extensive distribution networks and marketing campaigns, the more heavily financed films tend to cross national borders with greater ease. We must be mindful of Jigna Desai's suggestion that even in pirated forms "those films most likely to circulate transnationally are those that are more 'Western friendly', adopting familiar genres, narratives, or themes in their hybrid productions" (Desai 2004: 45). Such films function as what Desai calls "tasty, easily swallowed, apolitical global cultural morsels" (Desai 2004: 90)—in other words, cinematic Mcnuggets.

Yet, despite these commercial constraints, there has been, in recent years, a significant increase in accessibility to all kinds of media. Whereas in the nineteenth and twentieth centuries, immigration brought greater numbers of people together in a physical convergence that greatly facilitated cultural contact and exchange, in the twenty-first century, convergence is becoming ever more virtual, not only in technological terms as the coming together of different media in a single site, but also in the increasing mediatization of cultural interaction. The shocks and stimuli that Georg Simmel and Walter Benjamin located in the modern city are now conveyed largely through global media such as cinema, television, and the internet. Postmodern *flâneurs* now scroll, rather than stroll, and the signs that bombard them come primarily in the form of product placements and spam.

The globalization of film culture that was prefigured by the development and international dissemination of the video cassette recorder in the 1970s and 1980s has seen its most transformative aspects come to spectacular fruition in the rise of digital technology and the DVD. In their history of the first decade of the video cassette recorder, Gladys D. Ganley and Oswald Ganley have noted that within ten years of the commercial availability of VCRs "representative specimens of the entire spectrum of programming available in democracies [had] penetrated into even the most restrictive nations" (Ganley and Ganley 1987: xi). It was this technology that lay the groundwork for the emergence of transnational cinema as the destabilizing force that it has become by providing what we can retrospectively recognize as a low-tech precursor to the genuinely revolutionary impact of digital video production, projection, and reproduction. The falling cost of digital filmmaking equipment, which enables individuals to shoot and edit their own films on personal computers without studio backing, has facilitated the rise of a culture of access that functions as a delegitimating shadow of the official film cultures of most nation-states as they have been determined by the processes of screening, censorship, rating, and critique. Digital technology in all its aspects has enabled a growing disregard for national boundaries as ideological and aesthetic checkpoints by a range of legal and extra-legal players, and has functioned to disrupt and decentralize the forces that have, heretofore, maintained strict control over the representational politics of the cinematic public sphere.

Consequently, an important aspect of the impact of digital distribution as a catalytic component of transnational cinema is the extent to which these developments fundamentally compromise the effectiveness of all types of state or official censorship. As the availability of works by previously marginalized filmmakers increases, these once silenced voices will be able to make their concerns known with an immediacy and straightforwardness previously unavailable to all but the most unchallenging cultural insiders or the most fecklessly audacious outlaws. This new culture of access has also been fostered by the decreasing levels of commercial success that an "independent" film has to achieve in order to recoup its basic production costs, as the means of reproduction become less cost intensive and the capacity of the internet and other emerging media technologies to provide free advertising is exploited with growing levels of sophistication by minority filmmakers and producers. Although it must not be forgotten that there are still vast numbers of people across the globe who do not have direct access to new media, it is certainly true that as filmmaking becomes more accessible to disenfranchized cultural groups and distribution channels become even more flexible, cinema will become increasingly prominent as a means of global legitimation and cultural critique.

Motion Pictures: Film, Migration and Diaspora

Fundamental to the kinds of cultural critique made possible by widening accessibility are cinematic depictions of people caught in the cracks of globalization. Transnational subjects from all levels of the social hierarchy are finding themselves occupying the center of the frame in a growing number of widely seen films. Transnational distribution in its many forms unmoors films from their immediate contexts, thereby allowing them to circulate much more freely than ever before, i.e., to "migrate." This migratory potential is apparent not only in the very fact of the greater availability of a wider range of films to a wider range of audiences, but in the prominence of migration and diaspora as themes within transnational cinematic texts themselves.

The figure of the cosmopolite is being complicated and broadened as migrants and other displaced people acquire the means to insert themselves and their particular experiences of transnational consciousness and mobility into the spaces of cinematic representation and legitimation, necessitating the reconceptualization of naturalized senses of "home." Ironically, however, immigration as the search for a new "home" undermines the immigrant's potential for cosmopolitan identification in the very act of instantiating it. More often than not, transnational cinema's narrative dynamic is generated by a sense of loss. The lingering appeal of notions of cultural authenticity and normative ideas of "home" prompts filmmakers to explore the ways in which physical mobility across national borders necessarily entails significant emotional conflict and psychological adjustment. As Hamid Naficy writes of what he calls "accented cinema," "Loneliness is an inevitable outcome of transnationality, and it finds its way into the desolate structures of feeling and lonely diegetic characters" (Naficy 1999: 55).

As a figure within cinematic productions, the image of the displaced person grounds the transnational both thematically and in terms of global awareness. In such works, loss and deterritorialization are often represented not as transitional states on the transnational subject's path to either transcendence or tragedy, but instead as more or less permanent conditions—as, for example, in the film *Blackboards* (Samira Makhmalbaf, 2000), which depicts a group of nomads forced to travel ceaselessly throughout Kurdistan on the Iran–Iraq border. In much transnational cinema, identities are necessarily deconstructed and reconstructed along the lines of a powering dynamic based on mobility. A soldier deployed in a distant country is in many ways as much a displaced person as an immigrant who migrates in search of a better life. Such a sense of being "out of place" figures strongly, for instance, in Claire Denis's 2000 film *Beau Travail*, in which members of the French Foreign Legion stationed in Ethiopia appear adrift both in relation to the local residents who observe their strange ways with bemusement, and in their failure to establish cohesive relationships among themselves.

In the diasporic imagination, a psychological investment in mobility is usually counteracted by the emotional construction of a homeland, which provides a foundational narrative of departure and a validating promise of return. The 2003 film *Goodbye Lenin* (Wolfgang Becker) showed that even the fall of the Berlin Wall generated a diasporic nostalgia of sorts, as illustrated by the mother's desire for the privations of life in the former East Germany. Indeed, in many films that can be fruitfully considered from a transnational perspective, identification with a "homeland" is experienced and represented as a crisis. However, rather than being something that is simply transcended or jettisoned as the narrative unfolds, national identity often becomes a placeholder for idealized sites of cultural memory and imagined social security. In these films nostalgia for the mother country offers a tenuous refuge, which is constantly challenged by the constraints and attractions of life in the adopted country, often felt most acutely by the second generation. For example, in films such as *Bend it Like Beckham* (Gurinder Chadha, 2002) and *East is East* (Damien O'Donnell, 1999), first-generation South Asian immigrants in Great Britain struggle to impose an all-embracing identification with and allegience to a homeland that, for their children, is less meaningful than the reality of day-to-day existence in the United Kingdom. Similarly, in Mathieu Kassovitz's much discussed 1995 film *La Haine*, young second-generation immigrants from North Africa, West Africa, and Eastern Europe reject the traditional values of their families in order to embrace a "French" youth culture inspired by the global fashion for violent Hollywood films and rap music.

As a lived condition, diasporic identification entails an imaginative leap beyond the particulars of one's own experience. It functions as the postnational version of the "imagined community" that Benedict Anderson famously theorized[1] and that Arjun Appadurai invoked when he suggested that "as groups move yet stay linked to one another through sophisticated media capabilities [,] . . . ethnicity, once a genie contained in the bottle of some sort of locality (however large), has now become a global force, forever slipping in and through the cracks between states and borders" (Appadurai 1996: 41). Given this interstitiality, it is not surprising that so many films that problematize national or cultural identity take place in the "non-places" of the postindustrial landscape—airports, highways, high-rise hotels, and even the ultimate "non-place," cyberspace—those in-between spaces where people are spending an increasing amount of time and forming some of their most significant relationships (Augé 1995). As human networks are increasingly connected by nodes and hubs, a term like "on location" actually highlights the dislocation of most films from any representational relationship to or acknowledgement of the economic "home" that is making it possible. The phrase "there's no place like home" becomes very hollow indeed when so many films are being made (without necessarily being set) in places like Toronto, Canada and Cape Town, South Africa simply because of the ability of these cities to stand in for the "homes" that are no longer being called upon to represent themselves either because they are unionized and/or too expensive or because they are no longer capable of standing in for a former version of themselves. Moreover, the reliance on Computer-Generated Images (CGI) to create realistic backdrops for the action depicted in a growing number of films further problematizes any connection between the places films depict and the places where they are made.

Ironically, at the same time that capital, merchandise, information and images are circulating more freely around the globe, it has been argued that restrictions on the movements of people—from jet-setters to labor migrants and asylum seekers—are tightening up (see Vertovec and Cohen 1999: xiii). These transnational subjects, victims of what Slavoj Zizek terms the difference between "those who 'circulate capital' and those 'whom capital circulates,'" are increasingly figured as capital's by-products or, in the logic of planned obsolescence, refuse hauled or blown around from one dumping ground to the next.[2] As Hamid Naficy has written,

> The key words summarizing this postindustrial system—globalization, privatization, diversification, deregulation, digitization, convergence, and consolidation—are all associated with centralization of the global economic and media powers in fewer and more

powerful hands. However, this market-driven centralization masks a fundamental opposing trend at social and political levels, that is, the fragmentation of nation-states and other social formations, and the scattering, often violent and involuntary, of an increasing [. . .] number of people from their homelands and places of residence—all of which are driven by divergence, not convergence.

(Naficy 1999: 127)

This divergence serves to drive people apart economically and politically at the very moment that they are brought together physically and virtually. Paul Virilio opposes what he calls "residents," whom he defines "not [as] those who are stuck at home, but those who are everywhere at home thanks to their cell phones" to "nomads," who "are at home nowhere: homeless, migrants who only have a jalopy to live in."[3] This dichotomy is emblematized in the Steven Spielberg film *The Terminal* (2004), in which Tom Hanks plays a man from a fictional East European country who is forced to live in a New York airport when his passport is invalidated. When a flight attendant, played by Catherine Zeta-Jones, sees the security pager that airport officials have made him wear, she believes it to be a cell phone like the one she carries with her: what, for her, enables a kind of hyper-mobility, for him represents imprisonment. She is an itinerant "resident," always on the move yet "everywhere at home," whereas he is an immobilized nomad.

As some boundaries disappear, others spring up in their place. The drive to distinguish among groups never truly disappears; it just gets displaced periodically to reflect the shifting geopolitical landscape. For example, with the blurring of national boundaries that accompanied the huge expansion of the European Union in 2004, tirades against asylum seekers reached near fever pitch in countries such as Britain and France ("Old Europe"), whose national newspapers braced their readers against the impending arrival of "floods" of immigrants from former Eastern bloc countries ("New Europe"). Etienne Balibar has spoken of a "potential 'European apartheid': the dark side, as it were, of the emergence of the 'European citizen.'"[4] This dynamic is thematized in the film *Last Resort* (Pawel Pavlikovsky, 2000), in which a woman from the former Soviet Union is detained in an asylum center after being abandoned by her mail-order fiancé while attempting to immigrate to the United Kingdom. Another film, *Dirty Pretty Things* (Stephen Frears, 2002), focuses on the traffic in human organs to which some migrant workers are forced to submit in order to survive in the UK. The experimental film *La Vie nouvelle* (Philippe Grandrieux, 2002) is a hallucinogenic depiction of Eastern European sex workers in France whose objectification is allegorized in images that evoke vampirism and the Holocaust.

Reflecting the complex political dynamics of transnational cinema, one of the most important aspects of the essays in this collection is their refusal to fashion it into or champion it as a utopian discourse. The Coca-colonization of global marketing, the homogenization effected by mass culture, relies even more fundamentally on the gaps that divide worker-producers from consumers. By refusing to privilege either the top (as do traditional champions of capitalism) or the bottom (as do various forms of Marxism and socialism), transnationalism unfolds as an essentially self-motivated, and apparently amoral, cultural force. Just as postmodernism emerged as a stylistic (or superstructural) response to the economic contingencies of advanced capitalism, so transnationalism both reflects and mediates power relations in the postindustrial, digital age. It prompts us to ask: is the world really "borderless"? There is an upstream and a downstream to the flows of capital, which are not boundless and oceanic, but instead channeled with great precision from the large work forces in the "south" and the "east" toward company headquarters in the "north" and the "west." This movement is explicitly invoked in the film *Poniente* (Chus

Gutiérez, 2002), which depicts the exploitation of migrant laborers who have come from Morocco and Sub-Saharan Africa to work in Spain, the "West" of the film's title. In one scene, tomato growers claim that the price controls placed on their crop by the European Union is forcing them to lower wages, underscoring the fact that bureaucratic unity among European producers is underpinned, in this case, by the stark division between the African workers and their Spanish employers. This film illustrates the failure of the digital revolution to transform the workplace into a virtual space for manual laborers, the vast majority of the world's workers, whose digits remain firmly attached to their hands.

TOURISTS AND TERRORISTS: Pontecorvo at the Pentagon

In a variety of formal and ideological registers, transnational cinema reflects and thematically mediates the shifting material and ideological conditions that constitute global culture. The diverse politics of this mediation are rendered singularly transparent when cinema is called upon to represent real-world attempts to shift political conditions by extreme measures. For example, the screening of Gilles Pontecorvo's 1963 anticolonial epic *The Battle of Algiers* at the Pentagon on August 27, 2003 during the Iraq War (see, for example, slate.msn.com/id/2087628; *The New York Times*, September 7, 2003; and *The Washington Post*, October 31, 2003) revealed the heterogeneous, and indeed, at times internally contradictory, nature of transnational cinema. The fact that the film's ideological power could be appreciated and appropriated by ostensibly opposing interests reveals the dialectical tension that powers transnationalism as a synthesis of the social and conceptual forces that have preceded it.

A significant result of the transnationalization of film culture is the unparalleled impact it has had on the production and availability of documentary films and other forms of "committed" cinema. Although documentaries have been the primary mode of expression for many if not most "non-Western" or minority filmmakers for decades, for most of cinema history documentaries have been almost completely unavailable on any consistent basis to all but the most privileged of audiences. Recently, however, a growing number of documentarians are finding that the problems with lack of access to avenues for dissemination of their work that have plagued them for decades are being eased both by the explosion of television channels and film festivals desperate for increasingly specialized product and by new developments in digital technology. Greater distribution opportunities have even given new life to "popular" and "agit-prop" documentary as a form of political critique, as has been made particularly clear in the global stardom of the documentarian Michael Moore (the blatantly ideological straightforwardness of whose work, few would argue, relies upon the illusion of directorial objectivity).

Moore's film *Fahrenheit 9/11* was the most widely circulated filmic response to the 2001 terrorist attack on the World Trade Center (not to mention the most financially successful documentary ever made), and brought to the fore film's potential to engage with the complex issue of terrorism. In both their execution and in the counter-response(s) that they legitimate, terrorism and other types of politically motivated violence function as the limit cases, the negative underbelly, of transnationalism. It is in its depiction of terrorism that commercial cinema comes closest to offering its most ideologically revelatory and analytically transparent imagery and narrative constructions. The conflation of terrorism with banditry and illicit moneymaking in many U.S. and European films makes clear the ideologically determined resistance of commercial cinema to the recognition of radical political commitment under any category other than those of greed and fanaticism. To be sure, 9/11 as a terrorist event is so potent an instantiation of a transnational counternarrative to notions of American exceptionalism that it has so far been beyond the commercializing reach of the Hollywood dream machine. At the same time, the rhetorical deployment and exploitation of 9/11 and the subsequent Iraq war by political officials and some elements of the American media created a polarizing discourse that turned all U.S. citizens into potential victims and all "foreigners" into potential victimizers: in other words, every tourist venturing into the U.S. became a potential terrorist.

Hollywood as the standard-bearer for popular film as a world system has so far proven itself capable of coopting the forces of hybridity and difference effectively enough to avoid breakdown or the significant loss of its global hegemony. In order to maintain its homogenizing imperative, it must consistently neutralize transnational cinema's more fundamentally destabilizing potential. It has traditionally done this by constructing non-Western subjects as "others" and by rendering the markers of non-Western cultural identity as "exotic." The significance of crossing borders varies according to the identity of the traveler, most often along color-coded, gendered, and religious lines. For example, in U.S. and European films, white women travelers are usually positioned as tourists, while white male travelers are presented as either figures of salvation or as James Bond-like adventurers. Non-Western European and non-north American women or women of color, on the other hand, are usually represented as immigrants, while men of color are increasingly depicted as terrorists. If a white male traveler acts violently, it is likely to be in the guise of an action hero, with whom audiences are meant to identify, while similar actions performed by a brown-skinned character are usually signs of the violence and villainy that the narrative is devoted to eradicating. As the film franchise *Mission Impossible* makes clear, subterfuge and disguise may be associated either with an "international man of mystery" or with an international terrorist, according to the vagaries of pigmentation.

For instance, because of its status as an ideologically unstable site within the touristically fetishized space of "The British Isles," the ambivalence with which the situation in Northern Ireland has been dealt cinematically (see, for example, Jim Sheridan's *In the Name of the Father* or Neil Jordan's *The Crying Game*) reflects the general reluctance of Western elites to complicate the racial indexicality of the term "terrorist" as a marker for the potential contagion of "Third World" and implicitly religious alterity. Similarly, the infrequency with which global sites other than European ones are used as the backdrop for Western romances reflects the covert positioning of non-white (and especially Muslim) spaces as essentially dangerous and unstable. This positioning makes the terrorist and his Euro-American and, most frequently, white counterpart, the adventurer, signature figures for cinematic depictions of contact with the non-Western world.

As the essays in this collection ultimately suggest, and as scores of transnational films have illustrated in various generic modes, leaving one's homeland entails leaving behind both physically and emotionally the familiarity that home implies. This leave-taking often entails, to use Freud's term, a becoming-*unheimlich* both to oneself and to those who are variously invested in the diasporic subject's remaining recognizable. The argument is often made that if the citizen is by definition the subject who must be recognized, transnationalism can quickly lead to the production of subjects who are, in many ways, beyond recognition. Regardless of the ultimate tenability of this position, it is certainly no coincidence that transnational awareness is coming to the fore at the very moment when "cosmopolitanism" is becoming one of the key tropes for contemporary identity. As the primary artistic instantiation of cosmopolitanism, cinema itself is at home everywhere, and unlike the immigrant, the terrorist, or the refugee, must imagine itself as a welcome guest.

Notes

1   See Benedict Anderson, *Imagined Communities*, revised edition (London: Verso, 1991).
2   Slavoj Zizek, *Welcome to the Desert of the Real* (London: Verso, 2002), p. 83.
3   Paul Virilio and Sylvère Lotringer, *Crepuscular Dawn*, trans. Mike Taormina (New York: Semiotext[e], 2002), pp. 70 and 71.
4   Etienne Balibar, *Politics and the Other Scene* (London: Verso, 2002), p. ix.

PART ONE

FROM NATIONAL TO TRANSNATIONAL CINEMA

Introduction

The essays in this section provide a historical and conceptual overview of the shift that is taking place in film studies from conceptions of cinema and cinema history grounded in ideas of national identity to recognition and deployment of a new paradigm. This paradigm is one that recognizes the heuristic (and affective) force of the concept of "national" cinema, while emphasizing the complex constructions of identity, citizenship, and ethics both represented on screen and created in the film industry's transnational networks of production, distribution and reception. As the writers whose work we include in this section make clear, one of the central aspects of transnationalism as a critical discourse is its dialectical engagement with—rather than simple rejection of—ideas of the national. Yet, at the same time, these essays reflect the degree to which concepts like Third Cinema, postcolonial cinema, and world cinema have been conceptual way stations on the path to recognition of the globalizing imperative that has always been a signal component of cinematic production and of the cinematic imagination. Although all of these writers accept the practical necessity of national identity and self-recognition, they each consider the ways in which notions of the national can serve to obscure awareness of the often mystified and ideologically determined dynamics of national culture and authenticity.

In his essay "The Limiting Imagination of National Cinema," Andrew Higson explores and finally rejects the notion of the "national" as the master term in considering the contemporary politics of "world" cinema. By both deploying and contesting Benedict Anderson's notion of "imagined communities" which "imagines the nation as limited, with finite and meaningful boundaries," Higson suggests that "when describing a national cinema, there is a tendency to focus only on those films that narrate the nation as just this finite, limited space, inhabited by a tightly coherent and unified community, closed off to other identities besides national identity." By way of a carefully proposed set of questions that he presents to nationalist thinking, and an essentially deconstructive engagement with the arguments of those critics who have attempted to answer them, Higson concludes that a stable notion of the national cannot fully or even adequately account for the fundamental role played by globalization in much if not most contemporary film production and reception. As Higson makes clear, now more than ever the national is fully imbricated within the transformative and, for the national subject, often destabilizing dynamics of modernity and transcultural contact.

Alternatively, by way of an examination of African film, still perhaps the most underviewed body of cinema both within African nation-states and internationally, David Murphy argues for the continued use value of postcolonialism as a framework for considering the cultural dynamics of modernity in a postnational context. Murphy considers the ways in which the concept of "authenticity" has, on the one hand, served to prevent the collapse of cultural distinctiveness into a blandly universalizing notion of world cinema, while at the same time valorizing problematic notions of an essential African alterity and exoticism and of Africa as a cultural space that is fundamentally unreadable for Westerners. In a passage that is very suggestive for considerations of transnational cinema in general, Murphy writes that "[c]ultural influence is not simply a one way street with the West influencing the rest. Africa and the West are not mutually exclusive worlds that possess their own authentic and unchanging identities: they are hybrid entities that influence and modify each other, and this process of exchange applies to cinema (although in the current world order, the West remains the dominant force in this process of hybridization)." Murphy's essay makes clear that transnationalism need not be considered a strict alternative to or rejection of postcolonialism (just as it is not a rejection of the national), but instead builds upon and extends postcolonialism's critical force.

Ella Shohat also offers a critique of homogenizing discourses of postcolonial identity, but from a feminist perspective. In her essay "Post–Third-Worldist Culture: Gender, Nation and the Cinema," she examines the complexity of global networks of domination in the transnational era, which finds forceful articulation in films and videos by independent women filmmakers. Such works recognize both the impact of the colonial legacy on feminism and the importance of feminist critiques of racialized inequality. Shohat argues that these works "challenge the masculinist contours of the 'nation' in order to continue a feminist decolonization of Third-Worldist historiography, as much as they continue a multicultural decolonization of feminist historiography." Shohat at once emphasizes the particularities and diversity of local struggles for gender equality, and recuperates gender and sexuality from the universalizing narratives of national history, in an attempt to open up an alternative critical space within "this historical moment of intense globalization and immense fragmentation."

The final essay in this section also insists upon the pivotal role of gender in filmic representations of postcolonial society. In "Bombay Boys and Girls: The Gender and Sexual Politics of Transnationality in the New Indian Cinema in English," Jigna Desai traces the emergence of the new wave of English-language cinema from India's "cosmopolitan transnational middle class," which both represents and appeals to South Asian diasporic communities. These independent, low-budget films present an alternative to the dominant "Bollywood" model, both in the way they are produced and in terms of their alternative gender politics. Desai argues that "the socio-economic power relations between diasporas and nation-states are highly gendered and sexualised," and the films she analyzes illustrate this imbrication by offering a critique of narratives of heteronormative romance that allegorize the complex relations between diasporic communities and the Indian nation-state.

The Limiting Imagination of National Cinema

1

ANDREW HIGSON

In 1989, I published an essay about national cinema in *Screen* (Higson 1989).[1] Ten years on, much of what I wrote still seems valid, but there are also some issues I would want to reconsider. One of the problems with that essay is that I was very much extrapolating from my knowledge of just one national cinema (British cinema). As Stephen Crofts has suggested, scholarly work on national cinema often operates from a very limited knowledge of the immense diversity of world cinemas (Crofts 1993: 60–1). In my case, there is undeniably a danger that my essay transformed a historically specific Eurocentric, even Anglocentric version of what a national cinema might be into an ideal category, a theory of national cinema in the abstract that is assumed to be applicable in all contexts.

'When is a cinema "national"?', asks Susan Hayward (1993: 1). As if in answer, Crofts delineates several different types of 'national' cinema that have emerged in different historical circumstances (1993, 1998). They have performed quite distinct functions in relation to the state. They have had very different relationships to Hollywood. Divergent claims have been made for them. They adopt a range of formal and generic characteristics. They are 'national' cinemas in a variety of ways. Faced with such variety, a single, all-encompassing grand theory may be less useful than more piecemeal historical investigations of specific cinematic formations. How have specific national cinemas been defined as such, for instance? How have they come to be understood as national cinemas, in what historical circumstances? How have politicians, trade organisations, distributors, critics, historians, journalists and audiences demarcated one national cinema from another? How has a particular body of films or a particular economic infrastructure come to be seen as embodying a distinct national cinema? Which strands or traditions of cinema circulating within a particular nation-state are recognised as legitimate aspects of the national cinema? How have particular policies and practices been mobilised in the name of particular national cinemas?

While these are undoubtedly important questions, and while I have attempted to explore some of them elsewhere, I do in fact want to deal with some of the more abstract and theoretical issues here.[2] First, I want to revisit the idea that the modern nation, in Benedict Anderson's terms, is an imagined community (Anderson 1983). Second, I want to reconsider the traditional idea of the 'national' as a self-contained and carefully demarcated experience. In particular, I want to suggest that the concept of the 'transnational' may be a subtler means of describing cultural and economic formations that are rarely contained by national boundaries. Third, I want to examine John Hill's argument that the concept of national cinema is of vital importance at the level of state policy, particularly as a means of promoting cultural diversity and attending to national specificity (Hill 1992, 1996). For better or worse, I will again be drawing examples from the British context.

My intention overall is to question the usefulness of the concept of national cinema. It is clearly a helpful taxonomic labelling device, a conventional means of reference in the complex debates about cinema, but the process of labelling is always to some degree tautologous, fetishising the national rather than merely describing it. It thus erects boundaries between films produced in different nation-states although they may still have much in common. It may therefore obscure the degree of cultural diversity, exchange and interpenetration that marks so much cinematic activity.

The nation as imagined community

Following Anderson (1983), it is now conventional to define the nation as the mapping of an imagined community with a secure and shared identity and sense of belonging, on to a carefully demarcated geo-political space. The nation, from this perspective, is first forged and then maintained as a bounded public sphere. That is to say, it is public debate that gives the nation meaning, and media systems with a particular geographical reach that give it shape. Those who inhabit nations with a strong sense of self-identity are encouraged to imagine themselves as members of a coherent, organic community, rooted in the geographical space, with well-established indigenous traditions. As David Morley and Kevin Robins put it, 'the idea of the "nation" . . . involve|s| people in a common sense of identity and . . . work|s| as an inclusive symbol which provides "integration" and "meaning"' (1990: 6).

National identity is, in this sense, about the experience of belonging to such a community, being steeped in its traditions, its rituals and its characteristic modes of discourse. This sense of national identity is not of course dependent on actually living within the geo-political space of the nation, as the émigré experience confirms. Thus some diasporic communities, uprooted from the specific geo-political space of the nation or the homeland, still share a common sense of belonging, despite – or even because of – their transnational dispersal. On the one hand community, on the other, diaspora. On the one hand, modern nations exist primarily as imagined communities. On the other, those communities actually consist of highly fragmented and widely dispersed groups of people with as many differences as similarities and with little in the sense of real physical contact with each other. If this is the case, it follows that all nations are in some sense diasporic. They are thus forged in the tension between unity and disunity, between home and homelessness. Nationhood thus answers to 'a felt need for a rooted, bounded, whole and authentic identity' (Morley and Robins 1990: 19).

The public sphere of the nation and the discourses of patriotism are thus bound up in a constant struggle to transform the facts of dispersal, variegation and homelessness into the experience of rooted community. At times, the experience of an organic, coherent national community, a meaningful national collectivity, will be overwhelming. At other times, the experience of diaspora, dislocation and de-centredness will prevail. It is in times such as these that other allegiances, other senses of belonging besides the national will be more strongly felt.

It is widely assumed that the rituals of mass communication play a central role in re-imagining the dispersed and incoherent populace as a tight-knit, value-sharing collectivity, sustaining the experience of nationhood. But is that collectivity necessarily national? Consider three prominent media experiences that might be seen at one level as enabling the British to imagine themselves as a distinctive national community. First, consider the funeral of Diana, Princess of Wales, which of course became a major media event in which millions participated. Second, consider the consistent ratings success of long-running, home-grown, British-based soap operas depicting everyday inner-city life. Programmes such as *Coronation Street* and *EastEnders* are of course routinely transmitted on a nationwide basis by British broadcasters with at least some sense of a public service remit. Third, consider the immense success at the box-office and subsequently on video and the small screen of a handful of 'typically British' films of the 1990s, among them *Four Weddings and a Funeral* (1994), *The Full Monty* (1997) and *Shakespeare in Love* (1998), all of them British-produced and British-set. Each of these media events has had repercussions far greater than mere viewing figures suggest, given their wide discussion in print, on television, on the Internet and through word-of-mouth.

But are these media events best understood as national phenomena? For a start, there are always dissenters. Some Britons did not mourn Diana's death or participate in the media event of her funeral. Some Britons don't watch soaps, go to the cinema, or take any interest in popular culture. Nor do they recognise themselves in films like *Four Weddings* or *The Full Monty*, or feel interpellated by the invitation through such texts or viewing experiences to share in a collective sense of national identity. Second, the audiences for all three cited events were by no means simply national. To talk about these events as global phenomena would surely be an overstatement, but they undoubtedly were, and in some cases continue to be, considerable transnational experiences. Third, there is of course no guarantee that all audiences will make sense of these experiences in the same way, since audiences will translate each experience into their own cultural frames of reference, using them in different contexts and for different ends.

Fourth, the 'national' audience for a film like *The Full Monty* also 'gathers' to watch non-indigenous films, especially Hollywood films. On the one hand, their coming together for a Hollywood film surely underlines the transnational experience of the 'imagined community', rather than a solely national experience. On the other hand, it is clear that American films play a strong role in the construction of cultural identity in the UK. Fifth, the community that we might imagine 'gathered' around, say, the exhibition and dissemination of *The Full Monty* is always a fortuitous, contingent, abstract amalgam of dispersed and specific audiences or cultural subjects that have come together for a very specific event. At the end of this particular experience or event, the imagined community disperses again, while other communities reassemble quite differently for other relatively fleeting experiences. Such communities are rarely self-sufficient, stable or unified. They are much more likely to be contingent, complex, in part fragmented, in part overlapping with other senses of identity and belonging that have more to do with generation, gender, sexuality, class, ethnicity, politics or style than with nationality. The sense of community, of shared experiences and common identities that was mobilised around the death of Diana, for instance, was clearly mobilised beyond the boundaries of the nation. National identity did not always or necessarily come into it.

Thus in some quarters, the popular groundswell of empathy registered as feminism or sister-liness; in other quarters, or even at the same time, it took the shape of anti-authoritarian and especially republican principles.

The 'imagined community' argument, in my own work as much as anywhere else, is not always sympathetic to what we might call the contingency or instability of the national. This is precisely because the nationalist project, in Anderson's terms, imagines the nation as limited, with finite and meaningful boundaries. The problem is that, when describing a national cinema, there is a tendency to focus only on those films that narrate the nation as just this finite, limited space, inhabited by a tightly coherent and unified community, closed off to other identities besides national identity. Or rather, the focus is on films that seem amenable to such an interpretation. The 'imagined community' argument thus some-times seems unable to acknowledge the cultural difference and diversity that invariably marks both the inhabitants of a particular nation-state and the members of more geo-graphically dispersed 'national' communities. In this sense, as with more conservative versions of the nationalist project, the experience and acceptance of diversity is closed off. This seems particularly unfortunate as modern communication networks operate on an increasingly transnational basis and cultural commodities are widely exchanged across national borders.

The media are vital to the argument that modern nations are imagined communities. But contemporary media activity is also clearly one of the main ways in which transnational cultural connections are established. Hollywood of course is one of the longest standing and best organised media institutions with a transnational reach capable of penetrating even the most heavily policed national spaces. Should this fact be celebrated or bemoaned? As Hollywood films travel effortlessly across national borders, they may displace the sort of 'indigenous' films that might promote and maintain specific national identities. On the other hand, the entry of 'foreign' films into a restricted national market may be a powerful means of celebrating cultural diversity, transnational experiences and multinational identities. Certain British films may have been identified as projecting a core sense of national identity – the consensus films made at Ealing Studios and elsewhere in the latter half of the Second World War, for instance – but it is equally possible to identify 'British' films that seem to embrace the transnational or even quite self-consciously to dissolve rather than to sustain the concept of the nation.[3]

Nationalism and transnationalism

In 'The Concept of National Cinema' (Higson 1989), I suggested that national cinemas were the product of a tension between 'home' and 'away', between the identification of the homely and the assumption that it is quite distinct from what happens elsewhere. In this sense, there are two central conceptual means of identifying the imaginary coherence or specificity of a national cinema. On the one hand, a national cinema seems to look inward, reflecting on the nation itself, on its past, present and future, its cultural heritage, its indigenous traditions, its sense of common identity and continuity. On the other hand, a national cinema seems to look out across its borders, asserting its difference from other national cinemas, proclaiming its sense of otherness.

The problem with this formulation is that it tends to assume that national identity and tradition are already fully formed and fixed in place. It also tends to take borders for granted and to assume that those borders are effective in containing political and economic developments, cultural practice and identity. In fact of course, borders are always leaky and there is a considerable degree of movement across them (even in the most authoritarian states). It is in this migration, this border crossing, that the transnational emerges. Seen in this light, it is difficult to see the indigenous as either pure or stable. On the contrary, the degree of cultural cross-breeding and interpenetration, not only across borders but also within them, suggests that modern cultural formations are invariably hybrid and impure. They constantly mix together different 'indigeneities' and are thus always re-fashioning themselves, as opposed to exhibiting an already fully formed identity.

The cinemas established in specific nation-states are rarely autonomous cultural industries and the film business has long operated on a regional, national and transnational basis. The experience of border crossing takes place at two broad levels. First there is the level of production and the activities of film-makers. Since at least the 1920s, films have been made as co-productions, bringing together resources and experience from different nation-states. For even longer, film-makers have been itinerant, moving from one production base to another, whether temporarily or on a more permanent basis. When a German director like E.A. Dupont is based in England, and makes an Anglo-German co-production simultaneously in English and German (Atlantic, 1929), can it usefully be called a British film?[4] When a British director like Alan Parker makes a Hollywood film about an Argentinean legend (Evita, 1996), to which nation should the film be attributed? When a British director teams up with an American producer, a multinational cast and crew, and American capital, to adapt a novel about the contingency of identity by a Sri Lankan-born Canadian resident (The English Patient, 1996), can its identity be called anything other than transnational?

The second way in which cinema operates on a transnational basis is in terms of the distribution and reception of films. On the one hand, many films are distributed far more widely than simply within their country of production. Occasionally, even the small, 'home-grown', indigenous film can become an international box-office phenomenon given the right backing and promotional push. On the other hand, when films do travel, there is no certainty that audiences will receive them in the same way in different cultural contexts. Some films of course are physically altered for different export markets, whether in terms of subtitling, dubbing, re-editing or censorship. But even where they are not altered, audiences can still take them up in novel ways.

The debates about national cinema need to take greater account of the diversity of reception, the recognition that the meanings an audience reads into a film are heavily dependent on the cultural context in which they watch it. The movement of films across borders may introduce exotic elements to the 'indigenous' culture. One response to this is an anxious concern about the effects of cultural imperialism, a concern that the local culture will be infected, even destroyed by the foreign invader. A contrary response is that the introduction of exotic elements may well have a liberating or democratising effect on the local culture, expanding the cultural repertoire. A third possibility is that the foreign commodity will not be treated as exotic by the local audience, but will be interpreted according to an 'indigenous' frame of reference; that is, it will be metaphorically translated into a local idiom.[5]

Cultural diversity and national specificity: a matter of policy

One of the ways in which the nation talks to itself, and indeed seeks to differentiate itself from others, is in terms of state policy. The fear of cultural and economic imperialism has of course had a major impact on state policy in a great many different nations. Consequently, if the concept of national cinema is considered troublesome at the level of theoretical debate, it is still a considerable force at the level of state policy. One of the problems with legislating for a strong and healthy national cinema untroubled by foreign interlopers is that national legislation can rarely have more than a cosmetic effect on what is really a problem of the international capitalist economy. One of the solutions is that even governments occasionally operate on a transnational basis, notably in terms of the pan-European media funding infrastructure established under the auspices of the European Union and the Council of Europe.

Even so, there is no denying that at the level of policy the concept of national cinema still has some meaning, as governments continue to develop defensive strategies designed to protect and promote both the local cultural formation and the local economy. Such developments have traditionally assumed that a strong national cinema can offer coherent images of the nation sustaining the nation at an ideological level, exploring and celebrating what is understood to be the indigenous culture. Of equal importance today is the role that cinema is felt able to play in terms of promoting the nation as a tourist destination, to the benefit of the tourism and service industries. Also at the economic level, governments may legislate to protect and promote the development of the local media industries. They may encourage long-term investment (often from overseas). They may create the conditions that might generate significant export revenue. And they may seek to maintain an appropriately skilled domestic workforce in full employment.

To promote films in terms of their national identity is also to secure a prominent collective profile for them in both the domestic and the international marketplace, a means of selling those films by giving them a distinctive brand name. In this respect, it is worth noting how national labels become crucial at prestigious prize-giving ceremonies, such as the Oscars, for the kudos that can spill over from successful films on to their assumed national base. Note for instance the way in which the British press celebrated the success of films like *Chariots of Fire* (1981), *The English Patient* and *Shakespeare in Love* as British films, even though they all depended on significant amounts of foreign investment.

Given that the nation-state remains a vital and powerful legal mechanism, and given the ongoing development of national media policies, it remains important to conduct debate at that level and in those terms. It would be foolish in this context to attempt to do away altogether with the concept of national cinema. Yet it is important to ask to what precisely the concept refers, what sorts of cultural developments it can embrace and what it makes difficult. The implication of what I have argued so far is that the concept of national cinema is hardly able to do justice either to the internal diversity of contemporary cultural formations or to the overlaps and interpenetrations between different formations. This is surely true if we define a national cinema as one that imagines, or enables its audiences to imagine, a closed and coherent community with an already fully formed and fixed indigenous tradition. Ironically, it is very often the case that a government that legislates for a national cinema, or a pressure group that lobbies for such legislation, is in fact advancing an argument for cultural diversity. Those western European nations, for instance, that have erected defensive mechanisms in their own marketplace and economy against an apparently imperialist Hollywood have almost invariably done so as a means of promoting a film culture and a body of representations other than those that Hollywood can offer. ⟵——

Given the extent to which state media policy is still overwhelmingly defined in nationalist terms, it may then make sense to continue to argue for a national cinema precisely as a means of promoting cultural difference. A government-supported national cinema may be one of the few means by which a film culture not dominated entirely by Hollywood can still exist. This is an argument that John Hill has developed, with specific reference to British cinema. He suggests that the case for a national cinema is best made in terms of 'the value of home-grown cinema to the cultural life of a nation and, hence, the importance of supporting indigenous film-making in an international market dominated by Hollywood' (Hill 1992: 11). Such a statement of course begs the question of what exactly the value of that home-grown cinema is. This is particularly pressing in the light of the argument that the presence and popularity of Hollywood films in Britain is in itself a means of ensuring a populist diversity within British culture, a valuable means of broadening the British cultural repertoire.

Hill however is dismissive of the claim that the presence of Hollywood films within British culture should be seen as a potential democratisation of that culture. He argues that national cinemas have a much greater potential to act as forces for diversity and for the re-fashioning of the national cultural formation. 'It is quite possible to conceive of a national cinema', he writes, 'which is none the less critical of inherited notions of national identity, which does not assume the existence of a unique, unchanging "national culture", and which is capable of dealing with social divisions and differences' (Hill 1992: 16). In other words, to question tradition and to embrace cultural difference is not necessarily to reject altogether the idea of a national cinema that can speak eloquently to a multicultural audience. On the contrary, Hill argues, it is important that a national cinema is maintained in Britain, one that is 'capable of registering the lived complexities of British "national" life' (Hill 1996: 111). Hill suggests that this was precisely the national cinema that Britain enjoyed in the 1980s, when 'the "Britishness" of British cinema . . . was neither unitary nor agreed but depended upon a growing sense of the multiple national, regional and ethnic identifications which characterised life in Britain in this period' (Hill 1999: 244).

Is this a sufficient reason for persevering with the concept of national cinema? In fact, it seems to me that Hill is arguing less for a national cinema than for what might be called a critical (and implicitly left-wing) cinema, a radical cinema, or as he puts it, a cinema 'characterised by questioning and inquiry' (Hill 1992: 17). His concern is to ensure that the range of cultural representations available to audiences is not restricted by the operations of the marketplace. In this respect, as he puts it, 'The case for a national cinema . . . may be seen as part of a broader case for a more varied and representative range of film and media output than the current political economy of the communications industries allows' (Hill 1992: 18).

There are two problems with formulating a defence of national cinema in these terms. First, in order to promote a cinema characterised by questioning and inquiry is it necessary to do so on national grounds? A critical cinema surely need not be nationally based in its funding, its textual concerns or its reception. Likewise, cultural diversity within a national film-culture may just as easily be achieved through encouraging a range of imports as by ensuring that home-grown films are produced. Second, the British films of the 1980s that Hill favours are by no means the full range of British-made films produced in that decade, but those whose radical subject-matter and critical approach appeal to his own ideological preferences. Most histories of national cinema have of course been written in this way. Canons of critically favoured home-grown films are created to the neglect of other films circulating within the film culture, whether home-grown or imported. The formation of such canons also tends to overlook the relative popularity of the canonical films with 'national' audiences. As far as Hill is concerned, 'the most interesting type of British cinema, and the one which is most worthy of support' does not 'exemplify . . . the virtues and values of Britain'. Instead, what he calls for is 'the provision of diverse and challenging representations adequate to the complexities of contemporary Britain' (Hill 1992: 18–19).

What sort of cinema does this imply? It seems to me that it is really a call for a very specific type of film: social dramas set in contemporary Britain, attending to the specificities of multiculturalism and employing a more or less realist mode of representation. It is thus hardly surprising that Hill's book on British cinema in the 1980s presents the British costume dramas and heritage films of the period as of less *relevance* than the films of Ken Loach, Stephen Frears and Isaac Julien. It is not necessarily the case, however, that audiences will find more relevance in contemporary dramas than in period films. Nor is it the case that only British-made or British-set films can address matters of importance or value to audiences in Britain. After all, questions of gender, sexuality and ethnicity, for instance, can be addressed in very poignant ways in displaced or exotic settings, whether the displacement is in terms of period or geography. In this sense, films by a Spike Lee, a Jane Campion or an Emir Kusturica can make what Hill describes as 'a valuable contribution to British cultural life' (Hill 1992: 17). The case for supporting a home-grown cinema, it seems to me, is thus weakened rather than strengthened by Hill's call for a critical cinema that promotes cultural diversity.

Given his emphasis on national specificity, there is even a sense in which Hill's argument depends on a rather enclosed sense of the national, in which borders between nations are fully capable of restricting transnational flow. He does of course argue that films made in a particular nation-state need not necessarily invoke homogenising national myths and may precisely be sensitive to social and cultural differences and to the plurality of identities *within* that state. He seems less sensitive to the hybrid or the transnational, however. Central to his argument is the distinction between a cinema that indulges in homogenising national myths and one that 'works with or addresses nationally specific materials' (Hill 1992: 16). It is a distinction he draws from the work of Paul Willemen, who argues that a nationally specific cultural formation need not necessarily be characterised by a preoccupation with national identity (Willemen 1994). As Willemen points out, the discourses of nationalism will always try to repress the complexities of and internal differences within a nationally specific cultural formation. But he also argues that a cinema that attempts to engage with the nationally specific need not be a nationalist cinema.

The terms in which Hill and Willemen make this distinction seem to me confusing and therefore problematic because they persist in using the concept of the national. Willemen is of course right to insist that 'national boundaries have a significant structuring impact on . . . socio-cultural formations' (Willemen 1994: 210). We cannot therefore simply dismiss the category of the nation altogether, but nor should we assume that cultural specificity is best understood and addressed in national terms. To persist, as Hill does, in referring to a 'nationally specific' cinema that deals with 'national preoccupations' (Hill 1992: 11) within 'an identifiably and specifically British context' (Hill 1992: 16) seems once more to take national identity, and specifically Britishness, for granted. It seems to gloss over too many other questions of community, culture, belonging and identity that are often either defiantly local or loosely transnational. Concepts like 'national life' and 'national culture' thus seem destined to imply a homogenising and enclosing tendency.

Conclusion

I stated at the outset of this chapter that I wanted to question the usefulness of the concept of national cinema. It would be impossible – and certainly unwise – to ignore the concept altogether: it is far too deeply ingrained in critical and historical debate about the cinema, for a start. Even so, as Crofts has argued, it is important to question 'the ongoing critical tendency to hypostatize the "national" of national cinema' (1993: 61). The questions I have posed above suggest that it is inappropriate to assume that cinema and film culture are bound by the limits of the nation-state. The complexities of the international film industry and the transnational movements of finance capital, film-makers and films should put paid to that assumption. Should policy then be developed to ensure that cinema can operate at a national level? On the basis of the British experience, I have suggested that to make assumptions about national specificity is to beg too many questions. In other political circumstances, however, it may be that lobbying or legislating for a national cinema will usefully advance the struggle of a community for cultural, political and economic self-definition. As Crofts points out, in some contexts it may be necessary to challenge the homogenising myths of national cinema discourse; in others, it may be necessary to support them (1993: 62).

Are the limits of the national the most productive way of framing arguments about cultural diversity and cultural specificity? It is certainly valid to argue for a film culture that accommodates diverse identities, images and traditions, and it is undoubtedly important to promote films that deal with the culturally specific. But it doesn't seem useful to me to think through cultural diversity and cultural specificity in solely national terms: to argue for a national cinema is not necessarily the best way to achieve either cultural diversity or cultural specificity. In any case, the contingent communities that cinema imagines are much more likely to be either local or transnational than national.

Notes

1 This was an early version of material subsequently revised in Higson 1995, in which I explore some of the ways in which British cinema has been constructed as a specifically national cinema. See also three other papers in which I discuss the concept of national cinema: Higson 1997, 2000a and 2000b.
2 I look at some of the ways in which British cinema has been constructed as a national cinema in Higson 1995 and 2001; Higson and Maltby 1999 look at the development of a pan-European, transnational cinema in the 1920s and 1930s.
3 For a more detailed version of this argument, see Higson 2000b.
4 For a discussion of Dupont's career in Britain in the late 1920s, see Higson 1999.

5 For enlightening discussions of this process of cultural translation, see Bergfelder 1999a and 1999b.

Bibliography

Anderson, B. (1983) *Imagined Communities: Reflections on the Origins and Spread of Nationalism*, London: Verso.

Ashby, J. and Higson, A. (eds) (2000) *British Cinema, Past and Present*, London: Routledge.

Bergfelder, T. (1999a) 'The Internationalisation of the German Film Industry in the 1950s and 1960s', unpublished Ph.D. thesis, Norwich: University of East Anglia.

—— (1999b) 'Negotiating Exoticism: Hollywood, Film Europe and the Cultural Reception of Anna May Wong', in A. Higson and R. Maltby (eds).

Bondebjerg, I. (ed.) (2000) *Moving Images, Culture and the Mind*, Luton: University of Luton Press/John Libby Media.

Briggs, A. and Cobley, P. (eds) (1997) *The Media: An Introduction*, London: Addison Wesley Longman.

Crofts, S. (1993) 'Reconceptualising National Cinema/s', *Quarterly Review of Film and Video* 14, 3: 49–67.

—— (1998) 'Concepts of National Cinema', in J. Hill and P. Church Gibson (eds).

Hayward, S. (1993) *French National Cinema*, London: Routledge.

Higson, A. (1989) 'The Concept of National Cinema', *Screen* 30, 4: 36–46.

—— (1995) *Waving The Flag: Constructing a National Cinema in Britain*, Oxford: Clarendon Press.

—— (1997) 'Nationality and the Media', in A. Briggs and P. Cobley (eds).

—— (1999) 'Polyglot Films for an International Market: E. A. Dupont, the British Film Industry, and the Idea of a European Cinema', in A. Higson and R. Maltby (eds).

—— (2000a) 'National Cinemas, International Markets, Cross-Cultural Identities', in I. Bondebjerg (ed.).

—— (2000b) 'The Instability of the National', in J. Ashby and A. Higson (eds).

—— (2001) *English Heritage, English Cinema*, Oxford: Oxford University Press.

Higson, A. and Maltby, R. (eds) (1999) *'Film Europe' and 'Film America': Cinema, Commerce and Cultural Exchange, 1920–1939*, Exeter: Exeter University Press.

Hill, J. (1992) 'The Issue of National Cinema and British Film Production', in D. Petrie (ed.).

—— (1996) 'British Film Policy', in A. Moran (ed.).

—— (1997) 'British Cinema as National Cinema: Production, Audience and Representation', in R. Murphy (ed.).

—— (1999) *British Cinema in the 1980s*, Oxford: Oxford University Press.

Hill, J. and Church Gibson, P. (eds) (1998) *The Oxford Guide to Film Studies*, Oxford: Oxford University Press.

Moran, A. (ed.) (1996) *Film Policy: International, National and Regional Perspectives*, London: Routledge.

Morley, D. and Robins, K. (1990) 'No Place like Heimat: Images of Home(land) in European Culture', *New Formations* 12: 1–23.

Murphy, R. (ed.) (1997) *The British Cinema Book*, London: BFI.

Perrie, D. (ed.) (1992) *New Questions of British Cinema*, London: BFI.

Willemen, P. (1994) 'The National', in P. Willemen, *Looks and Frictions: Essays in Cultural Studies and Film Theory*, London/Bloomington: BFI/Indiana University Press.

Africans Filming Africa: Questioning Theories of an Authentic African Cinema

2

DAVID MURPHY

[. . .]

The cinema of sub-Saharan Africa began to emerge in the early 1960s, at the height of the process of decolonization. During the colonial era, cinematic images of Africa had been dominated by countless jungle epics, from the *Tarzan* series to *The African Queen* (1951) and the various adaptations of H. Rider Haggard's deeply racist 1885 novel, *King Solomon's Mines*.[1] Effectively, Western cinematic representations of Africa helped to reinforce the dominant Hegelian vision of Africa as a continent with no history and no culture.[2] Therefore, it came as no surprise that African filmmakers in the 1960s and 1970s set out to counter such demeaning and caricatural representations of Africa. At the second meeting of the federation of African filmmakers (FEPACI) in Algiers in 1975, this commitment to the development of an African cinema that would be radically different to previous cinematic representations of Africa was made explicit: not only should African films represent Africa from an African point of view, but they should also reject commercial, Western film codes.[3] However, many African directors have retreated somewhat from such radical calls over the past two decades, worrying far more about the problems of forging a popular African cinema and creating a viable African film industry. The reality of 'Africans filming Africa' has not produced a unified, 'authentic' African cinema. Rather, it has produced a series of complex and often contradictory visions of the continent. Therefore, it is one of the aims of this article to examine the representation of Africa in a number of African films in order to explore the different assumptions and concerns that emerge from these works. The films to be discussed are Djibril Diop Mambety's *Touki-Bouki* (Senegal, 1973), Ousmane Sembene's *Xala* (Senegal, 1974), and Souleymane Cissé's *Yeelen* (Mali, 1987), three radically different works with contrasting visions of Africa: *Touki-Bouki* is experimental and non-realistic; Sembene's film is deeply political and satirical; and *Yeelen* employs a mythical structure to explore the role of knowledge and power in Bambara society.

The second aim of this article is closely linked to the first: namely, to address the critical reception of African films, focusing in particular on the Western critic's relationship to African cinema. A great number of critics, both from Africa and the West, have argued, with differing degrees of subtlety and from varying standpoints, that the modern Western critic continues to be trapped within the Hegelian world-view that imagines Africa as a primitive and incomprehensible 'other.' I am in complete agreement with those who argue that the

Western critic must be sensitive to differing cultural values when dealing with African culture. However, to follow theorists such as Christopher Miller in calling for critics to interpret African culture from 'an authentically African point of view, interpreting African experience in *African terms*, perceiving rather than projecting' is another matter entirely (Miller 1990: 1). In the course of this article, I will argue against all notions of 'authenticity,' whatever their philosophical or ideological basis: in my view, there is no 'authentic' Africa, nor is there an 'authentic' West. This article will also engage with the issues raised by postcolonial theory, examining their relevance to the interpretation not only of African cinema, but contemporary African culture generally.

As sub-Saharan Africa was one of the last regions in the world to produce its own cinematic images, it probably should come as no surprise that critics have applied themselves so readily to the manner in which a 'true' African cinema should differ from other cinemas. For some Western critics, the emergence of African cinema was the source of a grave disappoint-ment. These critics did not know exactly what this cinema should be like, but they knew they wanted it to be radically different from everything that had come before. As the critic Serge Daney has claimed, a certain type of Western critic had been vaguely expecting African cinema to be a non-intellectual, all-singing, all-dancing extravaganza (Daney 1979). What room do such views leave for the films of Ousmane Sembene and Med Hondo which sought to produce a radical critique of independent African societies? The articulate and socially committed cinema represented by these directors was simply too 'Western' for these critics.

However, there were just as many left-wing critics, both African and Western, who readily saw such radical African films as defining the 'true' African cinema.[4] The mood of revolutionary optimism which accompanied the process of decolonization saw the birth of the theory of what was to become known as 'Third Cinema,' which was first developed in South America and which stressed the political function of cinema.[5] Those critics who have advocated the theory of a 'Third Cinema' have stressed that 'authentic' Third World films must abandon the structures and thematic concerns of commercial Western cinema. This ideological impera-tive is clearly at the heart of Sembene's work, and he has often stressed the need to move away from the preoccupations of Western cinema and, more particularly, from its stereotypical images of Africa. However, does this mean that Sembene's work is 'authentically' African? If it is 'authentically' African, should we then consider the experimental and dreamlike films of Djibril Diop Mambety, which are primarily concerned with cultural issues, to be somehow less African? Or what of the mythical structure of Souleymane Cissé's *Yeelen*?

Debates upon the nature of African cinema have too often been trapped within a reductive opposition between Western and African culture. This argument proposes that an 'authentic' African film must not only exclude all things European or Western, but must also set itself up in opposition to them. If we follow this argument to its logical conclusion, then all African films are 'inauthentic' or 'Western' simply because cinema was first invented in the West. However, if we remove this strict opposition between the West and the rest of the world, we get a much better view of the way in which different cultures interact with and influence one another. Cultural influence is not simply a one-way street with the West influencing the rest.[6] Africa and the West are not mutually exclusive worlds that possess their own authentic and unchanging identites: they are hybrid entities that influence and modify each other, and this process of exchange applies to cinema (although in the current world order, the West remains the dominant force in this process of hybridization).

I would now like to look more closely at the three films under discussion, beginning with two Senegalese films: Sembene's *Xala* and Mambety's *Touki-Bouki*. These two films provide a very useful point of departure for this discussion, as they are both films that portray post-independence Senegalese society in the early 1970s. However, the two directors represent their country in radically different ways. *Xala* is a Marxist-inspired attack on the neocolonial state, and it has been hailed as a classic example of 'Third Cinema.' *Touki-Bouki*, on the other hand, is a complex and confusing meditation on culture, modernity and alienation, and it was immediately greeted by many critics as Africa's first genuine *avant-garde* movie.

Xala is essentially the satirical story of El Hadji Abdou Kader Bèye, a businessman who has just acceded to the Dakar Chamber of Commerce with his Senegalese colleagues, replacing their white French counterparts. On this very same day, El Hadji is to marry his third wife. As both a businessman and a respectable Muslim, El Hadji would appear to have reached the top of the social ladder. However, disaster strikes on his wedding night, when he is struck down with the *xala*, the curse of impotence. His impotence eventually leads him to financial ruin and personal humiliation at the hands of a group of beggars who turn out to be responsible for the curse. The political symbolism is plain to see: the neocolonial bourgeoisie are presented as an impotent class whose downfall will be brought about by the destitute and the oppressed of their society.

Such a militant approach was lauded by critics in the heyday of Third Cinema in the 1970s (Gabriel 1982: 77–86). However, in the sceptical 1980s and 1990s, poststructuralism, with its distrust of totalizing meta-narratives (and Marxism chief amongst them), had become the dominant critical credo. This has led to Sembene's films being attacked by critics such as Olivier Barlet and Kenneth Harrow, who characterize them as being based on a series of simplistic oppositions: West versus Africa, urban versus rural, rich versus poor, etc.[7] Harrow's critique of Sembene's film *Camp de Thiaroye* is a particularly pernicious example of such criticism (Harrow 1995). Sembene's insistence on the oppressive nature of the French colonial regime in this film is interpreted by Harrow as an instance of the former's adherence to the rules of Marxist reasoning, with its alleged dependence on simplistic, binary opposites. Harrow conveniently omits any references to the numerous scenes in which Sembene clearly shows that it is African soldiers who are guarding the camp in which the *tirailleurs sénégalais* are imprisoned. Equally, citing what he sees as other cases of oppressor/victim relationships in Sembene's work, Harrow neglects to mention the film *Emitaï*, in which African colonial troops shoot unarmed African villagers.

Although Sembene's work is highly political, with more than a touch of didacticism, I believe that Barlet and Harrow present a wildly inaccurate picture of his films. It is true that *Xala* does not hide its socialist agenda, but it also presents an extremely complex vision of Senegalese society, addressing questions of gender as well as social, cultural, economic and political factors. The film is not a simplistic work of propaganda: it is deeply concerned with the rituals and symbols of Senegalese society, particularly those of the emerging urban bourgeoisie.

One of the most effective ways in which the film examines these issues is through the use of costume. In this respect, El Hadji's third wife, Ngoné, is a particularly useful example. She is introduced to the spectator at the wedding reception, where she is wearing a Western-style wedding dress. As she arrives, the camera moves in for a closeup of the wedding cake, on top of which we see a plastic model of a white bride and groom. The incongruity of the whole wedding becomes apparent in this one image. Aspiring to Western middle-class standards involves copying the Western marriage down to the last detail, including the white wedding dress that has no place in either Islamic or African animistic practices.

Ngoné's real value to El Hadji is shown in the scene where the matchmaker prepares the bride for the consummation of the marriage. This scene makes it clear that Ngoné is merely a sexual object that El Hadji has acquired. As the matchmaker undresses her and gives her advice on how to fulfil her 'traditional' duties as a wife, we see a nude photograph of Ngoné on the wall in the background. Shot in profile, showing Ngoné's bare back and a glimpse of one of her breasts, the photograph acts as a sexual promise of what the marriage is supposed to bring to El Hadji. The eroticized Ngoné of the photograph is the one that he is marrying. As the matchmaker finishes speaking, Ngoné turns around and we see her bare breasts, which are mostly hidden in the 'tasteful' photograph. El Hadji is about to realize his wish: the image is about to take flesh (until the *xala* strikes, that is). This commodification of Ngoné is evident from the extravagances of the wedding reception and the presents which are lavished upon her as part of her dowry. Chief amongst these presents is the car. As El Hadji arrives at Ngoné's house to consummate the marriage after he has been temporarily cured, he pauses to kiss the ribbon on the car. He believes that he will finally be able to enjoy his new possession but is once again left disappointed, as this time Ngoné is having her period. In *Xala*, money, sexual politics, Islamic culture and animism are all jumbled together in a complex mix of rituals and symbols. It is not Western influence that Sembéne rejects (as Barlet and Harrow suggest) but Western capitalism.

As I have already argued, the reductive opposition between Africa and the West merely produces a sterile stand-off between the different cultural influences which are so clearly present in African films, and no more so than in Mambety's work. Mambety borrows heavily from Western experimental films in *Touki-Bouki*, but in the process he creates something radically different, adapting such models to his own culture. In fact, *Touki-Bouki* can be read as an exploration of the cultural encounter between the West and Africa. The film tells the tale of a young Senegalese couple, Mory and Anta, who long to escape from their home town of Dakar to the promised land of France, where they hope to find the money that will allow them to return rich and famous to their homeland.

As we see in the opening sequence of the film, Mambety uses a complex array of imagery to reflect this contradictory pull between France and Africa. He deliberately plays around with the standard binary opposition between Africa and the West. In a static, medium-distance shot, we see a small boy riding on an ox's back, slowly advancing across the open savannah towards the camera. On the soundtrack, we hear what seems to be a 'traditional' African tune, played on a wind instrument. The spectator is led to expect a tale of rural Africa, perhaps even a tale of a simple, African past. However, as boy and beast move into the foreground, the sound of an engine revving up begins to vie with and eventually to dominate the sound of the music. The image then cuts to a shot of Mory, the male hero of the story, riding along on his motorbike. Filmed from the position of a pillion passenger over Mory's shoulder, the shot conveys a sense of speed and exhilaration far removed from the peace and calm of the preceding rural imagery. Time and location are fragmented as the spectator is shaken out of his/her original expectations and thrust into a tale of modern Africa, complete with motorbikes, motorways and machinery.

Despite the sudden intrusion of modern, technological artifacts, a visual link to the preceding rural scene remains in the shape of an ox's skull attached to the front of Mory's motorbike. In fact, the horns of the skull act as a sort of frame through which we observe the rapidly passing urban landscape. Essentially, Mambety provides us with a vision of an Africa in which the 'modern,' technological world is to be found side by side with the 'traditional,' rural world. As one of the characters in the film puts it, Mory is unsure whether he is driving an ox or a motorbike. He is the hybrid product of two vastly different cultures. The meeting of Africa and the West has created a new reality, sometimes exciting and dynamic, sometimes menacing and destructive. In many ways, Mambety's cinema itself stands as an example of the diversity and richness of this new culture, while also warning of its dangers.

Mambety rejects the openly political and social considerations of many African filmmakers of the 1970s, including Sembene. Indeed, in one highly significant scene early in the film, Mory is attacked by a group of young, left-wing intellectuals who despise him for his apolitical, amoral lifestyle. This scene can be read as Mambety thumbing his nose at those who would have him present a political agenda in his films. Equally, the figure of the postman who wanders aimlessly through the film appears to be a sideswipe at the figure of the postman in Sembene's film *Mandabi*, who is portrayed as someone who 'delivers' hope in the form of the film's political message of social solidarity. These anti-political elements do not mean that Mambety's films are not political, simply that he sees the world primarily in terms of culture rather than politics.

For the Western spectator, the narratives of *Xala* and *Touki-Bouki* reveal certain recognizable elements. *Xala* works broadly within a social realist framework, using a number of Brechtian symbolic devices. One can also readily identify the influence of a number of experimental Western movies on *Touki-Bouki*: firstly, one could mention *Easy Rider* and its psychedelic tale of the adventures of two drug-fuelled bikers; we might also think of Nicholas Roeg's films, especially *Performance*, and their blurring of identity, location, gender and time.

A number of African critics have reacted angrily to the cataloguing of Western influences in African cinema. In fact, many critics have convincingly argued that African cinema has borrowed heavily from the oral tradition (Barlet 1996: 157–99; Diawara 1996: 209–18). For example, both *Xala* and *Touki-Bouki* reproduce elements of traditional 'trickster' tales.[8] The archetypal 'trickster' narratives are those concerning *Leuk-le-lièvre*, the African forefather of the 'Brer Rabbit' character in the tales of the American South. Indeed, the title *Touki-Bouki*, which means 'the hyena's voyage,' evokes another staple character of the 'trickster' tale, the hyena; in West African folk tradition, the hyena, regarded as a cunning, deceitful animal that cannot be trusted, plays the role often attributed to the fox in the West. As in these traditional 'trickster' tales, the protagonists in both films are set a number of challenges with a prize waiting at the end. In *Touki-Bouki*, Mory and Anta deceive a number of hapless victims only to see the prize of their glorious journey to France ruined by Mory's last-minute change of heart. In *Xala*, El Hadji becomes the hapless victim, rather than the perpetrator, of deceit and cunning as he is set a number of tasks to overcome his impotence. A man who has callously deceived people in the past, El Hadji is forced to meet the fate that he has doled out to others.

However, the exploration of cinematic links to orality often overlooks the fact that African cinema, while providing a certain continuity with elements of the oral tradition, also constitutes a major rupture with that tradition. Cinema literally introduces a different way of seeing and representing the world to the stories of the *griot*, the guardian of the spoken word in Africa: a film, with its particular emphasis on spatial and temporal representation, introduces radically different questions to the oral performances of a *griot*. The oral tradition informs the work of African directors such as Sembene, Mambety and Cissé, but it cannot be cited as the sole determining factor in the production of African cinematic representations. If elements of orality are used in African films, they must be adapted to the expressive potential of the cinema as a medium. Equally, it is wrong to assume that African cinema audiences can only understand films that work within the structures of their own oral tradition. For generations now, Africans have been viewing Kung Fu movies and Indian melodramas, although they often respond to these films as though attending an oral performance (jumping up and down, clapping, imitating the actors). The relationship between the paying cinema spectator and a film, and the relationship between listener and storyteller, are vastly different. For example, films cannot engage in a dialogue with members of the audience as happens in a traditional oral performance. Above all, it should not be forgotten that films are commercial enterprises. One must pay to enter the cinema: it is not a 'traditional' communal gathering.

The examination of the final film under discussion here, *Yeelen* (1987), made by the Malian director, Souleymane Cissé, will focus on critical reactions rather than detailed analysis of the film itself. Cissé had begun his career with social realist films in the mode of Sembene, but *Yeelen* marked a major departure with its exploration of mythology and the supernatural in a rural African society. The first African film to win a prize at the Cannes Film Festival, and also a popular success in Europe, it has been the focus of intense critical debate. Some critics see *Yeelen* as the first genuine example of a truly African film both in terms of its style and content, while others have denounced it for reproducing the anthropological gaze and pandering to exotic Western stereotypes of Africa.[9] However, critics have managed to agree on one point at least: namely, that the film is very complex, and deeply embedded in the culture of the Bambara people of the Western Sudan, particularly the rituals of the secret society of the Komo.

The film takes place at an unspecified moment in the precolonial era, and it tells the story of Nianankoro, son of one of the elders of the Komo. Nianankoro, an adept of the society, is impatient at having to wait to learn the secrets of the Komo, so he steals one of the sacred fetishes and flees his homeland. However, he is eventually tracked down by his father, and in the film's final showdown, both father and son are killed. Despite the mythical trappings of the story, Cissé has consistently argued that *Yeelen* is, in fact, his most politicized work, and not simply an escape into a glorified African past. Far from pandering to the exotic fantasies of the West, the film attempts to explore a 'modernist' vision of Bambara culture, which stresses the power of so-called traditional cultures to modify and develop rather than act as endless repetitions of themselves.

The film criticizes the abuse of power and knowledge by the elders of the Komo, and it presents the ultimate act of transgression in revealing their supernatural power both to Nianankoro and to the cinema spectator. Much has been written about Cissé's meticulous recreation of the rituals of the Komo, particularly in the long scene in which we see the elders of the Komo venting their anger against Nianankoro.[10] However, is it absolutely necessary to understand the intricacies of the Komo in order to understand the film's discussion of the wresting of power and knowledge from what is presented as an oppressive and corrupt elite? Certain African critics have lambasted their Western counterparts for their 'misreadings' of *Yeelen*, which they see as the result of their ignorance of Bambara culture.[11] It is indeed salutary that Western critics, with our tendency to universalize our own experience, should be reminded of the cultural specificity of African cultural artefacts. However, speaking as a Western critic, I feel that I am in good company in not understanding the full complexities of the Komo. For a start, Africans other than Bambaras might be a bit nonplussed at certain points in the film. In fact, even Bambaras cannot be expected to understand all of the film's many-layered symbols, for the simple reason that only a select few are supposed to know all seven levels of the Komo. In this context, one simply cannot posit an accurate and 'authentic' African interpretation of the film against which one can oppose a simplistic, Western version. In fact, the film provides sufficient information within its narrative structure for viewers to comprehend the most important elements of the story. For example, in the scene featuring the rituals of the Komo, the anger of the elders and their fear at the potential loss of their privileged position is clear to the average, film-literate spectator. The film may imitate the complex structures of Bambara mythology, but its cinematic narrative retains more than enough 'legibility' as a film for the uninitiated cinema spectator to interpret the basic story.

It is not my purpose here to encourage 'universalist' readings of African films. On the contrary, I am in favour of using a cultural materialist framework that attempts to situate a film within its specific cultural context, and Western critics should indeed investigate the structures of Bambara society when examining *Yeelen*. However, I feel it is vital to reject the notion that only Africans can 'accurately' interpret African texts. The assumption on the part of Christopher Miller (quoted at the beginning of this article), that there is an *authentic* African point of view to which the Western critic should vainly aspire, is vitally flawed. While one cannot but accept that an African critic may very well have a different set of assumptions from the Western critic, there is absolutely no means of establishing the existence of a single, unified African view on African issues. The Western critic will always display some degree of 'ethnocentrism,' and this must be taken into account when appraising his/her work, but it should in no way be used to disqualify such work. In fact, as Mikhail Bakhtin has argued, an outsider's view of a culture can be deeply enriching for both parties:

> *Creative understanding* does not renounce itself, its own place and time, its own culture; and it forgets nothing. In order to understand, it is immensely important for the person who understands to be *located outside* the object of his/her creative understanding – in time, in space, in culture. In the realm of culture, outsideness is a most powerful factor in understanding . . . We raise new questions for a foreign culture, ones that it did not raise for itself; we seek answers to our own questions in it; and the foreign culture responds to us by revealing to us its new aspects and new semantic depths. Without *one's own* questions one cannot creatively understand anything other or foreign.
>
> (Quoted in Willemen 1989: 26)

Attempts to understand 'others' must be accompanied by a recognition of our own cultural specificity.

Each of the three films discussed in this article presents a different cinematic and ideological vision of Africa. Therefore, what conclusions can we draw about the category of 'African cinema'? The filmmaker and critic James Potts has noted the tendency within Africa and the West to make sweeping generalizations about the nature of 'black' or 'African cinema.' Not only do such arguments neglect the vast cultural diversity of the African continent, but they also assume that it is possible to create radically different film 'languages.' Having worked as a technical adviser on film projects in Ethiopia and Kenya over a five-year period, Potts was able to experience the problems of filmmaking in Africa first-hand. This leads him to argue that the technical limitations within which African filmmakers are forced to work can be shown to impose an aesthetic on a film far more readily than do the director's ethnic origins. Essentially, Potts believes that we do not yet have the theoretical basis to talk about national or ethnic film styles. Instead, he proposes an approach that attempts to negotiate the relationship between the 'universal' and the 'local' aspects of filmmaking:

> I still prefer to think that film-making is a form of universal speech – not so much a 'Visual Esperanto' as a developing visual language with a rich variety of dialects and idiolects which contain both alien and indigenous elements. These elements must be studied more closely and made more explicit if genuine intercultural communication is to take place.
>
> (Potts 1979: 81)

I believe that this approach allows us to develop a more complex vision of African cinema, viewing it in terms of its ability to adapt and modify established film codes from around the world. Therefore, the category of African cinema should be used descriptively rather than prescriptively: one cannot force the cinema of an entire continent to adhere to some preordained programme.

This is even more true when one attempts to create intercontinental categories: for example, as was argued above, most theorists of 'Third Cinema' sought to characterize the cinematic production of the entire Third World, not just Africa, as revolutionary and fundamentally opposed to Western hegemony, both in terms of style and content, a characterization that simply did not reflect reality (and which also grossly over-simplified the nature of 'Western' cinema).[12] I believe that the category of the post-colonial offers a better framework within which to examine the cinematic production of those countries that were formerly colonies of the Western imperial powers. As with all categories and schools, critics are not in complete agreement as to the definition of 'post-colonialism.' In fact, one cannot speak of post-colonialism as a single entity, as it comprises critics working from vastly different critical perspectives, from Marxists to feminists to post-structuralists. Essentially, post-colonialism applies these different approaches in an exploration of the links between cultures that have experienced colonization by one of the Western powers. However, as many critics have pointed out, post-colonialism runs the danger of viewing a nation's entire history through the prism of the colonial encounter, tying the former colonizer and the former colonized together in a permanent if reluctant embrace.

This has led a number of critics to reject post-colonial theory, claiming that it is distinctly Eurocentric in its approach, precisely because of its privileging of the colonial era. Aijaz Ahmad argues this case in the following quotation:

> In periodizing our history in the triadic terms of precolonial, colonial and postcolonial, the conceptual apparatus of 'postcolonial criticism' privileges as primary the role of colonialism as the principle of structuration in that history, so that all that came before colonialism becomes its own prehistory and whatever comes after can only be lived as infinite aftermath. That may well be how it appears to those who look at that history from the *outside* – to those, in other words, who look at the former colonies in Asia and Africa from *inside* the advanced capitalist countries – but not to those who live *inside* that history.
>
> (Ahmad 1996: 280–81; my italics)

Essentially, Ahmad accuses 'postcolonial theory' of maintaining the colonial paradigm in which Africa (and Asia) are viewed as the object of Western actions rather than as active participants in the making of their own history. As a Marxist, Ahmad believes that it is the fact of 'capitalist modernity' and its implications for African and Asian societies that links their literatures and cultures together. While recognizing the value and power of 'postcolonialism' as a category, he rightly warns that when applied too loosely it becomes mere jargon.

However, it is a gross simplification to say that all post-colonial theory is merely obsessed with the relationship between Africa and its former colonial masters. In fact, post-colonial theory has been greatly effective in forging links across the 'peripheral,' formerly colonized world, bypassing the 'centres' of Western power altogether. This forging of links along the periphery highlights the structures of power in the modern world. Such a move is particularly welcome in African cultural studies: it is all too common for African films and novels from different ends of the continent to be thrown together on the basis that they express some form of common, authentic African identity. In contrast, post-colonialism explores links between African cultures in the light of their shared history of colonial exploitation and their rebellion against this oppression (without assuming that this shared experience is identical in every African state). The three African films discussed in this article could all be fruitfully analysed within a post-colonial critical framework that seeks to explore cultural and political forces in a world that remains dominated by Western capital: the examination of neo-colonial Africa in Xala and Touki-Bouki is plain to see, but Yeelen, with its desire to present an African vision of modernity, can equally be argued to be challenging Western perceptions of knowledge in Africa. As Homi K. Bhabha has argued: 'Postcolonial criticism bears witness to the unequal and uneven forces of cultural representation involved in the contest for political and social authority within the modern world order' (Bhabha 1994: 171). I believe that this fact alone makes the post-colonial an extremely useful and strategic critical term in the analysis of contemporary African culture.

References

Ahmad, Aijaz. 1996. The politics of literary postcoloniality. In *Contemporary Postcolonial Theory: a Reader*, ed. by Padmini Mongia, pp. 276–93, London: Arnold.

Bakari, Imruh, and Mbye Cham (eds). 1996. *African Experiences of Cinema*, London: British Film Institute.

Barlet, Olivier. 1996. *Les Cinémas en Afrique noire: le regard en question*, Paris: L'Harmattan.

Bhabha, Homi K. 1994. The postcolonial and the postmodern: the question of agency. In his *The Location of Culture*, pp. 171–97, London and New York: Routledge.

Bory, Jean-Louis. 1968. La nouvelle arme du tiers monde. *Nouvel Observateur* (28 October–3 November): 50–51.

Cameron, Kenneth M. 1994. *Africa on Film: Beyond Black and White*, New York: Continuum.

Cham, Mbye Boubacar. 1982. Ousmane Sembene and the aesthetics of oral African traditions, *Africana Journal* 13 (1–4): 24–40.

Copans, Jean (ed). 1975. *Anthropologie et impérialisme*, Paris Maspéro.

Daney, Serge. 1979. *Ceddo* (O. Sembene), *Cahiers du cinéma* 304: 51–53.

Diawara, Manthia. 1992. *African Cinema: Politics and Culture*, Bloomington: Indiana University Press.

——. 1996. Popular culture and oral traditions in African film. In *African Experiences of Cinema*, ed. by Imruh Bakari and Mbye Cham, pp. 209–18. London: British Film Institute.

Gabriel, Teshome H. 1982. *Third Cinema in the Third World: the Aesthetics of Liberation*, London: Bowker.

Gentile, Philip. 1995. In the midst of secrets: Souleymane Cissé's Yeelen. *Iris: A Journal of Theory on Image and Sound* 18: 125–35.

Harrow, Kenneth W. 1995. *Camp de Thiaroye*: who's that hiding in those tanks and how come we can't see their faces? *Iris: A Journal of Theory on Image and Sound* 18: 147–52.

Kariithi, Nixon K. 1995. Misreading culture and tradition: Western critical appreciation of African films. In *Africa and the Centenary of Cinema/L'Afrique et le centenaire du cinéma*, ed. by Gaston Kaboré, pp. 166–87. Paris: Présence Africaine.

Miller, Christopher L. 1990. *Theories of Africans: Francophone Literature and Anthropology in Africa*. Chicago and London: University of Chicago Press.

Potts, James. 1979. Is there an international film language? *Sight and Sound* 48 (2): 74–81.

Solanas, Fernando and Octavio Getino. 1971. Towards a Third Cinema. *Afterimage* 3: 16–35.

Ukadike, Nwachukwu Frank. 1994. *Black African Cinema*. Berkeley, Los Angeles, London: University of California Press.

Willemen, Paul. 1989. The Third Cinema question: notes and reflections. In *Questions of Third Cinema*, ed. by Jim Pines and Paul Willemen, pp. 1–29. London: British Film Institute.

Notes

1 There have been three Hollywood versions of Haggard's 1885 novel (1937, 1950, 1987), and there have been countless versions of the the Tarzan story from the 1920s to the 1980s. See Cameron (1994).

2 Anthropological films provide the other main source of cinematic representations of Africa. The problematic relationship between colonialism and the anthropological project in Africa (with many colonial administrators also working as anthropologists) has been well documented (Copans 1975). Anthropological films have been criticized for presenting an image of Africa as primitive and ahistorical. Essentially, they are argued to be 'external' representations of Africa. Even the work of the French filmmaker Jean Rouch, which seeks to problematize this anthropological gaze, has been accused of producing films in which Africans remain objects of Western discourse rather than autonomous subjects.

3 The full text of the Algiers charter on African cinema is to be found in Bakari (1996: 27–30).

4 The French journalist Jean-Louis Bory championed 'radical' African films in his column in the *Nouvel Observateur* (Bory 1968). One of the most influential works on the theory of 'Third Cinema' is Gabriel (1982).

5 For an example of Third Cinema theory, see Solanas and Getino (1971). The article was originally published in Spanish in 1969.

6 A fascinating example of the circulation of cultural influences can be found in the work of the late Japanese director, Akira Kurosawa. His early films were heavily influenced by American westerns. Then, as Kurosawa became an established figure in world cinema, his films in turn became models for American directors to copy. African cinema has not yet reached a prominent cultural position within the Western world (not even on the arthouse circuit) that would allow it to influence a generation of aspiring Western filmmakers.

However, in other cultural spheres, African cultural influence is clearly visible. For example, African/black music is recognized as a major influence on the development of Western popular music since the 1950s.

7 Throughout his book, Barlet (1996) continually refers to Sembene as a filmmaker who rejects the influence of the West in his films.

8 For a discussion of orality in relation to Sembene's work, including analysis of 'trickster' narratives, see Cham (1982).

9 Manthia Diawara praises *Yeelen* for creating an African cinema which 'obeys the *mise-en-scène* of the oral tradition' (Diawara 1992: 164). Nwachukwu Frank Ukadike also praises the film's inventiveness in imitating the structures of orality, but he is wary of the film's 'universalism,' which is seen to be the result of the targetting of 'foreign' (i.e. Western) audiences (Ukadike 1994: 254–62).

10 For example, see Philip Gentile's examination of the film's depiction of the rituals of the Komo (Gentile 1995).

11 For instance, see the scathing comments made by Nixon K. Kariithi about Western 'misreadings' of *Yeelen* and other African films (Kariithi 1995).

12 In his excellent introduction to *Questions of Third Cinema*, Paul Willemen expresses similar doubts about the homogenous and over-simplified picture of Third World Cinema that was emerging from the work of critics such as Teshome Gabriel (Willemen 1989: 15–17).

Post–Third-Worldist Culture: Gender, Nation, and the Cinema

3

ELLA SHOHAT

At a time when the *grands récits* of the West have been told and retold ad infinitum, when a certain postmodernism (Lyotard) speaks of an "end" to metanarratives, and when Fukayama speaks of an "end of history," we must ask: precisely whose narrative and whose history is being declared at an "end"?[1] Hegemonic Europe may clearly have begun to deplete its strategic repertoire of stories, but Third-World peoples, First-World minoritarian communities, women, and gays and lesbians have only begun to tell, and deconstruct, theirs. For the "Third World," this cinematic counter-telling basically began with the postwar collapse of the European empires and the emergence of independent nation-states. In the face of Eurocentric historicizing, the Third World and its diasporas in the First World have rewritten their own histories, taken control over their own images, spoken in their own voices, reclaiming and reaccentuating colonialism and its ramifications in the present in a vast project of remapping and renaming. Third-World feminists, for their part, have participated in these counternarratives, while insisting that colonialism and national resistance have impinged differently on men and women, and that remapping and renaming is not without its fissures and contradictions.

Although relatively small in number, women directors and producers in the "Third World" already played a role in film production in the first half of this century: Aziza Amir, Assia Daghir, and Fatima Rushdi in Egypt; Carmen Santos and Gilda de Abreu in Brazil; Emilia Saleny in Argentina; and Adela Sequeyro, Matilda Landeta, Candida Beltran Rondon, and Eva Liminano in Mexico. However, their films, even when focusing on female protagonists, were not explicitly feminist in the sense of a declared political project to empower women in the context of both patriarchy and (neo)colonialism. In the postindependence or post-revolution era, women, despite their growing contribution to the diverse aspects of film production, remained less visible than men in the role of film direction. Furthermore, Third-Worldist revolutionary cinemas in places such as China, Cuba, Senegal, and Algeria were not generally shaped by an anticolonial feminist imaginary. As is the case with First-World cinema, women's participation within Third-World cinema has hardly been central, although their growing production over the last decade corresponds to a worldwide burgeoning movement of independent work by women, made possible by new, low-cost technologies of video communication. But quite apart from this relative democratization through technology, postindependence history, with the gradual eclipse of Third-Worldist nationalism and the growth of women's grass roots local organizing, also helps us to understand the emergence of what I call "post–Third-Worldist"[2] feminist film and video.

Here, I am interested in examining recent feminist film and video work within the context of post–Third-Worldist film culture as a simultaneous critique both of Third-Worldist anticolonial nationalism and of First-World Eurocentric feminism. Challenging white feminist film theory and practice that emerged in a major way in the 1970s in First-World metropolises, post–Third-Worldist feminist works have refused a Eurocentric universalizing of "woman-hood," and even of "feminism." Eschewing a discourse of universality, such feminisms claim a "location,"[3] arguing for specific forms of resistance in relation to diverse forms of oppression. Aware of white women's advantageous positioning within (neo)colonialist and racist systems, feminist struggles in the Third World (including that in the First World) have not been premised on a facile discourse of global sisterhood, and have often been made within the context of anticolonial and antiracist struggles. But the growing feminist critique of Third-World nationalisms translates those many disappointed hopes for women's empowerment invested in a Third-Worldist national transformation. Navigating between the excommunication as "traitors to the nation" and "betraying the race" by patriarchal nationalism, and the imperial rescue fantasies of clitoridectomized and veiled women proffered by Eurocentric feminism, post–Third-Worldist feminists have not suddenly metamorphosized into "Western" feminists. Feminists of color have, from the outset, been engaged in analysis and activism around the intersection of nation/race/gender. Therefore, while still resisting the ongoing (neo)colonized situation of the "nation" and/or "race," post–Third-Worldist feminist cultural practices also break away from the narrative of the "nation" as a unified entity so as to articulate a contextualized history for women in specific geographies of identity. Such feminist projects, in other words, are often posited in relation to ethnic, racial, regional, and national locations.

[. . .]

Rather than merely "extending" a preexisting First-World feminism, as a certain Euro-"diffusionism"[4] would have it, post–Third-Worldist cultural theories and practices create a more complex space for feminisms open to the specificity of community culture and history. To counter some of the patronizing attitudes toward (post)Third-World feminist filmmakers—the dark women who now also do the "feminist thing"—it is necessary to contextualize feminist work in national/racial discourses locally and globally inscribed within multiple oppressions and resistances. Third-World feminist histories can be understood as feminist if seen in conjunction with the resistance work these women have performed within their communities and nations. Any serious discussion of feminist cinema must therefore engage the complex question of the "national." Third-Worldist films are often produced within the legal codes of the nation-state, often in (hegemonic) national languages, recycling national intertexts (literatures, oral narratives, music), projecting national imaginaries. But if First-World filmmakers have seemed to float "above" petty nationalist concerns, it is because they take for granted the projection of a national power that facilitates the making and the dissemination of their films. The geopolitical positioning of Third-World nation-states continues to imply that their filmmakers cannot assume a substratum of national power.

Here, I am interested in examining the contemporary work of post–Third-Worldist feminist film- and videomakers in light of the ongoing critique of the racialized inequality of the geopolitical distribution of resources and power as a way of looking into the dynamics of rupture and continuity with regard to the antecedent Third-Worldist film culture. These texts, I argue, challenge the masculinist contours of the "nation in order to continue a feminist decolonization of Third-Worldist historiography, as much as they continue a multicultural decolonization of feminist historiography. My attempt to forge a "beginning" of a post–Third-Worldist narrative for recent film and video work by diverse Third-World, multicultural, diasporic feminists is not intended as an exhaustive survey of the entire spectrum of generic practices. Rather, by highlighting works embedded in the intersection between gender/sexuality and nation/race, this essay attempts to situate such cultural practices. It looks at a moment of historical rupture and continuity, when the macronarrative of women's liberation has long since subsided yet sexism and heterosexism prevail, and in an age when the metanarratives of anticolonial revolution have long since been eclipsed yet (neo)colonialism and racism persist. What, then, are some of the new modes of a multicultural feminist aesthetics of resistance? And in what ways do they simultaneously continue and rupture previous Third-Worldist film culture?

The Eclipse of the Revolutionary Paradigm

Third-Worldist films by women assumed that revolution was crucial for the empowering of women, that the revolution was integral to feminist aspirations. Sarah Maldoror's short film *Monangambe* (Mozambique, 1970) narrates the visit of an Angolan woman to see her husband who has been imprisoned by the Portuguese, while her feature film *Sambizanga* (Mozambique, 1972), based on the struggle of the MPLA in Angola, depicts a woman coming to revolutionary consciousness. Heiny Srour's documentary *Saat al Tahrir* (The Hour of Liberation, Oman, 1973) privileges the role of women fighters as it looks at the revolutionary struggle in Oman, and her *Leila wal dhiab* (Leila and the Wolves, Lebanon, 1984) focuses on the role of women in the Palestine Liberation Movement. Helena Solberg Ladd's *Nicaragua Up From the Ashes* (U.S., 1982) foregrounds the role of women in the Sandanista revolution. Sara Gomez's well-known film *De cierta manera* (One Way or Another, Cuba, 1975), often cited as part of the late 1970s and early 1980s Third-Worldist debates around women's position in revolutionary movements, interweaves documentary and fiction as part of a feminist critique of the Cuban revolution. From a decidedly pro-revolutionary perspective, the film deploys images of building and construction to metaphorize the need for further revolutionary changes. Macho culture is dissected and analyzed within the overlaid cultural histories (African, European, and Cuban), in terms of the need to revolutionize gender relations in the postrevolution era.

Already in the late 1960s and early 1970s, in the wake of the Vietnamese victory over the French, the Cuban revolution, and Algerian independence, Third-Worldist film ideology was crystallized in a wave of militant manifestos—Glauber Rocha's "Aesthetic of Hunger," (1965), Fernando Solanas and Octavio Getino's "Towards a Third Cinema," (1969), and Julio García Espinosa's "For an Imperfect Cinema" (1969)—and in declarations from Third-World film festivals calling for a tricontinental revolution in politics and an aesthetic and narrative revolution in film form.[5] Within the spirit of a politicized auteurism, Rocha demanded a "hungry" cinema of "sad, ugly films"; Solanas and Getino urged militant guerrilla documentaries; and Espinosa advocated an "imperfect" cinema energized by the "low" forms of popular culture. But the resistant practices of such films are neither homogeneous nor static; they vary over time, from region to region, and, in genre, from epic costume drama to personal small-budget documentary. Their aesthetic strategies range from "progressive realist" to Brechtian deconstructivist to avant-gardist, tropicalist, and resistant postmodern.[6] In their search for an alternative to the dominating style of Hollywood, such films shared a certain preoccupation with First-World feminist independent films which sought alternative images of women. The project of digging into "herstories" involved a search for new cinematic and narrative forms that challenged both the canonical documentaries and mainstream fiction films, subverting the notion of "narrative pleasure" based on the "male gaze." As with Third-Worldist cinema and with First-World independent production, post–Third-Worldist feminist films and videos conduct a struggle on two fronts, at once aesthetic and political, synthesizing revisionist historiography with formal innovation.

The early period of Third-Worldist euphoria has given way to the collapse of Communism, the indefinite postponement of the devoutly wished "tricontinental revolution," the realization that the "wretched of the earth" are not unanimously revolutionary (nor necessarily allies to one another), the appearance of an array of Third-World despots, and the recognition that international geopolitics and the global economic system have forced even the "Second World" to be incorporated into transnational capitalism. Recent years have even witnessed a crisis around the term "Third World" itself; it is now seen as an inconvenient relic of a more militant period. Some have argued that Third-World theory is an open-ended ideological interpellation that papers over class oppression in all three worlds, while limiting socialism to the now nonexistent second world.[7] Three-worlds theory not only flattens heterogeneities, masks contradictions, and elides differences, but also obscures similarities (for example, the common presence of the "Fourth-World," or indigenous, peoples in both "Third-World" and "First-World" countries). Third-World feminist critics such as Nawal El-Saadawi (Egypt), Vina Mazumdar (India), Kumari Jayawardena (Sri Lanka), Fatima Mernissi (Morocco), and Lelia Gonzales (Brazil) have explored these differences and similarities in a feminist light, pointing to the gendered limitations of Third-World nationalism.

But even within the current situation of "dispersed hegemonies" (Arjun Appadurai),[8] the historical thread or inertia of First-World domination remains a powerful presence. Despite the imbrication of "First" and "Third" worlds, the global distribution of power still tends to make the First-World countries cultural "transmitters" and the Third-World countries "receivers." (One byproduct of this situation is that First-World "minorities" have the power to project their cultural productions around the globe). While the Third World is inundated with North American films, TV series, popular music, and news programs, the First World receives precious little of the vast cultural production of the Third World, and what it does receive is usually mediated by multinational corporations.[9] These processes are not entirely negative, of course. The same multinational corporations that disseminate inane blockbusters and canned sitcoms also spread Afro-diasporic music, such as reggae and rap, around the globe. The problem lies not in the exchange but in the unequal terms on which the exchange takes place.[10]

At the same time, the media-imperialism thesis, which was dominant in the 1970s, needs drastic retooling. First, it is simplistic to imagine an active First World simply forcing its products on a passive Third World. Second, global mass culture does not so much replace local culture as coexist with it, providing a cultural lingua franca remarked by a "local" accent.[11] Third, there are powerful reverse currents as a number of Third-World countries (Mexico, Brazil, India, Egypt) dominate their own markets and even become cultural exporters.[12] We must distinguish, furthermore, between the ownership and control of the media—an issue of political economy—and the specifically cultural issue of the implications of this domination for the people on the receiving end. The "hypodermic needle" theory is as inadequate for the Third World as it is for the First: everywhere spectators actively engage with texts, and specific communities both incorporate and transform foreign influences.[13] In a world of transnational communications, the central problem becomes one of tension between cultural homogenization and cultural heterogenization, in which hegemonic tendencies, well-documented by Marxist analysts like Mattelart and Schiller, are simultaneously "indigenized" within a complex, disjunctive global cultural economy. At the same time, discernible patterns of domination channel the "fluidities" even of a "multipolar" world; the same hegemony that unifies the world through global networks of circulating goods and information also distributes them according to hierarchical structures of power, even if those hegemonies are now more subtle and dispersed.

Although all cultural practices are on one level products of specific national contexts, Third-World filmmakers (men and women) have been forced to engage in the question of the national precisely because they lack the taken-for-granted power available to First-World nation-states. At the same time, the topos of a unitary nation often camouflages the possible contradictions among different sectors of Third-World society. The nation states of the Americas, of Africa and Asia often "cover" the existence, not only of women, but also of indigenous nations (Fourth World) within them. Moreover, the exaltation of "the national" provides no criteria for distinguishing exactly what is worth retaining in the "national tradition." A sentimental defense of patriarchal social institutions simply because they are "ours" can hardly be seen as emancipatory. Indeed, some Third-World films criticize exactly such institutions: *Xala* (1990) criticizes polygamy; *Finzan* (1989) and *Fire Eyes* (1993) critique female genital mutilation; films like *Allah Tanto* (1992) focus on the political repression exercised even by a pan-Africanist hero like Sekou Touré; and Sembene's *Guelwaar* (1992) satirizes religious divisions within the Third-World nation. Third, all countries, including Third-World countries, are heterogeneous, at once urban and rural, male and female, religious and secular, native and immigrant. The view of the nation as unitary muffles the "polyphony" of social and ethnic voices within heteroglot cultures. Third-World feminists, especially, have highlighted the ways in which the subject of the Third-World nationalist revolution has been covertly posited as masculine and heterosexual. Fourth, the precise nature of the national "essence" to be recuperated is elusive and chimerical. Some locate it in the precolonial past, or in the country's rural interior (e.g., the African village), or in a prior stage of development (the preindustrial), or in a non-European ethnicity (e.g., the indigenous or African strata in the nation-states of the Americas); and each narrative of origins has had its gender implications. Recent debates have emphasized the ways in which national identity is mediated, textualized, constructed, "imagined," just as the traditions valorized by nationalism are "invented."[14] Any definition of nationality, then, must see nationality as partly discursive in nature, must take class, gender, and sexuality into account, must allow for racial difference and cultural heterogeneity, and must be dynamic, seeing "the nation" as an evolving, imaginary construct rather than an originary essence.

The decline of the Third-Worldist euphoria, which marked feminist films like *One Way or Another*, *The Hour of Liberation*, and *Nicaragua Up From the Ashes*, brought with it a rethinking of political, cultural, and aesthetic possibilities, as the rhetoric of revolution began to be greeted with a certain skepticism. Meanwhile, the socialist-inflected national-liberation struggles of the 1960s and 1970s were harassed economically and militarily, violently discouraged from becoming revolutionary models for postindependence societies. A combination of IMF pressure, cooptation, and "low-intensity warfare" obliged even socialist regimes to make a sort of peace with transnational capitalism. Some regimes repressed those who wanted to go beyond a purely nationalist bourgeois revolution to restructure class, gender, religion, and ethnic relations. As a result of external pressures and internal self-questioning, the cinema also gave expression to these mutations, with the anticolonial thrust of earlier films gradually giving way to more diversified themes and perspectives. This is not to say that artists and intellectuals became less politicized but that cultural and political critique took new and different forms. Contemporary cultural practices of post–Third-World and multicultural feminists intervene at a precise juncture in the history of the Third World.

Third Worldism Under Feminist Eyes

Largely produced by men, Third-Worldist films were not generally concerned with a feminist critique of nationalist discourse. It would be a mistake to idealize the sexual politics of anticolonial Third-Worldist films like the classic Battle of Algiers, for example. On one level, it is true that Algerian women are granted revolutionary agency. In one sequence, three Algerian women fighters are able to pass for Frenchwomen and, consequently, slip through the French checkpoints with bombs in their baskets. The French soldiers treat the Algerians with discriminatory scorn and suspicion but greet the Europeans with amiable "bonjours." The soldiers' sexism leads them to misperceive the three women as French and flirtatious when, in fact, they are Algerian and revolutionary. The Battle of Algiers thus underlines the racial and sexual taboos of desire within colonial segregation. As Algerians, the women are the objects of the military as well as the sexual gaze; they are publicly desirable for the soldiers, however, only when they masquerade as French. They use their knowledge of European codes to trick the Europeans, putting their own "looks" and the soldiers' "looking" (and failure to see) to revolutionary purpose. (Masquerade also serves the Algerian male fighters, who veil as Algerian women to better hide their weapons.) Within the psychodynamics of oppression, the colonized knows the mind of the oppressor, while the converse is not true. In The Battle of Algiers, the women deploy this cognitive asymmetry to their own advantage, consciously manipulating ethnic, national, and gender stereotypes in the service of their struggle.

On another level, however, the women in the film largely carry out the orders of the male revolutionaries. They certainly appear heroic, but only insofar as they perform their sacrificial service for the "nation." The film does not ultimately address the two-fronted nature of their struggle within a nationalist but still patriarchal revolution.[15] In privileging the nationalist struggle, Battle of Algiers elides the gender, class, and religious tensions that fissured the revolutionary process, failing to realize that, as Anne McClintock puts it, "nationalisms are from the outset constituted in gender power" and that "women who are not empowered to organize during the struggle will not be empowered to organize after the struggle."[16] The final shots of a dancing Algerian woman waving the Algerian flag and taunting the French troops, accompanied by a voice-over announcing: "July 2, 1962: Independence. The Algerian Nation is born," has the woman "carry" the allegory of the "birth" of the Algerian nation. But the film does not raise the contradictions that plagued the revolution both before and after victory. The nationalist representation of courage and unity relies on the image of the revolutionary woman precisely because her figure might otherwise evoke a weak link, the fact of a fissured revolution in which unity vis-a-vis the colonizer does not preclude contradictions among the colonized.

Third-Worldist films often favored the generic and gendered space of heroic confrontations, whether set in the streets, the casbah, the mountains, or the jungle. The minimal presence of women corresponded to the place assigned to women both in the anticolonialist revolutions and within Third-Worldist discourse, leaving women's homebound struggles unacknowledged. Women occasionally carried the bombs, as in *Battle of Algiers*, but only in the name of a "Nation." More often, women were made to carry the "burden" of national allegory: the woman dancing with the flag in *Battle of Algiers*, the Argentinian prostitute whose image is underscored by the national anthem in *La Hora de las Hornos* (The Hour of the Furnaces), the mestiza journalist in *Cubagua*, as embodiment of the Venezuelan nation, or scapegoated as personifications of imperialism, for example, the allegorical "whore of Babylon" figure in Rocha's films. Gender contradictions have been subordinated to anticolonial struggle: women were expected to "wait their turn."

A recent Tunisian film, *Samt al Qusur* (The Silence of the Palace, 1994) by Moufida Tlatli, a film editor who had worked on major Tunisian films of the postindependence, "Cinema Jedid" (New Cinema) generation, and who has now directed her first film, exemplifies some of the feminist critiques of the representation of the "nation" in the anticolonial revolutionary films. Rather than privileging direct, violent encounters with the French, which would necessarily have to be set in male-dominated spaces of battle, the film presents 1950s Tunisian women at the height of the national struggle as restricted to the domestic sphere. Yet, it also challenges middle-class assumptions about the domestic sphere as belonging to the isolated wife-mother of a (heterosexual) couple. *The Silence of the Palace* focuses on working-class women, the servants of the rich, pro-French Bey elite, subjugated to hopeless servitude, including at times sexual servitude, but for whom life outside the palace, without the guarantee of shelter and food, would mean the even worse misery of, for example, prostitution. Although they are bound to silence about what they see and know within the palace, the film highlights their survival as a community. As an alternative family, their emotional closeness in crisis and happiness and their supportive involvement in decision-making show their ways of coping with a no-exit situation. They become a nonpatriarchal family within a patriarchal context. Whether through singing as they cook for an exhibitionist banquet, through praying as one of them heals a child who has fallen sick, or through dancing and eating in a joyous moment, the film represents women who did not plant bombs but whose social positioning turns into a critique of failed revolutionary hopes as seen in the postcolonial era. The information about the battles against the besieging French are mediated through the radio and by vendors, who report to the always "besieged" women on what might lead to an all-encompassing national transformation.

Yet, this period of anticolonial struggle is framed as a recollection narrative of a woman singer, a daughter of one of the female servants, illuminating the continuous pressures exerted on women of her class. (With some exceptions, female singers/dancers are still associated in the Middle East with being just a little above the shameful occupation of prostitution.) The gendered and classed oppression that she witnessed as an adolescent in colonized Tunisia led her to believe that things would be different in an independent Tunisia. Such hopes were encouraged by the promises made by the middle-class male intellectual, a tutor for the Bey's family, who suggests that in the new Tunisia not knowing her father's name will not be a barrier for establishing a new life. Their passionate relationship in the heat of revolution, where the "new" is on the verge of being born, is undercut by the framing narrative. Her fatherless servant-history and her low status as a singer haunt her life in the post-independence era; the tutor lives with her but does not marry her, yet gives her the protection she needs as a singer. The film opens on her sad, melancholy face singing a famous Um Kulthum song from the 1960s, "Amal Hayati" (The Hope of My Life). Um Kulthum, an Egyptian, was the leading Arab singer of the twentieth century. Through her unusual musical talents—including her deep knowledge of "fusha" (literary) Arabic—she rose from her small village to become "kawkab al sharq" (the star of the East). Her singing accompanied the Arab world in all its national aspirations and catalyzed a sense of Arab unity that managed to transcend, at least on the cultural level, social tensions and political conflicts. She was closely associated with the charismatic leadership of Gamal Abdul Nasser and his anti-imperial pan-Arab agenda, but the admiration, respect, and love she elicited continued well after her death in 1975. Um Kulthum's transcendental position, however, has not been shared by many female singers or stars in the Arab world.

The protagonist of *The Silence of the Palace* begins her public performance at the invitation of the masters of the palace. This invitation comes partly because of her singing talent but no less because of the sexual advances she begins to experience as soon as one of the masters notices that the child has turned into a young woman. The mother who manages to protect her daughter from sexual harassment is herself raped by one of the masters. On the day of the daughter's first major performance at a party in the palace, the mother dies of excessive bleeding from medical complications caused by aborting the product of the rape. In parallel scenes, the mother shouts from her excruciating pain and the daughter courageously cries out the forbidden Tunisian anthem. The sequence ends with the mother's death and with her daughter leaving the palace for the promising outside world of young Tunisia. In post-independent Tunisia, the film implies, the daughter's situation has somewhat improved. She is no longer a servant but a singer who earns her living, yet needs the protection of her boyfriend against gender-based humiliations. Next to her mother's grave, the daughter articulates, in a voice-over, her awareness of some improvements in the conditions of her life in comparison with that of her mother. The daughter has gone through many abortions, despite her wish to become a mother, in order to keep her relationship with her boyfriend—the revolutionary man who does not transcend class for purposes of marriage. At the end of the film, she confesses at her mother's grave that this time she cannot let this piece of herself go. If, in the opening, the words of Um Kulthum's song relay a desire for the dream not to end—"Khalini, gambak, khalini/ fi hudhni albak, khahlini/ oosibni ahlam bik/ Yaret Zamani ma yesahinish" (Leave me by your side/ in your heart/ and let me dream/ wish time will not wake me up)—the film ends with an awakening to hopes unfulfilled with the birth of the nation. Birth, here, is no longer allegorical as in *The Battle of Algiers*, but concrete, entangled in taboos and obstacles, leaving an open-ended narrative, far from the euphoric closure of the Nation.

The Cinema of Displacement

Third-World nationalist discourse has often assumed an unquestioned national identity, but most contemporary nation-states are "mixed" formations. A country like Brazil, arguably

Third World in both racial terms (a *mestizo* majority) and economic ones (given its economically dependent status), is still dominated by a Europeanized elite. The U.S., a "First-World" country, which always had its Native American and African American minorities, is now becoming even more "Third Worldized" by waves of postindependence migrations. Contemporary United States life intertwines First- and Third-World destinies. The song "Are My Hands Clean," by Sweet Honey in the Rock, traces the origins of a blouse on sale at Sears to cotton in El Salvador, oil in Venezuela, refineries in Trinidad, factories in Haiti and South Carolina. Thus, there is no Third World, in Trinh T. Minhha's pithy formulation, without its First World, and no First World without its Third. The First-World/Third-World struggle takes place not only *between* nations but also *within* them.

A number of recent diasporic film and video works link issues of postcolonial identity to issues of post–Third-Worldist aesthetics and ideology. The Sankofa production *The Passion of Remembrance* (1986) by Maureen Blackwood and Isaac Julien thematizes post–Third-Worldist discourses and fractured diasporic identity—in this case, Black British identity—by staging a "polylogue" between the 1960s black radical as the (somewhat puritanical) voice of nationalist militancy and the "new," more playful voices of gays and lesbian women, all within a derealized reflexive aesthetic. Film and video works such as Assia Djebar's *Nouba Nisa al Djebel Chenoua* (The Nouba of the Women of Mount Chenoua) (1977), Lourdes Portillo's *After the Earthquake* (1979), Lucia Salinas's *Canto a la Vida* (Song to Life) (1990), Mona Hatoum's *Measures of Distance* (1988), Pratibha Parmar's *Khush* (1991), Trinh T. Minh-ha's *Surname Viet Given Name Nam* (1989) and *Shoot for the Content* (1991), Prajna Paramita Parasher and Den Ellis's *Unbidden Voices* (1989), Lucinda Broadbent *Sex and the Sandinistas* (1991), Mona Smith's *Honored by the Moon* (1990), Indu Krishnan's *Knowing Her Place* (1990), Christine Chang's *Be Good My Children* (1992), Teresa Osa and Hidalgo de la Rivera's *Mujeria* (1992), Marta N. Bautis's *Home is the Struggle* (1991) break away from earlier macronarratives of national liberation, re-envisioning the nation as a heteroglossic multiplicity of trajectories. While remaining anticolonialist, these experimental films call attention to the diversity of experiences within and across nations. Since colonialism had simultaneously aggregated communities fissured by glaring cultural differences and separated communities marked by equally glaring commonalities, these films suggest, many Third-World nation-states were highly artificial and contradictory entities. The films produced in the First World, in particular, raise questions about dislocated identities in a world increasingly marked by the mobility of goods, ideas, and peoples attendant with the "multinationalization" of the global economy.

Third Worldists often fashioned their idea of the nation-state according to the European model, in this sense remaining complicit with a Eurocentric Enlightenment narrative. And the nation-states they built often failed to deliver on their promises. In terms of race, class, gender, and sexuality, in particular, many of them remained, on the whole, ethnocentric, patriarchal, bourgeois, and homophobic. At the same time, a view of Third-World nationalism as the mere echo of European nationalism ignores the international realpolitik that made the end of colonialism coincide with the beginning of the nation-state. The formation of Third-World nation-states often involved a double process of, on the one hand, joining diverse ethnicities and regions that had been separate under colonialism, and, on the other, partitioning regions in a way that forced regional redefinition (Iraq/Kuwait) and a cross-shuffling of populations (Pakistan/India, Israel/Palestine). Furthermore, political geographies and state borders do not always coincide with what Edward Said calls "imaginary geographies," whence the existence of internal emigres, nostalgics, rebels (i.e., groups of people who share the same passport but whose relations to the nation-state are conflicted and ambivalent). In the postcolonial context of a constant flux of peoples, affiliation with the nation-state becomes highly partial and contingent.

While most Third-Worldist films assumed the fundamental coherence of national identity, with the expulsion of the colonial intruder fully completing the process of national becoming, the postnationalist films call attention to the fault lines of gender, class, ethnicity, region, partition, migration, and exile. Many of the films explore the complex identities generated by exile—from one's own geography, from one's own history, from one's own body—within innovative narrative strategies. Fragmented cinematic forms homologize cultural disembodiment. Caren Kaplan's observations about a reconceived "minor" literature as deromanticizing solitude and rewriting "the connections between different parts of the self in order to make a world of possibilities out of the experience of displacement,"[17] are exquisitely appropriate to two autobiographical films by Palestinians in exile, Elia Suleiman's *Homage by Assassination* (1992) and Mona Hatoum's *Measures of Distance. Homage by Assassination* chronicles Suleiman's life in New York during the Persian Gulf War, foregrounding multiple failures of communication: a radio announcer's aborted efforts to reach the filmmaker by phone; the filmmaker's failed attempts to talk to his family in Nazareth (Israel/Palestine); his impotent look at old family photographs; and despairing answering-machine jokes about the Palestinian situation. The glorious dream of nationhood and return is here reframed as a Palestinian flag on a TV monitor, the land as a map on a wall, and the return (*awda*) as the "return" key on the computer keyboard. At one point, the filmmaker receives a fax from a friend, who narrates her family history as an Arab-Jew, her feelings during the bombing of Iraq and Scud attacks on Israel, and the story of her displacements from Iraq, through Israel/Palestine, and then on to the U.S.[18] The mediums of communication become the imperfect means by which dislocated people struggle to retain their national imaginary, while also fighting for a place in a new national context (the U.S., Britain), in countries whose foreign policies have concretely impacted on their lives. *Homage by Assassination* invokes the diverse spatialities and temporalities that mark the exile experience. A shot of two clocks, in New York and in Nazareth, points to the double time-frame lived by the diasporic subject, a temporal doubleness underlined by an intertitle saying that, due to the Scud attacks, the filmmaker's mother is adjusting her gas mask at that very moment. The friend's letter similarly stresses the fractured space-time of being in the U.S. while identifying with relatives in both Iraq and Israel.

In *Measures of Distance*, the Palestinian video and performance artist Mona Hatoum explores the renewal of friendship between her mother and herself during a brief family reunion in Lebanon in the early 1980s. The film relates the fragmented memories of diverse generations: the mother's tales of the "used-to-be" Palestine, Hatoum's own childhood in Lebanon, the civil war in Lebanon, and the current dispersal of the daughters in the West. (It should be noted that the cinema, from *The Sheik* through *The King and* I to *Out of Africa*, has generally preferred showing Western women travelers in the East rather than Eastern women in the West.) As images of the mother's handwritten Arabic letters to the daughter are superimposed over dissolves of the daughter's color slides of her mother in the shower, we hear an audiotape of their conversations in Arabic, along with excerpts of their letters as translated and read by the filmmaker in English.

The voice-over and script of *Measures of Distance* narrate a paradoxical state of geographical distance and emotional closeness. The textual, visual, and linguistic play between Arabic and English underlines the family's serial dislocations, from Palestine to Lebanon to Britain, where Mona Hatoum has been living since 1975, gradually unfolding the dispersion of Palestinians over very diverse geographies. The foregrounded letters, photographs, and audiotapes call attention to the means by which people in exile negotiate cultural identity. In the mother's voice-over, the repeated phrase "My dear Mona" evokes the diverse "measures of distance" implicit in the film's title. Meanwhile, background dialogue in Arabic, recalling their conversations about sexuality and Palestine during their reunion, recorded in the past but played in the present, parallels shower photos of the mother, also taken in the past but looked at in the present. The multiplication of temporalities continues in Hatoum's reading of a letter in English: to the moments of the letter's sending and its arrival is added the moment of Hatoum's voice-over translation of it for the English-speaking viewer. Each layer of time evokes a distance at once temporal and spatial, historical and geographical; each dialogue is situated, produced, and received in precise historical circumstances.

The linguistic play also marks the distance between mother and daughter, while their separation instantiates the fragmented existence of a nation. When relentless bombing prevents the mother from mailing her letter, the screen fades to black, suggesting an abrupt end to communication. Yet the letter eventually arrives via messenger, while the voice-over narrates the exile's difficulties of maintaining contact with one's culture(s). The negotiation of time and place is here absolutely crucial. The videomaker's voice-over reading her mother's letters in the present interferes with the dialogue recorded in the past in Lebanon. The background conversations in Arabic give a sense of present-tense immediacy, while the more predominant English voice-over speaks of the same conversation in the past tense. The Arabic speaker labors to focus on the Arabic conversation and read the Arabic scripts, while also listening to the English. If the non-Arabic speaking spectator misses some of the film's textual registers, the Arabic-speaking spectator is overwhelmed by competing images and sounds. This strategic refusal to translate Arabic is echoed in Suleiman's *Homage by Assassination* where the director (in person) types out Arab proverbs on a computer screen, without providing any translation. These exiled filmmakers thus cunningly provoke in the spectator the same alienation experienced by a displaced person, reminding us, through inversion, of the asymmetry in social power between exiles and their "host communities." At the same time, they catalyze a sense of community for the minoritarian speech community, a strategy especially suggestive in the case of diasporic filmmakers, who often wind up in the First World precisely because colonial/imperial power has turned them into displaced persons.

Measures of Distance also probes issues of sexuality and the female body in a kind of self-ethnography, its nostalgic rhetoric concerned less with the "public sphere" of national struggle than with the "private sphere" of sexuality, pregnancy, and children. The women's conversations about sexuality leave the father feeling displaced by what he dismisses as "women's nonsense." The daughter's photographs of her nude mother make him profoundly uncomfortable, as if the daughter, as the mother writes, "had trespassed on his possession." To videotape such intimate conversations is not a common practice in Middle Eastern cinema or, for that matter, in any cinema. (Western audiences often ask how Hatoum won her mother's consent to use the nude photographs and how she broached the subject of sexuality.) Paradoxically, the exilic distance from the Middle East authorizes the exposure of intimacy. Displacement and separation make possible a transformative return to the inner sanctum of the home; mother and daughter are together again in the space of the text.

In Western popular culture, the Arab female body, whether in the form of the veiled, barebreasted women who posed for French colonial photographers or the Orientalist harems and belly dancers of Hollywood film, has functioned as a sign of the exotic. But rather than adopt a patriarchal strategy of simply censuring female nudity, Hatoum deploys the diffusely sensuous, almost pointillist images of her mother naked to tell a more complex story with nationalist overtones. She uses diverse strategies to veil the images from voyeuristic scrutiny: already hazy images are concealed by text (fragments of the mother's correspondence, in Arabic script) and are difficult to decipher. The superimposed words in Arabic script serve to "envelop" her nudity. "Barring" the body, the script metaphorizes her inaccessibility, visually undercutting the intimacy verbally expressed in other registers. The fragmented nature of existence in exile is thus underlined by superimposed fragmentations: fragments of letters, dialogue, and the mother's *corps morcelle* (rendered as hands, breasts, and belly). The blurred and fragmented images evoke the dispersed collectivity of the national family itself.[19] Rather than evoke the longing for an ancestral home, *Measures of Distance*, like *Homage by Assassination*, affirms the process of recreating identity in the liminal zone of exile.[20] Video layering makes it possible for Mona Hatoum to capture the fluid, multiple identities of the diasporic subject.

Interrogating the Aesthetic Regime

Exile can also take the form of exile from one's own body. Dominant media have long disseminated the hegemonic white-is-beautiful aesthetic inherited from colonialist discourse, an aesthetic which exiled women of color from their own bodies. Until the late 1960s, the overwhelming majority of Anglo-American fashion journals, films, TV shows, and commercials promoted a canonical notion of beauty within which white women (and, secondarily, white men) were the only legitimate objects of desire. In so doing, the media extended a longstanding philosophical valorization of whiteness. European writing is replete with homages to the ideal of white beauty, implicitly devalorizing the appearance of people of color. For Gobineau, the "white race originally possessed the monopoly of beauty, intelligence and strength."[21] For Buffon, "[Nature] in her most perfect exertions made men white."[22] Fredrich Bluembach called White Europeans "Caucasians" because he believed that the Caucusus mountains were the original home of the most beautiful human species.[23]

[. . .]

The hegemony of the Eurocentric gaze, spread not only by First-World media but even at times by Third-World media, explains why *morena* women in Puerto Rico, like Arab-Jewish (Sephardi) women in Israel, paint their hair blond, and why Brazilian TV commercials are more suggestive of Scandinavia than of a black-majority country, and why "Miss Universe" contests can elect blond "queens" even in North African countries, and why Asian women perform cosmetic surgery in order to appear more Western. (I am not questioning the partial "agency" involved in such transformations but highlighting the patterns informing the agency exercised.) Multicultural feminists have criticized the internalized exile of Euro-"wannabees" (who transform themselves through cosmetic surgery or by dying their hair) while at the same time seeking an open, nonessentialist approach to personal aesthetics. The mythical norms of Eurocentric aesthetics come to inhabit the intimacy of self-consciousness, leaving severe psychic wounds. A patriarchal system contrived to generate neurotic self-dissatisfaction in *all* women (whence anorexia, bulimia, and other pathologies of appearance) becomes especially oppressive for women of color by excluding them from the realms of legitimate images of desire.

[. . .]

The existential life of the racialized body has been harsh, subject not only to the indignities of the auction block, to rape, branding, lynching, whipping, stun gunning, and other kinds of physical abuse but also to the kind of cultural erasure enailed in aesthetic stigmatization. Many Third-World and minoritarian feminist film and video projects offer strategies for coping with the psychic violence inflicted by Eurocentric aesthetics, calling attention to the sexualized/racialized body as the site of both brutal oppression and creative resistance. Black creativity turned the body, as a singular form of "cultural capital," into what Stuart Hall calls a "canvas of representation."[24] A number of recent independent films and videos—notably Ayoka Chenzira's *Hairpiece: A Film for Nappy-Headed People* (1985), Ngozi A. Onwurah's *Coffee Coloured Children* (1988), Deborah Gee's *Slaying the Dragon* (1988), Shu Lea Cheang's *Color Schemes* (1989), Pam Tom's *Two Lies* (1989), Maureen Blackwood's *Perfect Image?* (1990), Helen Lee's *Sally's Beauty Spot* (1990), Camille Billop's *Older Women and Love* (1987), and Kathe Sandler's *A Question of Color* (1993)—meditate on the racialized/sexualized body in order to narrate issues of identity. These semiautobiographical texts link fragmented diasporic identities to larger issues of representation, recovering complex experiences in the face of the hostile condescension of Eurocentric mass culture. *Perfect Image?*, for example, satirizes the mass-mediated ideal of a "perfect image" by focusing on the representation and self-representation of two black British women, one light-skinned and the other dark, lampooning the system that generates self-dissatisfaction in very diverse women, all of whom see themselves as "too" something—too dark, too light, too fat, too tall. Their constant shifting of personae evokes a diversity of women, and thus prevents any essentialist stereotyping along color lines in the Afro-diasporic community.

Pathological syndromes of self-rejection—black skins/white masks—form the psychic fallout of racial hegemony. Given the construction of dark bodies as ugly and bestial, resistance takes the form of affirming black beauty. The Black Power movement of the 1960s, for example, transformed kinky hair into proud Afro hair. Sandler's *A Question of Color* traces tensions around color-consciousness and internalized racism in the African American community, a process summed up in the popular dictum: "If you're white, you're all right/if you're yellow, you're mellow/if you're brown, stick around/ but if you're black, stay back." (Such tensions formed the subject of Duke Ellington's musical composition "Black, Brown and Beige.") Hegemonic norms of skin color, hair texture, and facial features are expressed even within the community through such euphemisms as "good hair" (i.e., straight hair) and "nice features" (i.e., European-style features), and in inferentially prejudicial locutions like "dark *but* beautiful," or in admonitions not to "look like a Ubangi." The film registers the impact of the "Black is Beautiful" movement, while regarding the present moment as the contradictory site both of the resurgent Afrocentrism of some rap music along with lingering traces of old norms. One interview features a Nigerian cosmetic surgeon who de-Africanizes the appearance of black women, while the film reflects on the valorization of light-skinned black women in rap video and MTV. Sandler also probes intimate relations in order to expose the social pathologies rooted in color hierarchies; the darker-skinned feel devalorized and desexualized, the lighter-skinned—to the extent that their own community assumes they feel superior to it—are obliged to "prove" their blackness. Filtering down from positions of dominance, chromatic hierarchies sow tensions among siblings and friends, all caught by Sandler's exceptionally sensitive direction.

In all these films, internalized models of white beauty become the object of a corrosive critique. Not coincidentally, many of the films pay extraordinary attention to hair as the scene both of humiliation ("bad hair") and of creative self-fashioning, a "popular art form" articulating "aesthetic solutions," in Kobena Mercer's words, to the "problems created by ideologies of race and racism."[25] Already, since the Afro hair style of the late 1960s and 1970s but especially recently, there have been reverse currents linked to the central role of African Americans in mass-mediated culture: whites who thicken their lips and sport dreadlocks, fades, or cornrows. From a multicultural feminist perspective, these cross-cultural trans- formations (cosmetic surgery, dyeing the hair) on one level are exempla of "internal exile" or "appropriation." But on another level they evoke the possibility of an open, nonessentialist approach to looks and identity. Ayoka Chenzira's ten-minute animated short *Hairpiece: A Film for Nappy-Headed People* addresses hair and its vicissitudes in order to narrate African Americans' history of exile from the body as well as the utopia of empowerment through Afro-consciousness. In a dominant society where beautiful hair is that which "blows in the wind," *Hairpiece* suggests an isomorphism between vital, rebellious hair that refuses to conform to Eurocentric norms and the vital, rebellious people who "wear" the hair. Music by Aretha Franklin, James Brown, and Michael Jackson accompanies a collage of black faces (from Sammy Davis to Angela Davis). Motown tunes underscore a quick-paced visual inventory of relaxers, gels, and curlers, devices painfully familiar to black people, and particularly to black women. The film's voice-over and "happy ending" might seem to imply an essentialist affirmation of "natural African beauty," but as Kobena Mercer points out in another context, "natural hair" is not itself African; it is a syncretic construct.[26] Afro-diasporic hair styles, from the Afro to dreadlocks are not emulations of "real" African styles but rather neologistic projections of diasporic identity. The styles displayed at the film's finale, far from being examples of "politically correct" hair, rather assert a cornucopia of diasporic looks, an empowering expression of a variegated collective body. Satirizing the black internalization of white aesthetic models, the film provokes a comic catharsis for spectators who have experienced the terror and pity of self-colonization.[27]

Ngozi A. Onwurah's lyrical semiautobiographical film *Coffee Coloured Children*, meanwhile, speaks of the black body as hemmed in by racism. The daughter of a white mother and an absent Nigerian father, the film's narrator recalls the pain of growing up in an all-white English neighborhood. The opening sequence immediately demonstrates the kind of racist harass- ment the family suffered: a neo-Nazi youth defiles their front door with excrement, while the mother, in voice-over, worries about protecting her children from feeling somehow responsible for the violence directed at them. The narrative conveys the traumatic self-hatred provoked by imposed paradigms. In one scene, the daughter doffs a blonde wig and white makeup in front of a mirror, trying to emulate a desired whiteness. If *The Battle of Algiers* made the mirror a revolutionary tool, here, it becomes the speculum for a traumatized identity, literally that of a black skin masked with whiteness. The simple act of looking in a mirror is revealed to be multiply specular, as one looks even at oneself through the eyes of many others—one's family, one's peers, one's racial others, as well as the panoptic eyes of the mass media and consumerist culture. The scar inflicted on the victims of this aesthetic hegemony are poignantly suggested in a bath sequence in which the children, using cleaning solutions, frantically try to scrub off a blackness lived as dirt.[28] The narrator's voice-over relating the cleansing ritual is superimposed on a close shot of rapid scrubbing, blurred so as to suggest bleeding, an apt image for colonialism's legacy inscribed on the body of children, a testament to the internalized stigmata of a devastating aesthetic regime.

[. . .]

A discourse which is "purely" feminist or "purely" nationalist, I have tried to argue, cannot apprehend the layered, dissonant identities of diasporic or postindependent feminist subjects. The diasporic and post–Third-Worldist films of the 1980s and 1990s, in this sense, do not so much reject the "nation" as interrogate its repressions and limits, passing nationalist discourse through the grids of class, gender, sexuality, and diasporic identities. While often embedded in the autobiographical, they are not always narrated in the first person, nor are they "merely" personal; rather, the boundaries between the personal and communal, like the generic boundaries between documentary and fiction, the biographic and the ethnographic, are constantly blurred. The diary form, the voice-over, the personal written text, now bear witness to a collective memory of colonial violence and postcolonial displacement. While early Third-Worldist films documented alternative histories through archival footage, interviews, testimonials, and historical reconstructions, generally limiting their attention to the public sphere, the films of the 1980s and 1990s use the camera less as a revolutionary weapon than as a monitor of the gendered and sexualized realms of the personal and the domestic, seen as integral but repressed aspects of national history. They display a certain skepticism toward metanarratives of liberation but do not necessarily abandon the notion that emancipation is worth fighting for. Rather than fleeing from contradiction, they install doubt and crisis at their very core. Rather than a grand anticolonial metanarrative, they favor heteroglossic proliferations of difference within polygeneric narratives, seen not as embodiments of a single truth but rather as energizing political and aesthetic forms of communitarian self-construction.

Since all political struggle in the postmodern era necessarily passes through the simulacral realm of mass culture, the media are absolutely central to any discussion of post–Third-Worldist multicultural and transnational feminist practices. I have tried to link the often ghettoized debates concerning race and identity politics, on the one hand, and nationalism and postcolonial discourse, on the other, as part of an attempt to put in dialogue, as it were, diverse post–Third-Worldist feminist critiques. The global nature of the colonizing process and the global reach of the contemporary media virtually oblige the cultural critic to move beyond the restrictive framework of the nation-state. Within postmodern culture, the media not only set agendas and frame debates but also inflect desire, memory, and fantasy. The contemporary media shape identity; indeed, many argue that they now exist close to the very core of identity production. In a transnational world typified by the global circulation of images and sounds, goods, and peoples, media spectatorship impacts complexly on national identity, communal belonging, and political affiliations. By facilitating a mediated engagement with distant peoples, the media "deterritorialize" the process of imagining communities. And while the media can destroy community and fashion solitude by turning spectators into atomized consumers or self-entertaining monads, they can also fashion community and alternative affiliations. Just as the media can exoticize and disfigure cultures, they have the potential power not only to offer countervailing representations but also to open up parallel spaces for anti-racist feminist transformation. In this historical moment of intense globalization and immense fragmentation, the alternative spectatorship established by the kind of film and video works I have discussed can mobilize desire, memory, and fantasy, where identities are not only the given of where one comes from but also the political identification with where one is trying to go.

Notes

I would like to thank Robert Stam for generously allowing me to use some shared material from our coauthored book *Unthinking Eurocentrism* (New York: Routledge, 1994). I am also grateful to the editors of this volume, Chandra Talpade Mohanty and Jacqui Alexander, for their useful suggestions and insightful comments, and for their truly dialogical spirit.

1   Lyotard, despite his skepticism about "metanarratives," supported the Persian Gulf War in a collective manifesto published in *Liberation*, thus endorsing George Bush's metanarrative of a "New World Order."

2   I am proposing here the term "post–Third-Worldist" to point to a move beyond the ideology of Third Worldism. Whereas the term "postcolonial" implies a movement beyond anticolonial nationalist ideology and a movement beyond a specific point of colonial history, post–Third-Worldism conveys a movement "beyond" a specific ideology—Third-Worldist nationalism. A post–Third-Worldist perspective assumes the fundamental validity of the anticolonial movement, but also interrogates the fissures that rend the Third-World nation. See Ella Shohat, "Notes on the Post-Colonial," *Social Text*, nos. 31–32 (Spring 1992).

3   For more on the concept of "location," see, for example, Chandra Talpade Mohanty, "Feminist Encounters: Locating the Politics of Experience," *Copyright* 1 (Fall 1987); Michele Wallace, "The Politics of Location: Cinema/Theory/Literature/Ethnicity/Sexuality/ Me," *Framework* no. 36 (1989); Lata Mani, "Multiple Mediations: Feminist Scholarship in the Age of Multinational Reception," *Inscriptions* 5 (1989); and Inderpal Grewal, "Autobiographic Subjects and Diasporic Locations: *Meatless Days* and *Borderlands*" and Caren Kaplan, "The Politics of Location as Transnational Feminist Practice," in Inderpal Grewal and Caren Kaplan, *Scattered Hegemonies: Postmodernity and Transnational Feminist Practice* (Minneapolis: University of Minnesota Press, 1994).

4   See J. M. Blaut, *The Colonizer's Model of the World: Geographical Diffusionism and Eurocentric History* (New York and London: Guilford Press, 1993).

5   The various film festivals—in Havana, Cuba (dedicated to New Latin American cinema), in Carthage, Tunisia (for Arab and African cinemas), in Ougadoogoo, Burkino Faso (for African and Afro-diasporic cinemas)—gave further expression to these movements.

6   In relation to cinema, the term "Third World" has been empowering in that it calls attention to the collectively vast cinematic productions of Asia, Africa, and Latin America, as well as the minoritarian cinema in the First World. While some, such as Roy Armes (1987), define "Third-World cinema" broadly as the ensemble of films produced by Third-World countries (including films produced before the very idea of the "Third World" was current), others, such as Paul Willemen (1989), prefer to speak of "Third cinema" as an ideological project (i.e., as a body of films adhering to a certain political and aesthetic program, whether or not they are produced by Third-World peoples themselves). As long

as they are not taken as "essential" entities but as collective projects to be forged, both "Third-World cinema" and "Third cinema" retain important tactical and polemical uses for a politically inflected cultural practice. In purely classificatory terms, we might envision overlapping circles of denotation: 1) a core circle of "Third-Worldist" films produced by and for Third-World people (no matter where those people happen to be) and adhering to the principles of "third cinema"; 2) a wider circle of the cinematic productions of Third-World peoples (retroactively defined as such), whether or not the films adhere to the principles of third cinema and irrespective of the period of their making; 3) another circle consisting of films made by First- or Second-World people in support of Third-World peoples and adhering to the principles of third cinema; and 4) a final circle, somewhat anomalous in status, at once "inside" and "outside," comprising recent diasporic hybrid films (for example, those of Mona Hatoum or Hanif Kureishi), which both build on and interrogate the conventions of "third cinema." See Paul Willemen, "The Third Cinema Question: Notes and Reflections," in Jim Pines and Paul Willemen (eds) *Questions of Third Cinema* (London: BFI Pub., 1989); Shohat/Stam, *Unthinking Eurocentrism*.

7 See Aijaz Ahmad, "Jameson's Rhetoric of Otherness and the National Allegory," *Social Text* no. 17 (Fall 1987): 3–25; Julianne Burton, "Marginal Cinemas," *Screen* 26, nos. 3–4 (May–August 1985).

8 See Arjun Appadurai, "Disjuncture and Difference in the Global Cultural Economy," *Public Culture* 2, no. 2 (1990). A similar concept, "scattered hegemonies," is advanced by Inderpal Grewal and Caren Kaplan, who offer a feminist critique of global-local relations in their introduction to *Scattered Hegemonies*.

9 In the cinema, this hegemonizing process intensified shortly after World War I, when U.S. film distribution companies (and, secondarily, European companies) began to dominate Third-World markets, and was further accelerated after World War II, with the growth of transnational media corporations. The continuing economic dependency of Third-World cinemas makes them vulnerable to neocolonial pressures. When dependent countries try to strengthen their own film industries by setting up trade barriers to foreign films, for example, First-World countries can threaten retaliation in some other economic area such as the pricing or purchase of raw materials. Hollywood films, furthermore, often cover their costs in the domestic market and can, therefore, be profitably "dumped" on Third-World markets at very low prices.

10 Although direct colonial rule has largely come to an end, much of the world remains entangled in neocolonial globalization. Partially as a result of colonialism, the contemporary global scene is now dominated by a coterie of powerful nation-states, consisting basically of Western Europe, the U.S., and Japan. This domination is economic ("the Group of Seven," the IMF, the World Bank, GATT), political (the five veto-holding members of the UN Security Council), military (the new "unipolar" NATO), and techno-informational-cultural (Hollywood, UPI, Reuters, France Presse, CNN). Neocolonial domination is enforced through deteriorating terms of trade and the "austerity programs" by which the World Bank and the IMF, often with the self-serving complicity of Third-World elites, impose rules that First-World countries would themselves never tolerate.

11 For a similar argument, see Grewal and Kaplan's introduction to *Scattered Hegemonies*.

12 The Indian TV version of the *Mahabharata* won a 90 percent domestic viewer share during a three-year run, and Brazil's Rede Globo now exports its telenovelas to more than eighty countries around the world.

13 For Appadurai, the global cultural situation is now more interactive; the U.S. is no longer the puppeteer of a world system of images, but only one mode of a complex transnational construction of "imaginary landscapes." In this new conjuncture, he argues, the invention of tradition, ethnicity, and other identity markers becomes "slippery, as the search for certainties is regularly frustrated by the fluidities of transnational communication." See Appadurai, "Disjuncture and Difference in the Global Cultural Economy."

14 See Benedict Anderson, *Imagined Communities: Reflexions on the Origins and Spread of Nationalism* (London: Verso, 1983); and E. J. Hobsbawm and Terence Ranger, eds., *The Invention of Tradition* (Cambridge: Cambridge University Press, 1983).

15 Pontecorvo returned to Algiers in 1991 to make *Gillo Pontecorvo Returns to Algiers*, a film about the evolution of Algeria during the twenty-five years that have elapsed since *Battle of Algiers* was filmed, and focusing on such topics as Islamic fundamentalism, the subordinate status of women, the veil, and so forth.

16 Anne McClintock, "No Longer in a Future Heaven: Women and Nationalism in South Africa," *Transition*, no. 51 (1991): 120.

17 Caren Kaplan, "Deterritorializations: The Rewriting of Home and Exile in Western Feminist Discourse," *Cultural Critique*, no. 6 (Spring 1987): 198.

18 The friend in question is Ella Habiba Shohat.

19 Or as the letters put it: "This bloody war takes my daughters to the four corners of the world." This reference to the dispersion of the family, as metonym and metaphor for the displacement of a people, is particularly ironic given that Zionist discourse itself has often imaged its own national character through the notion of "the ingathering of exiles from the four corners of the globe."

20 In this sense, *Measures of Distance* goes against the tendency criticized by Hamid Naficy which turns nostalgia into a ritualized denial of history. See "The Poetics and Practice of Iranian Nostalgia in Exile," *Diaspora*, no. 3 (1992).

21 Quoted in Brian V. Street, *The Savage in Literature* (London: Routledge and Kegan Paul, 1975), p. 99.

22 Georges-Loins Leclerc de Buffon, *The History of Man and Quadrupeds*, trans. William Smellie (London: T. Cadell and W. Davies, 1812), p. 422.

23 George Mosse, *Toward the Final Solution: A History of European Racism* (London: Dent, 1978), p. 44.

24 Stuart Hall, "What Is This 'Black' in Black Popular Culture?" in Gina Dent, ed. *Black Popular Culture* (Seattle: Bay Press, 1992), p. 27.

25 Kobena Mercer, "Black Hair/Style Politics," *New Formations*, no. 3 (Winter 1987).

26 Ibid.

27 Not surprisingly, the film has been screened in museums and churches, and even for social workers and hair stylists, as a provocative contemplation of the intersection of fashion, politics, and identity.

28 This association is especially ironic given the colonial legacy of slavery and servitude in which black men (janitors) and women (maids) were obliged to clean up the "mess" created by white Europeans.

Bombay Boys and Girls: The Gender and Sexual Politics of Transnationality in the New Indian Cinema in English

4

JIGNA DESAI

[. . .]

Introduction

Although diasporas are articulated typically and largely as cultural and political derivatives of homelands, which are seen as the national origins of cultural authenticity, such formulations tend to ignore the larger economic significance of and political implications of diasporas. These limited formulations may align authority and power with the nation-state and suggest that diasporas are 'hailed by'[1] the narratives of the homeland nation-state that activate sentiments of nostalgia and belonging. However, these constructions illuminate neither the power relations that may exist between diasporas and homeland nation-states, especially between diasporas located in the economic North from nation-states in the economic South, nor the mutually constitutive and embedded relationship between homeland nation-states and diasporas. In general, South Asian diasporic communities, especially those located in the West, including Europe, North America, and Australia, have had a strong impact on South Asian nation-states. Therefore, focusing only on the homeland nation as origin of culture, tradition, and values and the state as authority and granter of citizenship can overshadow an examination of the economic and political power in relations between diasporic communities and nation-states.

In recent scholarship, there has been some attention to the ways in which transnational groups, including but not limited to diasporas, organise economically, socially, and politically across nation-states.[2] For example, scholars of migration studies have pointed out that many transnational communities play significant roles in influencing and supporting the political economy of the homeland nation-state through strategies such as remittance, investment, and lobbying.[3] Thus, diasporic communities with economic clout are able to make demands upon nation-states (whether in claims of rootedness, consumption of cultural goods, or access to special economic and political benefits). In the case of India, billions of dollars have been invested by Non-Resident Indians (NRIs). Postcolonial diasporas located in the economic North often act as transnational agents integral to globalisation processes in the economic South whose nation-states increasingly recognise diasporas. Recently within the context of transnationalism and globalisation, diasporas have been conceptualised as deterritorialised nations, unbounded from the territory associated with the nation-state. Probing how the nation-state as agent of authority acknowledges and empowers diasporic communities, bestowing on them legitimacy and membership, can further illuminate the relationship between diaspora and the nation-state. For example, analyses can emphasise how the state offers opportunities for dual citizenship or economic investment to deterritorialised nations as is the case with NRIs. Again, the Indian state identifies certain members of diaspora as desirable members of the deterritorialised nation to invest in government bonds, technology industries, and the development of nuclear capabilities.

From the development of state councils and academic centres on the diaspora to the prevalence of NRI characters in Bollywood cinema,[4] the nation-state advances its interest in diasporas in different modalities, articulating its varying relationships with diaspora based on contradictory and complementary interests. Since the structural adjustment policies of the 1980s and 1990s requiring India to 'liberalise' its economy by devaluing its currency, opening its markets to transnational and foreign corporations, and increasing its debt, the ideal diaspora is one that willingly exchanges economic and technological investments for national membership and state citizenship. However, diasporas may not always respond dutifully in their roles as sentimental benefactors. Additionally, homelands may resent their economic dependence on diasporic support.

In some cases, the nation-state has sought to disenfranchise those who might otherwise claim national membership, while in other cases it has been advantageous to make little or no distinction between those in diaspora and in the homeland, cultivating diasporic citizens under categories such as NRI and Person of India Origin (PIO). Those diasporic subjects who may be migrant workers, exiles, or refugees need not apply for cultural citizenship as deterritorialised nationals. In the case of India, the ideal diasporic subjects are frequently imagined as those privileged elites interested in infusing investments for economic and technological development in exchange for national membership and state citizenship. In her study of Chinese diasporas, Aihwa Ong describes these transnational subjects with political and economic privilege and with cultural, if not state, citizenship in multiple places as elite flexible citizens. Possessing capital and brokering flexible citizenship, these idealised diasporans blur the boundaries between diasporas and homeland under the name of the cosmopolitan transnational.

Currently, in media, academia, and policy, the nation-state relays its vision of ideal diasporic relations. Ample examples of these subjects are available in Bollywood cinema that portrays jet-setting families with mansions in India and Britain or the US. In films such as *Kuch Kuch Hota Hai*, *Dil to Pagal Hai*, *Yaadein*, and *Dil Chatha Hai*, the protagonists of the films are young and extremely wealthy, often of the transnational elite class. Desire is central here to constructions of diaspora. Multiple valences of desire, e.g. longing, belonging, and cultural and familial filiation are suggested through some connection to the homeland. Within Bollywood cinema, the deterritorialised nation is frequently sutured to the homeland nation-state through the gendered and sexualised cultural logic of transnationality[5] mobilised in the trope of the family. Often in Bollywood cinema, diasporic desires become framed within the heteronormative romance and become mapped as family and marriage (usually between the male NRI protagonist and the homeland heroine). In most narratives, the damsel is a pure and traditional virgin unsullied by Westernisation who 'reorients' the male NRI in his homeland and culture, thus reuniting the wayward capital of the male NRI with the proper object of desire.

New Wave Cinema

Recently, this transnational cosmopolitan class has emerged in South Asian metropolises due to economic liberalisation, namely in Mumbai[6] the cultural and economic capital of India. The urban transnational cosmopolitan class overlaps with but is not identical to the diasporic middle classes. Rachel Dwyer's study of romance in India[7] investigates the rise of this elite transnational class and the new middle class. She links together these classes and contrasts them to the older bourgeois who are the dominant class of the moment, simultaneously un-naming themselves and their privilege.[8] Dwyer describes the new middle class with its own structures of feelings and ideologies as distinct from the previous colonial and postcolonial dominant bourgeoisie. In addition to fluency in and frequent use of English, consumption of material leisure goods and services (including food, fashion, travel, and high priced commodities associated with the West) defines this new middle class as well as the cosmopolitan transnational class. Moreover, these groups share cultural capital and forward cultural and social values that challenge those of the national bourgeoisie.[9]

The youth (16–26 years) of this class have come of age during the emergence of these economic and political shifts due to globalisation, including increasing consumption of media, fashion, music, and mobility. An MTV generation familiar with DKNY, Blimpie, Nintendo, and vacations to the Seychelles, this group seems to seek the formation of its own public sphere through cultural production and consumption. Though dominant Indian cinema has registered these shifts, exhibiting the 'taste' and cultural capital of this class, this new middle class in India has also engendered other cultural production, in particular cinematic productions in English, foregrounding its own articulation of Indian culture. In the last decade, a new low-budget 'independent' cinema in English characterised by such films as Bombay Boys,[10] Split Wide Open,[11] and Hyderabad Blues[12] has emerged. In this essay, though I include brief descriptions of the major English films, I focus primarily on Bombay Boys.

Significantly, the language of this class and these recent films is English. While Indian literature in English has a long history due to the legacy of colonialism, popular Indian films in English are phenomena that are more recent. Similarly, while vernacular language films in Hindi, Tamil, Telegu, Malayalam, Punjabi, Gujarati, and Bengali are present in Indian cinema, English films have not developed a large audience. While South Asian diasporic films in English have received some crossover attention in India (from Merchant and Ivory productions to the films of Deepa Mehta, Mira Nair, and Gurinder Chadha), these films are nevertheless often viewed as diasporic films in terms of subject, financing, and production. The liberalisation of the Indian economy (and globalisation processes in general) has led to increasing use of English, not only as the language of capital, but also (mixed with vernacular languages) as part of everyday practices for the new urban classes. English used in conjunction with vernacular languages, especially Hindi, in this case functions as not only a marker, distinguishing the economic status of the new middle class, but its cultural status as well, suggesting ease in code—switching from English to other Indian languages.

For example, in *Split Wide Open*, the protagonist code switches from Hindi to English and back again depending primarily on the class of his addressee; so he directly addresses not only the NRI characters, but also the audience in English, while speaking Hindi with his 'sister' a homeless child.

Notably, these films rarely if ever depict conflict with the West. Instead, it is encounters with wealthy NRIs as diaspora, rather than with the West, which configure negotiations and constructions of modernity. Thus, modernity is not positioned as foreign to India; and, though it may not immediately seem authentic, modernity appears through class contradictions and conflicts in relation to the nation. The essay interrogates the representations of diaspora in these films in order to illuminate the political economy between diaspora and the nation-state, specifically from the vantage of this cosmopolitan transnational middle class. Consequently, these emerging films mark the increasing centrality of diaspora and the transnational class to the postcolonial nation-state due to the deterritorialisation of the nation and other global processes. Furthermore, I argue that discourses on diaspora, gender, and sexuality are those that most strongly configure modernity and the nation for these classes in the films. Specifically, examining the gendered and sexualised logics of transnationality in these films indicates that sexuality is most often the site marking and negotiating these class interests. In other words, I suggest that the socio-economic power relations between diasporas and nation-states are highly gendered and sexualised. To summarise, this essay examines both the production and the content of these films in order to analyse the gendered and sexual logics of transnationality between the diaspora and the cosmopolitan elite of the postcolonial nation-state.

These films depict the interests of a shifting middle class, one whose interests have supposedly been unmet by Indian national cinemas.[13] The emerging Indian cinema in English articulates the nationalist claims of a dominant but non-hegemonic class in India, one that is struggling to establish its own public culture. Simultaneously legitimating themselves while remaining unnamed (and almost invisible as the films feature very few cosmopolitan urban characters), the new middle class not only challenges the hegemony of the post-colonial bourgeoisie (symbolised in these discourses by the state and Bollywood), but also highly regarded diaspora hailed by the 'liberalised' postcolonial nation-state in structural adjustment and globalisation. The filmmakers also assert that these films challenge the aesthetics and content of dominant Indian cinemas. Kaizad Gustad,[14] the director of *Bombay Boys* explains:

> What started to happen in 1998 was that a lot of young Indian filmmakers had gone abroad and came back to India and figured Bollywood just didn't do it for them, perhaps because they were urban people and wanted more representation through a cinema that speaks their language. So in 1998 we had a series of films that came out of all this and bucked the trend.
>   They had low budgets and dealt with entirely new stories with an entirely new set of values.[15]

Gustad's comments most clearly foreground his perception of the inadequacy of national cinemas in expressing the cultural values of the new middle and the transnational cosmo-politan classes.[16] While Gustad frames the difference of this group demographically in terms of age (youth) and residence (urban), he clearly refers to the new middle class that is searching for its interests (new set of values) articulated in its own public sphere (cinema that speaks their language). Moreover, Gustad stresses that the transnational travel and experiences of this class are essential to the emergence of the new cinematic productions. Ironically, the transnational mobility seemingly engenders the possibility of expressing new Indian cultural values and experiences resulting from dissatisfaction with the conventions and ideologies of national cinemas. For example, Kaizad Gustad, a graduate of New York University film school, internationally financed Bombay Boys through friends, family, and credit cards. Gustad took four years to complete his first full-length feature film Bombay Boys with shooting in Mumbai and post-production in London. The low value of the rupee in relation to Western currencies allows low budget filmmakers to garner venture capital internationally for cinematic production in South Asia. Thus, many of the artists (for example, Kaizad Gustad, Nagesh Kukunoor, and Raul Bose) work and/or seek funding outside of India.

[. . .]

Written by Benegal and Chatterjee, produced by Anuradha Parikh-Benegal, adapted to screenplay by Farrukh Dhondy,[17] and also starring Rahul Bose, Split Wide Open (1999) focuses on the impact of globalisation on various characters in Bombay. Concentrating on Kut Price (KP), a former villager who tries to eke a living from the water trade (selling everything from access to municipal water to cases of Evian), the film touches on his relationships with other Bombayites including Didi (his sister), a ten-year-old flower seller who becomes a child sex -worker to a wealthy NRI, Nandita, a diasporic Londoner who hosts an anonymous sex discussion talk show, and a Christian priest who has same sex desires and taught the abandoned child KP English and survival skills. Portraying the contrasting and simultaneous worlds in which designer spring water and cell phones co-exist with a lack of portable water and exploited children, the film probes contemporary contestations of social and sexual mores, seeking to expose the bourgeoisie's and underworld's sexual and economic exploitations in Bombay.

[. . .]

Severe and perverse exploitation occurs (in Split Wide Open) at the hands of an NRI man posted to Bombay by a multinational corporation whose wealth and political power enable him to kidnap and sexually abuse pre-adolescent female street children; his paedophilia is discovered and then revealed by his NRI daughter on the show. When the common Indian man KP goes to rescue Didi from the lair of the paedophile, clutching her Toblerone box in one hand, she dismisses him asking if he can provide her with a television, food, and shelter, not to mention imported candy. The sexual predation by the diasporic elite upon the vulnerable populations of Mumbai (children, women, poor, abused, etc.) becomes a trope for many forms of exploitation in general. In other words, the disparity in economic and power relations between the nation-state in the South and the diasporas of the North occurs in the form of gender and sexual exploitation; additionally, these power imbalances are often represented in gendered and sexualised terms.[18] Split Wide Open, like other films, represents the economic, social, and political impact of globalisation, personified by the NRI transnational elite of the economic North), on the postcolonial nation-state as gendered and sexualised. Moreover, the most egregious abuse occurs by those with political immunity, patriarchal power, economic wealth, and a detachment from the family and nation, by those harbingers of globalisation—the diaspora and NRI.

Emerging around the same time as *Split Wide Open*, Kaizad Gustad's *Bombay Boys* and Nagesh Kukunoor's *Hyderabad Blues*[19] surprised the film industry with their popularity in the urban theatres. Originally scheduled to play the early afternoon matinee in Mumbai theatres, *Bombay Boys* by word of mouth and guerrilla publicity managed to secure top evening slots in a number of theatres within a few weeks of opening. The satirical *Bombay Boys* features three NRI Indian men returning to the homeland, searching for fame, fortune, family, and fulfilment in Mumbai. Suppressing the specificities of migration histories and politics, the film throws the three men together as representatives of diaspora, suggesting that diasporas are indistinguishable. The director, Kaizad Gustad himself a transnational cosmopolitan who grew up in Mumbai but travelled and lived throughout Europe, Australia, Asia, and North America, nevertheless seems to distinguish himself from his ignorant and naïve diasporic/NRI protagonists who are chewed up and spit out by Mumbai. Ultimately, all three boys flee their homeland forced away by their inability to handle the law, the underworld, and the city itself.

Atlanta resident Nagesh Kukunoor, the director and star of *Hyderabad Blues*, creates a wistful narrative of a young NRI's return to see his family after 12 years. The film centres on his coming to terms with his inability to accept social 'traditions' and practices, such as arranged marriages, that he confronts upon his return to Hyderabad. The film revolves around his expectations and behaviour upon meeting a Hyderabadi doctor with whom he falls in love. Kukunoor's second production *Rockford* is a coming of age narrative in which a young boy recounts the trials and tribulations of his first year at boarding school. Kukunoor's third film *Bollywood Calling*[20] though not a box office smash is an interesting satire of the Bollywood film industry.

Both *Bombay Boys* and *Hyderabad Blues* focus on the return of diasporic Indians or NRIs to their homeland. In the former, the director uses camp, emphasising an ironic but empathetic critique of this return, and employs the diasporic men as mechanisms to reveal the senti-mental, sordid, and sinister underbelly of Mumbai and its film industry. In the latter, the narrative mobilises the binary of modern and tradition, producing a denial of coevalness resulting from the displacement experienced in returning to Hyderabad. *Bombay Boys* avoids such evocations, painting Mumbai as a cosmopolitan world city, albeit with its own logic and practices around sex, drugs, alcohol, and culture. In comparison, Hyderabad functions the same as every city in India (despite its emergence as a centre of technology in India) and is circumscribed by class, caste, gender, and family practices that are critiqued from a neo-liberal Western vantage. Nevertheless, *Hyderabad Blues* too understands diaspora and nation-state through an analysis of gender and sexual norms—in this case of arranged and transnational marriages.

Filmi Fundas

While these films may not constitute a cinema in and of themselves, they nevertheless initiate a new Indian cinema that can be grouped together as a coherent category. The films *English August*, *Bombay Boys*, *Hyderabad Blues*, *Split Wide Open*, and *Rockford* along with *The Godmother* (a Hindi film starring Shahbana Azmi in a fictionalized depiction of a real Gujarati widow who replaces her husband as mafia don) toured together as an international film festival under the title Filmi Fundas (Film Fundamentals) in England and Australia. The popularity of the films created the possibility of imagining a new market, audience, and spectator for such films. *Hyderabad Blues* bills itself as the highest grossing small budget film in India; the film played to audiences in Mumbai for over seven months and in other cities like Hyderabad and Delhi for over six months. The financial success of *English August*, *Bombay Boys*, and *Hyderabad Blues* enabled the possibility of low budget 'independent' films to be made and marketed in India.

[. . .]

The group of films showcased as Filmi Fundas also led to the development of a manifesto.[21]

[. . .]

The Filmi Fundas Manifesto outlines the ideologies and guidelines of alternative cinematic production in India, more specifically emphasising 'independence' from the film studios and industries. The Filmi Fundas directors categorise themselves as independent filmmakers creating low budget movies initially financed by the filmmakers themselves rather than by the film industry.

[. . .]

These filmmakers attempt to distinguish themselves from the hegemony of Bollywood and vernacular cinema and that which they call parallel or art cinema. The manifesto elaborates its antidotes to what it identifies as the Bollywood formula of national Indian cinema —loosely scripted films with rehashed stories, high production costs, extradiegetic musical sequences, and an overabundance of slow pans typical of melodramas and epics. Moreover, the specified topical and aesthetic precepts target the most frequently cited characteristics distinguishing popular Indian cinema from Western cinema (the melodrama, the extradiegetic scenes set in picturesque foreign locations, and the musical sequences), suggesting the influence of Western cinema on those filmmakers. The manifesto also emphasises that the control of production remains with the director (rather than the financiers and producers) attempting to ensure that new stories are told without compromise. Simultaneously, the filmmakers eschew the social realist narratives or docu-dramas associated with parallel and even diasporic cinema, especially those depicting colonialism or the Raj. Evoking their sensibilities as those of a new middle class to whom extradiegetic song and dance numbers are signs of catering to the lower classes and older generations, these directors claim to tell new stories, presumably ones that relay the interests of the young new middle or transnational cosmopolitan class.

Notably, the manifesto collapses the distinction between diasporic and transnational Indian, requiring only that the director or content be of 'Indian origin.' In doing so, diasporic films and filmmakers are incorporated into the body of 'new Indian cinema.' Yet, the manifesto while distinguishing between this cinema and national cinemas, also differentiates itself from other diasporic productions such as Merchant and Ivory productions which often focus on the Raj, as well as Deepa Mehta's *Earth* and Mia Nair's *Kama Sutra* both of which take place before or during independence.[22] These filmmakers posit their texts as Indian and therefore within Indian cinema, thereby forwarding their challenge to other constructions of the nation (especially by those of the bourgeoisie and the diaspora). Furthermore, many of these filmmakers travel, work, and live abroad as well as in India, blurring the line between the diasporic and the transnational.

[. . .]

Sexual Orientations

Bombay Boys interweaves the return of three diasporic Indians or NRIs to Mumbai in its narrative.[23] Formerly Goan Christian Ricardo Fernandez (Rahul Bose) has come from Sydney to find his brother, though he also falls in love, Hindu Krishna Sahni (Naveen Andrews) from New York to find an acting career in Bollywood, and Parsi Xerxes Mistry (Alexander Gifford) from London to further his music, if not his sexual identity. The film with its quick edits, campy humour, and farcical plot incorporates romance, drugs, sex, films, and music in a staccato cut and mix narrative in order to portray the fast paced and modern life of Mumbai as a world city. With its satirical tone, *Bombay Boys* quippily critiques both the Orientalist ways in which travel to India is a spiritual journey in search of the self and the abandonment of family and cultural values in the homeland by diasporans. The first is discussed through the character of Xerxes and the latter through Ricardo;[24] both Ricardo and Xerxes together illustrate the ways in which diasporic desires become eroticised.

Bombay Boys reasserts and maintains the Bollywood trope of the family and the hetero-sexual romance as significant modes eroticising and domesticating diasporic desires. The trope of the family is also employed here in suturing diaspora to the homeland-nation-territory; more specifically it functions here to mark the desertion of the nation by diaspora. Accusations of being forgotten and abandoned are put forth by both the nation (family and neighbours) and the state (the police officer). These accusations hound Ricardo as he searches for his brother Roger who, after falling in with 'bad company' and drugs, has died alone and almost forgotten in the city. During his search, Ricardo is censured by Bombayites for abandoning his brother and his homeland. Their chastisement reflects a criticism of diasporic neglect and abdication of filial responsibility: 'You leave the country with your family, and come back looking for him. Why did you go away in the first place? Wasn't it fun out there?' The criticism suggests that while diasporas hail the homeland through nostalgia and return, they do so when convenient. The homeland nation's heralding of diaspora has little to do with the everyday lives and interests of the non-elite classes who are clearly critical of and ambivalent in regard to diaspora. The state in the form of the police too admonishes Ricardo, 'so you forgot him (since you lived abroad and he lived here). Know why people are lost? I think it's because we forget them. Completely.' The barrage of criticism inevitably indicates a resentment and recognition of the ways in which diasporic economic, cultural, and political capital brokers social power in the homeland. The broken family, in particular, becomes the trope of the deterritorialised diaspora's neglect of the homeland nation, particularly its most vulnerable members.

In contrast to the reunited family of Bollywood cinema, Ricardo proves himself inadequate, losing his brother and the object of his love Dolly. In the end, he must flee Mumbai, aban-doning the romance he has begun and leaving Dolly in the clutches of the mobster Mastana. Rejecting Bollywood romantic fantasies of the NRI hero rescuing the Indian damsel in distress, *Bombay Boys* subverts the narrative closure of the happily ever after between the wealthy masculine diaspora and the poor feminine nation-state. While the heterosexual relationship serves still to suture the masculine diaspora back to the feminine nation, it does so in complicated ways. The romance between Ricardo and Dolly hardly resembles those of dominant Bollywood cinema. In *Bombay Boys*, this relationship is satirised, as the heroine is not the chaste and innocent Hindu maiden, but the vampy and sassy Christian actress Dolly who is the mistress of Bollywood mobster-producer Mastana. In the film, Mastana ropes Ricardo and Xerxes into the shooting ending of his film *Mumbai Banditos* with Krishna. The three mounted on horses dressed as Parsi, Hindu, and Christian cowboys dispose of all the evil henchmen before they ride off into the sunset. These three Indian cowboys, however, are hardly heroic; in fact, they prove incapable and self-preserving, suggesting that they are far from the heroes of Bollywood cinema who would gladly risk their lives to prove their commitment and attachment to their families, loves, and homelands demonstrating their true Indian-ness. The film eschews dominant Bollywood narratives that usually forward the NRI male as retaining Indian values. In this film, the NRI men prove to be inadequate Indians and Bombay boys, as all (including Ricardo) choose to leave Dolly (Ricardo's girlfriend and Mastana's moll) to her fate in Bombay and Bollywood. (However, during the credits, we see Dolly holding a plane ticket presumably from Ricardo.)

But *Bombay Boys* has an ambivalent construction of women's power. In dominant constructions, the heroine provides the mechanism for inspiring and reasserting the hero's Indian-ness or cultural authenticity. While the film forwards a critique of the dependency of the nation on the diaspora, it does not make Dolly's escape contingent squarely on Ricardo. In fact, Dolly proves capable of protecting herself. Dolly is not the virgin maiden representing Indian tradition in the national imaginary, suggesting a different formulation of the feminine homeland nation, albeit characterised as the romantic prostitute with the heart of gold. Nevertheless, she provides a space of critique in regard to the heteronormative narrative that sutures and reunifies the diaspora and homeland nation through the tropes of family and marriage.

Dolly in part represents a different aspect of the Indian nation. Rather than returning to the fertile fields of a Punjabi village symbolizing the traditional culture and soil of the nation, a common trope of Bollywood cinema, the return in *Bombay Boys* is to the world city of Bombay or Mumbai. In dominant Indian cinema, the West marks the space of contamination and vice. This theme has been emphasised consistently and repeatedly in films. Bollywood film romances and 'happy endings' indicate the preservation of cultural values and authenticity despite the dangers of diasporic and Western contamination. Mumbai functions in contrast to Punjabi villages as a site already filled with vice and corruption. In this film, it is not Westernisation that sullied India but the cosmopolitan city itself that is a playground of capital, sex, alcohol and violence, one that is decidedly Indian. In this case, it is not the Western-residing protagonists contaminating Indian values and traditions; in fact, the boys prove overwhelmingly incapable and inadequately prepared for their return to India. Mumbai is no longer and has never been the site of unchanging Indian culture and traditions welcoming with open arms weary travellers from the West who have come to seek fame, fortune, and themselves in its Oriental mystique.

Bombay Boys satirises this travel from West to East (usually the Punjabi fields of the cultural heartland or mystical and spiritual Orient) through the inability of the three protagonists to negotiate the space of India—Mumbai. However, while other films have handled the topic of colonial and neo-colonial tourism, the difference in *Bombay Boys* is that all three characters are South Asian diasporic or NRIs. While the *South Asian* protagonist cannot travel to the mystic East to find himself, the diasporic Indian still has the possibility of doing so.

[. . .]

While India has functioned in the Orientalist imaginary as the site of spirituality, it has done so in contrast to the materiality of the West. In evoking Mumbai as a world city (an urban cosmopolitan metropolis albeit with disparities between poverty and wealth), the film upsets that binary. In this case, India does not function as escape from the excess of the West as drugs, sex, money, and vice too are rampant here. Any expectations of an idyllic and holy experience are out of place (and time) argues the film. This is the new Mumbai. In fact, Ricardo's quest for his brother and involvement with Mastana's moll, Dolly, exposes the underbelly of the cosmopolitan city, a city that challenges normal social activities beyond the naïve expectations of the diaspora. Transgressing sexual and normal social activities is entirely possible in Mumbai, which thwarts all Orientalist expectations in a land of tradition and repression, but deviancy results in consequences that surpass the boys' capabilities. Finally, hounded by Mastana and overcome by their run-ins with the law, the boys decide to leave Mumbai: 'We'll have to go away or this city's going to kill us.'

Conclusion

In the Bollywood films, often the economic wealth of NRI males engenders and enables access to the Indian girl-woman and nation whose value lies in her sense of tradition and her cultural authenticity. Bombay Boys, like Split Wide Open, in contrast to Bollywood cinema, portrays these relationships as exploitative and predatory, ones in which the feminine nation is taken advantage of by the masculine diaspora in the form of the male capital-wielding NRI. It is revealed that the Indian cowboys of Bombay Boys are hardly the capable and brave heroes that they are painted to be. (In contrast, the unnamed elite of the city, suggested by Mastana, Pesi and Xerxes' lover, manoeuvre through Bombay with similar interests, but with greater ease and grace, while the non-elite suggested by Ricardo's brother and Dolly are either lost or continue to survive, manoeuvring between the power of the diasporic and local capital.)

Bombay Boys, like many other recent films in English, characterises the vulnerability of the Indian nation through the figure of the (often sexually exploited) female and the abuse she suffers at the hands of the powerful NRI male. As discussed earlier, in Split Wide Open, the figure is the homeless girl-child who 'chooses' to trade sex for candy, clothes, and shelter with an NRI male. In Monsoon Wedding,[25] it is the girl-child who is molested by her rich NRI uncle, the patriarch and sugar daddy of the family who trades his American gained wealth for high status and, in this case, access to young children. In Bombay Boys, the romantic mobster's moll with the heart of gold, though abandoned by her NRI lover, sells herself in hope of making it big in Bollywood. While some of these figures emphasise the unequal power relations of these exploitations, others emphasise the increasing sexual agency of women. These gendered relationships challenge the heteronormative narratives of Bollywood, suggesting forces and fissures in the power relations between diaspora and the homeland nation. More importantly, Bombay Boys traces the class, gender, and sexual ideologies, in its understanding of the political economy and power relations between diaspora and postcolonial nation-state.

Bombay Boys and the new Indian cinema provide a critical perspective of diaspora from the position of the homeland nation-state, particularly from the new middle and transnational cosmopolitan classes. Its perspective relays the shifts and tensions in the postcolonial nation-state due to expansion of global capitalism and especially to NRI participation in the liberalisation of the economy encouraged by the Indian state. The Indian cinema in English, less interested in wooing overseas markets than its Bollywood counterparts or even *Monsoon Wedding*, suggests that there are alternative narratives of diaspora and nation besides that of the reunified family and the heteronormative romance that require attention; they offer ones that provide critiques of the gendered and sexualised power of diasporic transnational capital.

Notes

1 See Louis Althusser, 'Lenin and Philosophy and Other Essays'. London: Verso, 1971— specifically in regard to the interpellation of the subject who recognises himself when the law names and calls him.

2 Margaret Keck and Kathryn Sikkink, 'Activists Beyond Borders: Advocacy Networks in International Politics.' Ithaca: Cornell University Press, 1998 and Frederic Jameson and Masao Miyoshi 'The Cultures of Globalisation,' Durham, North Carolina: Duke University Press, 1998 are just two recent examples.

3 See the work of Linda Basch, Nina Glick Schiller, and Cristina Szanton Blanc, 'Nations Unbound: Transnational Projects, Postcolonial Predicaments, and the Deterritorialization Nation-States.' Langhorne, PA: Gordon and Breach Science Publishers, 1994 and Yossi Shain. 'Marketing the Democratic Creed Abroad: US Diasporic Politics in the Era of Multiculturalism,' *Diaspora* 3, 1, (1994) pp. 85–111 for example. However, other scholars have pointed out the dangers of overstating the impact and reach of transnational groups whether in the form of deterritorialised nations or as activist groups organised around environmental, feminist, or human rights.

4 My forthcoming research analyses the ways in which dominant Indian cinemas articulate and hail diasporic subjects. Specifically, it examines the cinema of the last decade to mark the changing representation of diasporas.

5 Aihwa Ong, 'Flexible Citizenship: The Cultural Politics of Transnationality.' Durham, NC: Duke University Press, 1999.

6 In 1996 the city officially changed its name in English from Bombay to Mumbai. Forwarded by Shiv Sena as part of their Hindutva agenda, Mumbai emphasises Marathi over English. I use both Bombay and Mumbai.

7 Rachel Dwyer, 'All You Want is Money, All You Need is Love: Sex and Romance in Modern India.' London: Cassell, 2000.

8 Rachel Dwyer too refers to Roland Barthes idea of ex-nomination by which the dominant bourgeoisie un-name their privilege and render their processes of normalisation invisible. Roland Barthes, 'Mythologies.' Selected and translated by Annette Lavers. London: Paladin, 1973.

9 In this discussion, I seek not to delineate an exact subgroup of the capital owning bourgeoisie in economic terms, but rather in cultural terms and therefore discuss the middle classes as incoherent categories, inclusive of a wide range of income and capital. Thus, what I emphasise are the competing claims to the nation and national culture posed through the rhetoric of modern and tradition by groups who identify different interests and tastes.

10 Kaizad Gustad, *Bombay Boys* 1998.

11 Dev Benegal, *Split Wide Open* 2000.

12 Nagesh Kukunoor, *Hyderabad Blues* 1998.

13 The filmmakers distinguish themselves from popular and art cinema rather than national cinema. My position argues against this kind of classification distinguishing between highbrow and lowbrow culture and instead emphasises the ways in which the emerging classes and audiences facilitate and consume new cinematic production. Hence, I refer to both parallel and popular cinema as national cinemas.

14 His short films *Corner Store Blues* (1994) and *Lost and Found* (1995) take place in the world cities of New York and Mumbai respectively. Gustad has also written a novel *Of No Fixed Address* (1998) based on travels from Bali and Paris to Sydney and New York. Kaizad Gustad, *Of No Fixed Address* New Delhi: Harper Collins, 1998.

15 Jeremy Kay, 'Filmi Fundas: The Other Face of Indian Cinema.' 15 January 2001. <http://www.6degrees.co.uk/en/2/200008ftfilmi.html>

16 Of course, Gustad's comment should not suggest homogenous viewing and interpretative practices for audiences of Bollywood or other Indian cinemas. Audiences create diverse and multiple modalities of meanings. Moreover, Bollywood cinema itself is hardly monolithic in its presentation of coherent constructions of diaspora. Nevertheless, it seems quite possible to identify dominant Bollywood discourses on diaspora.

17 Dhondy is known for his television and performance productions in England. He is also the author of *Bombay Duck*, a novel that like *Split Wide Open* is concerned in part with the exploitation of subaltern street children in India.

18 A similar take on the gendered and sexual logics of transnationalism is presented in Mira Nair's *Monsoon Wedding*, which also presents the older and rich NRI male character as predatory, exploitative, and dangerous to the daughters of the homeland. Mira Nair, *Monsoon Wedding* 2001.

19 *Bombay Boys* and *Hyderbad Blues* illustrate the folly of attempting to define diasporic versus Indian films. Both films are made by directors who lived abroad, financed with support from diasporic communities, and focus on the displacement experienced by NRI male protagonists upon travel or return to India. Both are also part of Filmi Fundas. None the less, distinctions are made between the two. I want to suggest that these films indicate the blurring between the diasporic and the transnational as present in the new middle class.

20 Nagesh Kukunoor, *Bollywood Calling* 2001.

21 'Filmi Fundas Manifesto.' http://bzine.bsee.com.au/entertainment/reviews goatsisland 2000.html#2 accessed 4 October 2001.

22 Rahul Bose who stars in several of these films, recently wrote, directed, and starred in his own *Everybody Says I'm Fine* due for release in 2002; he comments that this new cinema is categorically different from diasporic cinema in that it is about contemporary India by Indians, but a new generation that has absorbed MTV and other media. Rahul Bose, 'New Cinema and the Urban,' 'Bollywood and Beyond.' Lansing: Michigan State University and University of Michigan. 2–3 December 2001.

23 The men are presented in relation to the Indian nation, rather than state initially as they hold passports from the US, England, and Australia. In contrast to the Indian state's Person of Indian Origin Card scheme aimed at claiming Indian identified foreign citizens, the film emphasises their Western citizenship and lack of affiliation to the Indian state.

24 Krishna's character functions less as a vehicle for critiquing diasporic return than it does as a send-up of Bollywood itself.

25 Although technically not part of the Filmi Fundas, Mira Nair's film thematically resembles these other films. As a filmic production, however, it has much greater access to capital and circulation due to Nair being an established director in the West with much greater exposure in the Western art house circuits of distribution.

PART TWO

GLOBAL CINEMA IN THE DIGITAL AGE

Introduction

The essays in this section offer an overview of the ways in which the globalization of film culture has seen its most transformative aspects come to fruition in the evolution of digital technology and, correlatively, the new modes of transnational film and video distribution that these technologies have enabled. These essays explore the pros and cons of the imbrication of the discourses and practices of transnationalism within the corporate structures that have generated and maintained them. Each of these writers considers the extent to which digital technology and other technological developments, more thoroughly than any of the previous forms of film distribution and exhibition, unmoor films from their local contexts and their seemingly naturalized interpretive parameters. These developments then allow films, as cultural objects, to generate new types of community and identification.

Robert E. Davis's essay documents recent changes in the delivery methods of the film industry as it adapts to and appropriates the possibilities engendered by technological advances. These advances enable the temporal truncation of the economic "windows of exploitation" that ultimately determine the commercial success or failure of a popular film at a time when film piracy is a growing concern to the industry. Davis offers an overview of the production and distribution process, or what he calls "the motion picture value chain" that has characterized popular cinema for much of its history. He then explores the forces that are transforming that structure. The most notable of these, he argues, is the possibility of "the instantaneous worldwide release" or IWR and the advent and commercial maturation of VOD or Video on Demand. Both of these forces, Davis argues, are auguring a cinema landscape in which "perhaps in the near future that old movie advertising slogan, 'Coming soon to a theater near you,' will be revised to read, 'Coming soon to everyone, everywhere.'"

In an essay that further considers the capacity of digital technology to transform almost all aspects of film production and reception, Elana Shefrin analyzes the ways in which the internet and the World Wide Web can be used by filmmakers to foster new and more intensely interactive modes of fan culture and community. Through a consideration of director Peter Jackson's online colloquies with Tolkien fans during his making of the *Lord of the Rings* trilogy and George Lucas's more conflictual relation to the world of *Star Wars* fandom, Shefrin reveals how the internet can be used to create a global community of awareness, expectation, and legitimation for high-profile film productions long before the "finished" work is available on screen.

Finally, in contrast to some of the other pieces in this volume, John Hess and Patricia Zimmermann offer a celebratory analysis of the possibilities of transnational cinema in their consideration of the burgeoning world of alternative documentary filmmaking. By way of what they call a "polemical intervention into the emerging transnationalization of the world," Hess and Zimmermann argue that "[t]he concept of adversarial transnational documentaries wrenches the notion of the transnational away from its corporatist location, moving it instead into the disruptive realms of bodies, people, movements and representational practices that dislodge corporate influence by creating new places for social justice on a global scale." In a more overtly optimistic manner than many theorists of the transnational have been willing to essay, Hess and Zimmermann imagine transnational documentary as the exemplary site from which to imagine a leftist practice of cinematic and sociocultural aesthetics.

The Instantaneous Worldwide Release: Coming Soon to Everyone, Everywhere

5

ROBERT E. DAVIS

The film industry has been characterized by challenge and change throughout its history. From the patent trust as the industry was first developing through the advent of sound, the challenge of television, and the emergence of home video, the industry has responded and adapted. However, today the industry faces more technological changes than at any point in its history, changes occurring more rapidly than those the industry has faced in its past.

While the changes are very apparent to consumers on the creative front through the new images computer applications are enabling filmmakers to put on the screen, the changes that will most affect the industry's future are economic in nature. Specifically, these are changes in the distribution and marketing models the industry has followed for decades. There has been considerable coverage of these changes recently in the industry and business publications widely read by executives and content producers; however, scholarly research continues to focus on applying standardized marketing and economic models to the existing distribution structure. This paper examines technological innovations that will permit the industry to modify the delivery methods it uses to get its products to the consumers. As these new delivery systems become commonplace, it is hoped that their acceptance along with such introductory analyses as this paper will prompt more scholarly attention to the evolving role of science and technology in motion picture distribution methods.

On November 5, 2003, when *The Matrix Revolutions* opened simultaneously on movie screens in more than 100 countries at 1400 Greenwich Mean Time, the Warner Brothers publicity department heralded the moment as the "zero hour" when the earth became "Planet Matrix."[1] Although the film's instantaneous global opening was widely viewed as a public relations ploy in the promotion of another mega-budget Hollywood film, this release strategy could, in fact, be a strong indication of the future distribution model for motion pictures. As one journalist describes the situation, "The movie industry is on the verge of a major technological transition – one that seems likely to be a jump cut, rather than a slow fade."[2]

To comprehend fully the ramifications posed by the new technologies, an understanding of the life cycle of a feature film is necessary. A model useful in illustrating this concept is the motion picture value chain.[3] The first stage in the chain is the development stage in which an idea or script is pitched to a studio, producer, or network either as a stand-alone project or as a package with stars and a director attached to the script. The goal of the development process is to obtain a step deal which will provide financing for the development and writing of a shooting script over a series of four steps or phases from idea to story to draft script to shooting script. Once a studio or broadcast network agrees to commit a film to production, that script or project is said to have received a "greenlight" from the studio or network with production funds now made available. The project then enters preproduction, which is the planning stage that continues until the beginning of principal photography. The production stage includes all activities of principal photography while the postproduction stage includes the addition of elements such as music and sound effects as well as editing to produce the final film negative consumers will see in theaters. The film then enters the final stages of the value chain, which are distribution and exhibition. While a studio's marketing department becomes involved once a film receives a "greenlight" in development, the marketing function takes precedence throughout the film's distribution and exhibition stages.

The same major Hollywood studios have dominated the film industry for the past seventy-five years:

1930:	2005:
Paramount	Paramount (Viacom)
Warner Brothers	Warner Brothers (Time Warner/AOL)
Fox	Fox (News Corporation)
Universal	Universal (General Electric/NBC)
Columbia	Columbia (Sony)
MGM	MGM (Sony)
United Artists	United Artists (Sony)
RKO	Disney

The only substantial differences in the major studios in 1930 and the major studios in 2005 are that RKO ceased distributing films in the late 1950s, Disney began distributing its own product after having relied upon RKO and United Artists at different points in its history, and MGM acquired United Artists and was subsequently acquired by Sony. However, while the list from 2005 is very similar to the list from 1930, it is important to note that the studios today are subsidiaries of much larger media conglomerates (identified in parentheses).

One reason the list of major studios in 2005 is so similar to the list of seventy-five years ago is that these companies created and have perfected key competitive strategies difficult for new companies to emulate. One of these strategies identified as a barrier to entry into the motion picture industry is the expertise in marketing and distribution that these companies have developed.[4] They have the resources effectively to market their products and deliver several thousand prints of a film to theaters across the country for a simultaneous opening. This is no small task and even DreamWorks, with its strong capital base and creative alliances, does not distribute its own product; it relies on Universal for that function.[5] In fact, the studios increase their annual revenue by releasing independent films through their distribution machines both in the United States and abroad.

When examining the importance of the distribution and exhibition functions, it is imperative to look at the costs associated with these activities. The total cost of a finished film is the negative cost, which represents all costs associated with production of the film negative, plus the "P and A" costs, which represent prints, advertising, and related marketing expenses. Print costs reflect the expense of producing the copies of the film and shipping them to the theaters. These costs can become quite large, given the fact that a wide release of a film today means that it will open in 3,000 or more theaters on 4,000 or 5,000 screens on the same day.[6] Advertising costs obviously refer to the promotional costs associated with marketing the film. The following table illustrates the total cost of an average studio film in 2004 utilizing data from the Motion Picture Association of America (MPAA).

The Cost of an Average Studio Film:

Negative Cost	(cost of producing the film negative)	$63.6 million
P & A Cost	(prints and advertising)	$34.4 million
Total Cost		$98.0 million[7]

The figures indicate that the "P and A" costs, although down 12% from 2003, still represented 35% of the total cost of the average studio film in 2004. Obviously, the studios are receptive to anything that can help lower their costs in these areas. This is an important consideration that will ultimately influence these companies in their adoption of new distribution methods.

In terms of the revenue stream generated by films, a movie goes through a series of windows of exploitation. Until the 1950s, a film earned its revenue through its domestic theatrical release, its international theatrical release, and possibly theatrical re-releases. Eventually, studios began to sell or rent their films to television, which created an additional window of exploitation.

Within the last thirty years, more windows have opened, so that today a film moves through a whole series of revenue-producing opportunities. Until recent years, the progression began with the domestic theatrical release followed by the international theatrical release. A film next appeared on pay-per-view-television and four to six months later the film entered the home video market through VHS and DVD rentals and sales, followed by airings on premium cable television channels such as HBO, and finally broadcast television airings. The theatrical success or failure of a film determined its value in the subsequent markets which was a formula that was established with the advent of television and reinforced by the later development of the home video market.

In the mid and late 1990s, studios began to shrink the time intervals between the windows of exploitation. For example, the international release today is often simultaneous with the North American release. One reason is to diminish the time video pirates in certain international markets have to obtain and sell fraudulent copies in DVD and cassette formats prior to the film's appearance in theaters in those markets. The MPAA estimates that the U.S. studios are losing three billion dollars to piracy each year.[8]

However, as important as the piracy issue is, studios are also shrinking the time frame on international releases because of the increased revenue derived from international theatrical markets. According to MPAA data, for the first time in the year 2000, the seven major Hollywood studios obtained as much in gross revenue from international theatrical markets as they did from the North American box office.[9] According to MPAA figures, the studios' total global box in 2004 was 25.24 billion dollars, of which 15.7 billion dollars (or 62%) came from theaters outside North America.[10] With so much at stake from a financial standpoint, it is not surprising that studios are shrinking the interval between domestic and international theatrical release periods.

Similarly, as DVD sales began to surpass U.S. box office revenue for many films, the time interval between theatrical and DVD releases also began to shrink. The Ray Charles biopic, Ray, was still playing in 526 theaters at the time it was released on DVD.[11] Advertising for theatrical showings of the film at that time not only provided theater locations and show times, but also carried a promotion for the DVD. Ray earned $80 million during its first week of DVD sales, $6 million more than it had earned during its entire theatrical run.[12]

Considering the increased revenue that has resulted from shortening the intervals between the international and DVD windows, it is natural that studios will examine shortening the duration between all the windows of exploitation. Some executives are talking about the time when these traditional windows of exploitation will disappear completely.

In 1999, Ben Feingold, president of Columbia TriStar Home Video, stated, "There are inherent bottlenecks in the current system. There are only 26,000 theater screens and 30,000 video stores. Often, theaters are sold out, and video stores run out of copies. Digital technology will permit us to remove those bottlenecks."[13]

Mr. Feingold is referring to a concept that can best be described as an instantaneous worldwide release, or IWR, in which the studios will deliver movies digitally to theaters and homes simultaneously while also making copies available in video stores and retail outlets at the same time. While details such as pricing and piracy issues are currently being analyzed, it may not be long before anyone who wants to see a movie on opening day can do so in a variety of ways. Two pieces of the technological puzzle enabling the IWR to become reality are digital exhibition of films in theaters and video on demand for home viewing.

Despite all of film's technological advancements, motion pictures are still shown in most movie theaters on film stock. However, in the summer of 1999, Star Wars: Episode 1 – The Phantom Menace became the first motion picture in history to enjoy a commercial run using digital projection technology for a four-week engagement at two Los Angeles and two New Jersey theaters. A digital run of Tarzan followed the Star Wars engagement and Phil Barlow, executive vice president of the Walt Disney Motion Pictures Group, stated, "Digital exhibition is a major milestone in motion picture history and ranks alongside such other remarkable breakthroughs as sound, color, wide-screen formats, and digital sound" (Koseluk 1).

Studios stand to benefit the most from such technology. It is estimated they currently spend 1.5 billion dollars a year printing and shipping film stock worldwide, whereas digital delivery to theaters is estimated to cost the studios less than one hundred million dollars (Koseluk 1). Consumers will also benefit as digital exhibition will guarantee a sharper, crisper presentation throughout a film's entire theatrical run.

A major factor in this digital revolution will be exhibitors' willingness to convert to the new systems. A traditional film projector costs $35,000 whereas digital projectors cost $100,000 each; therefore, the capital investment involved in the transformation will be quite extensive, given the number of movie screens in existence (Koseluk 1). Muvico Theaters is a developer and owner of multiplex cinemas around the country. Known for its state-of-the-art design and exemplary customer service, the company is one of the few success stories in exhibition today. In an interview (20 Apr. 2000) with Hamid Hashemi, its founder and chief executive officer, I learned that all new construction includes projection rooms capable of easy conversion to digital projection.

While most exhibitors have long maintained the position that studios should share in the cost of the digital conversion, some exhibition companies have been proactive in securing digital projection and looking to a new business model to help fund the conversion and enhance profits. An example is Landmark Theaters which is installing digital projectors in its 58 theaters, representing over 200 screens, in 2005.[14] The company plans to utilize the projectors not only to show movies, but also to screen live concerts and sports events. This is a business model that may become more common as theater operators realize that the future economic situation may see them relying less on movies for their profits and more on other sources. Muvico is one of several chains incorporating restaurants, catering services, and meeting rooms into some of its larger facilities.

There is also an international move toward digital exhibition. In 2005, the Irish Film Board announced that it intends to take the lead in digital projection by replacing 35mm projectors with digital ones in all of its 500 theaters. The plan includes both the Republic of Ireland and Northern Ireland. In announcing the conversion, the Film Board noted that theaters will be able to download the latest releases via satellite and advantages include improved picture quality and the fact that theaters in small towns will be able to show the same films playing in large cities.[15]

The creative community in Hollywood is also monitoring the advent of digital exhibition. In a discussion with film director John Frankenheimer (14 Nov. 1998), I was exposed to another viewpoint on the evolving technology. He explained that when he started directing feature films in the late 1950s and early 1960s, studios were willing to wait to give a film time to build an audience. Then, once the advent of the opening weekend gross took hold, studios began to place more importance on getting the largest return as soon as possible. As he pointed out, when a film opens today on more than 3,000 screens on a given Friday, the studio marketing department already knows by late Friday night or Saturday morning whether or not the film met its Friday night projections. If it did not, executives often begin trimming the advertising budget immediately. Frankenheimer pointed out that in an era of digital projection, once a film does not perform at its expected level on its first Friday evening showing, the studio and/or exhibitor will simply flip a switch and replace the film with a more profitable film or a duplicate copy of a sold-out film. This change could conceivably take place before the original film's second Friday night showing.

In addition to this dramatic change in the way consumers may soon see movies in theaters, there are equally dramatic changes on the horizon in terms of home viewing. The most dramatic is the advent of video on demand (VOD) whereby consumers can view any movie they want to see, old or new, studio blockbuster or independent, domestic release or foreign film, at any time in their own homes either through cable television or by Internet download. With respect to cable television VOD, the technology exists, the carriers and infrastructure exist, and the customers who have it seem to enjoy it. In fact, based on early trials, the industry predicts consumers with VOD will spend significantly more money watching movies than they otherwise would, which translates into more revenue for Hollywood's studios.[16]

The only reason that VOD has not made more of an impact to this point has been lack of product availability. Initially, the studios, which once feared television and home video, feared VOD from a market control standpoint. They resented losing further control of the home video market to intermediaries such as cable television and telephone companies. Many studio executives, for example, apparently think Blockbuster has too much power in the home video arena and thereby feel its parent, Viacom-Paramount, has an unfair advantage in the home video marketplace.[17] However, acceptable profit sharing arrangements have been reached, and cable television VOD is in the process of becoming a mainstream home entertainment option.

One market segment in which the studios seem determined to retain as much control as possible is the Internet VOD marketplace. Sony, MGM, Paramount, Warner Brothers, and Universal offer movies for download through their movielink.com website, and they license films for download from Disney and other companies. The critical concern is the consumer's willingness to watch a feature film on a personal computer. In a 2001 report compiled by Forrester Research titled "Movie Distribution's New Era," it was reported that in a survey of entertainment executives (including representatives of studios, video retailers, cable system operators, and others), 65% thought cable television VOD would definitely affect their business practices over the next five years as against 47% for digital cinema, and 34% for Internet VOD.[18] However, as consumers embrace technology at a rapid rate, it is very likely that they will eventually routinely order films via download, paying a lower price for the option of seeing a film within a short, specified time span, or paying a higher price to make a DVD copy which will then be added to the consumer's library.

One certainty is that the technology for IWR exists and the time intervals between the windows of exploitation are shrinking. Despite some initial obstacles (primarily cost and piracy issues), the studios are poised to take advantage of the technology and increase the rate at which they receive returns for individual films. The studios today are components of much larger, vertically and horizontally integrated entertainment conglomerates. In addition to content production, these companies are engaged in such businesses as theater ownership, publishing, home video, television network ownership, computer online services, music (publishing, recording, and distribution), merchandising, retailing, and theme park operations. A current film can easily move through all the windows of exploitation while remaining firmly under the umbrella of the parent company. In the case of the Sony Corporation, which owns Columbia Pictures, MGM, and United Artists, it is possible for a consumer to purchase or rent a film produced by one of the company's subsidiaries and distributed by Columbia-TriStar Home Video for playing on a Sony DVD or VHS player for viewing on a Sony television monitor. Another option is for the consumer to download a movie from Movielink, of which Sony is part owner, for viewing on a Sony personal computer. Additionally, a consumer might purchase a video game based on one of the company's films for playing on a Sony Playstation unit.

In this age of multimedia entertainment super conglomerates, the studios have been relegated to the role of software managers. The individual pieces of software (the films) are now viewed from the standpoint of providing multiple profit centers to the company well beyond the revenue earned from theatrical showings.

The idea of generating more profits as quickly as possible while reducing costs is most appealing to studio executives. Therefore, it may be only a matter of time before the IWR becomes reality. John Cooke, executive vice president for corporate affairs for the Walt Disney Company, stated in a 1999 interview, "A movie could be premiered globally to an audience of one billion people on its opening day" (Koseluk 1). I will take Cooke's hypothesis a step further and propose that if the access charge to view the film (be it in a theater, rented from a video store, or viewed through VOD technology) were only one dollar and one hundred million people accessed the film on its opening day, then the film would earn one hundred million dollars in revenue in one day of release. Of course, my example is conservative since the access charge will certainly be more than one dollar.

The summer of 2001 saw the beginning of a heavy reliance on the concept of frontloading whereby the studio emphasizes earning as much revenue as possible during a film's opening weekend by concentrating advertising on that period alone. This practice, coupled with the studios currently shrinking the duration between the windows of exploitation, indicates they are already moving toward the IWR. The next logical step will be to focus on the film's opening day revenue. When one examines the potential advantages of such a distribution model, it is obvious that content producers, such as studios, will benefit by extracting profit at a much more rapid rate for their individual films while decreasing the time that pirates have to copy and exploit their work. They will also benefit by no longer having profit models for the subsequent windows of exploitation based on the initial theatrical release, and they will benefit from minimal time exposure to negative reactions to the film from critics and consumers.

Consumers will benefit by having more viewing options for a film available immediately upon its release. Additionally, consumers will enjoy improved quality in theatrical images throughout a film's entire theatrical release.

Independent filmmakers may also benefit from the IWR model by having more opportunity than ever before to showcase their work. Most studios have several hundred films in various stages of development at any given time, yet each company typically releases about 15 to 20 movies per year. In the era of the IWR, it seems possible that there will be opportunity and demand for more films than the major studios are capable of producing, leaving a gap that independent filmmakers can fill. The 2005 Sundance Film Festival saw a record number of 6,500 entries including features, shorts and documentaries, and a journalist noted that, "Inexpensive digital cameras, editing and effects software that run on laptop computers, and a new set of Internet and DVD based distribution mechanisms are cracking open the clubby Hollywood scene. Like all technological shifts, the digital cinema revolution is threatening the dominance of establishment powers, in this case, the major movie studios" (Kirsner D1).

In 2001, Greg Coote, executive chairman of Intertainer Asia, which has licensed the Sony VOD system for fifteen Asian territories including Singapore, New Zealand, Hong Kong, Korea, and Taiwan (with a potential customer base of 1.7 billion people), summed up the situation by saying, "Video on demand puts the whole entertainment business back to the consumer. It's an evolution as opposed to a revolution."[19] Although he was referring specifically to VOD, I think his point is applicable on a broader level in that the IWR is the next step, economically, in the evolution of delivering movies to the consumer. Therefore, perhaps in the near future that old movie advertising slogan, "Coming soon to a theater near you," will be revised to read, "Coming soon to everyone, everywhere."

Notes

1   Jonathan Bing and Dade Hayes, *Open Wide: How Hollywood Box Office Became a National Obsession* (New York: Miramax Books, 2004) 372.
2   Scott Kirsner, "Who Needs Hollywood Anymore?" *The Boston Globe*, 31 Jan. 2005: D1.
3   Warren F. Gulko and James B. Hunt, Project Report: *The Business of Films and Entertainment* (Wilmington: U. of North Carolina, 1998) 28.

4 Martin Dale, *The Movie Game: The Film Business in Britain, Europe and America* (London: Cassell, 1997) 31.

5 Andrew Hindes, "DreamWorks Sticks with Universal," *Microsoft National Broadcasting Company* 17 Apr. 2001, 17 Apr. 2001<http://www.msnbc.com/news/560663.asp>.

6 Rick Lyman, "Today's Box Office Trend: Fast and Furious," *Sun-Sentinel* (Fort Lauderdale, FL) 15 Aug. 2001: 1–2.

7 "U.S. Film Industry is Picture of Health – Officials," *The New York Times*, nytimes.com 15 Mar. 2005, 15 Mar. 2005 <http:nytimes.com/reuters/arts/entertainment-leisure-movies.html>.

8 "Anti-Piracy," *Motion Picture Association of America*, mpaa.org 15 Mar. 2005 <http://www.mpaa.org/anti-piracy/>.

9 Colin Brown and Mike Goodridge, "International Box Office Brings Home the Bacon for Hollywood," *Screen Daily* 9 Mar. 2001:1–2.

10 Dan Glickman, Presentation, "The Movie Industry is a Vital Part of the American Economy," *ShoWest Conference*, Paris Hotel, Las Vegas, 15 Mar 2005.

11 Lew Irwin, ed., "Still in Theaters, 'Ray' Has Fine Video Debut," *Studio Briefing – imdb.com* 3 Feb. 2005, 15 Mar. 2005 <http://www.imdb.com/news/sb/2005-02-03>.

12 Lew Irwin, ed., "See the Movie, Then Buy the DVD – Four Days Later," *Studio Briefing – imdb.com* 10 Feb. 2005, 15 Mar. 2005 <http://www.imdb.com/news/sb/2005-02-10>.

13 Chris Koseluk, "The Trend Is Near," Spec. issue of *Hollywood Reporter* (1999): 1.

14 Lew Irwin, ed., "Landmark Theaters to Go Digital," *Studio Briefing – imdb.com* 15 Mar. 2005, 16 Mar. 2005 <http://www.imdb.com/news/sb/2005-03-15>.

15 Lew Irwin, ed., "Ireland to be First Country to Go All Digital in Theaters," *Studio Briefing – imdb.com* 22 Mar. 2005, 22 Mar. 2005 <http://www.imdb.com/news/sb/2005-03-22>.

16 Ben Berkowitz, "Video on Demand Hits Roadblocks," MSNBC 7 Apr. 2001, 17 Apr. 2001 <http://www.msnbc.com/news/560174.asp>.

17 Vito J. Racanello, "Blockbusters? Hollywood, Cable Firms Finally Pose a Real Threat to the King of Video Chains," *Barron's* 27 Aug. 2001:17.

18 Ben Berkowitz, "Interest in Online Film is Little and Less, Say Two New Studies," *Inside.com* 12 Mar. 2001, 18 Apr. 2001, <http://www.inside.com/jcs?process...pod_id=10&uifiller+N$antiCacheRandom=8124>.

19 David Seguin, "Coote Spearheads Intertainer's VOD Launch in Asia," *Screendaily.com* 17 Apr. 2001, 18 Apr. 2001 <http://www.screendaily.com/shtml_files/newsletter_redirect.shtml>.

Lord of the Rings, Star Wars, and Participatory Fandom: Mapping New Congruencies Between the Internet and Media Entertainment Culture

6

ELANA SHEFRIN

[. . .]

Hollywood newcomer Peter Jackson and Hollywood legend George Lucas are both engaged in projects that are mapping out new congruencies between the Internet and media entertainment culture. Operating within the genre of science fiction/fantasy filmmaking, Jackson and Lucas share sophisticated abilities for combining technology and mythology in the creation of authentic, self-contained alternate universes. Both cinematic universes—Jackson's Middle-earth and Lucas's far-away galaxy—have generated immense fan bases that have swelled the ranks of loyal audiences and have ensured the commercial success of the two media franchises. Additionally, a growing number of "active" or "participatory" fans (Jenkins, 1992) are exhibiting a sense of ownership that includes an investment in the creative development of these universes. Internet clubs and Web sites have provided venues for fans to maintain heightened connections to the two media producers and their evolving franchises through social gossip, artistic production, and political activism. The differing styles that Jackson and Lucas have adopted with their online fan bases, and the consequential effects on the production, circulation, and consumption of their commercial offerings, provide us with two divergent models of interaction between popular representatives of media entertainment culture and Internet fan culture.

Jackson's project as the screenwriter-director-producer of J.R.R. Tolkien's (1954/1986) *Lord of the Rings* trilogy has developed over the past six years, beginning with the first screenplay draft in 1997. In an unprecedented feat, Jackson filmed three feature-length installments during a 15-month period from 1999 to 2001. These films, fortuitously bolstered by high sales figures and continuous production revisions, have been meted out on a yearly basis: *The Fellowship of the Ring* in December 2001, *The Two Towers* in December 2002, and *The Return of the King* in December 2003. Lucas, conversely, has been developing his legendary Hollywood status over the past 30 years. As the *auteur* and part owner of the *Star Wars* franchise, his roles have been variously configured. He did the screenwriting and directing of the original *Star Wars* (1977) film, and then became the screenwriter-producer of the second and third installments of the trilogy: *The Empire Strikes Back* (1980) and *The Return of the Jedi* (1983). Most recently, he has mirrored Jackson's credentials as the screenwriter-director-producer of three prequels: *Star Wars: Episode I – The Phantom Menace* (1999), *Star Wars: Episode II – The Attack of the Clones* (2002), and *Star Wars: Episode III*, (2005).

Although both filmmakers' releases in the year 2002—Jackson's *The Two Towers* and Lucas's *Attack of the Clones*—have been enjoying a commensurate economic popularity, their career trajectories over the past six years have not been similar. While Jackson has been consistently gaining prestige with critics and fans, Lucas has been buffeted by controversy, alternatively excoriated and praised. During that period of time, one of the major distinctions between the production styles of the two filmmakers has been in their relationships with online fan clubs and participatory fandom. *Lord of the Rings* fans have been actively courted by Jackson and New Line Cinema throughout all aspects of authoring, casting, filming, and marketing the trilogy. *Star Wars* fans, however, have been doubly offended by the actions of Lucas and Lucasfilm: on the one hand, their desires to be "consumer affiliates" in the cinematic production process have been generally ignored; on the other hand, their roles as "illegal pirates" of corporately-owned intellectual property have been overtly emphasized (Jenkins, 2003). Consequently, Jackson's and New Line Cinema's innovative strategies with online fans have been advantageous to Jackson's career, while causing raised expectations that have been detrimental to Lucas's career.

The two filmmakers' contrasting motivations, strategies, and trajectories can be effectively analyzed by applying Bourdieu's (1984, 1993a, 1993b, 1993c, 1998) theory of cultural production, which employs a game-playing terminology to illuminate the interaction between three "fields of practice": the artistic field, the field of power, and the field of class relations (1993a, p. 38). Bourdieu develops a social construct that is graphically illustrated as three co-existing, permeable fields. The artistic field is positioned within the larger field of power which, in turn, is positioned within the overarching field of class relations. To further substantiate the patterns of interaction among the three fields, Bourdieu places the artistic field at a *dominated* position within the field of power, but at a *dominant* position within the field of class relations. Clearly, with the advent of media entertainment conglomerates and the Internet, Bourdieu's fields of practice are becoming more permeable, with a two-way communicative flow between the dominant and dominated forces. Exemplifying a transmitting flow from the artistic field, cultural producers are gaining status in both personal and corporate fields of power. Exemplifying a receptive flow from the fields of power and class relations, media entertainment is splintered by social distinctions—from target audiences to niche markets—and hierarchized by economic potentials—from calculations of fan base spending power to predictions of worldwide market sales.

To some extent, the dominating effects of outside forces on a particular artistic field will depend upon the strategies employed and the alliances chosen by the cultural producers who are positioned within the field. Bourdieu's (1993a) construct can be augmented by Jenkins's (1992, 2003) ethnographic observations on the changing patterns of media entertainment culture, which present a cogent rationale for re-conceptualizing traditional producer-consumer alliances to include the participatory practices of active fans. This is particularly true within the cinematic field of Hollywood production, where "middle-brow art" carrying an aura of cultural legitimacy (Bourdieu, 1993c) is peddled to mass audiences and emulated throughout the global marketplace.

In mapping the congruencies between the Internet and media entertainment culture, this essay will explore the communicative flows between Bourdieu's three fields of practice—artistic, power, and class relations—at four procedural stages: pre-production, production, circulation, and consumption. It will be argued that the advent of the Internet and online fandom has "out-moded" the previous nature of those communicative flows and now supplies a strong link between the three fields. In characterizing the Internet as the site of a political struggle between utopian visions of participatory democracy and prevailing hierarchies of economic power, Harrison and Falvey's (2001) thesis-counterthesis model will be presented and applied. These authors' "pro" and "con" evaluation of Internet culture will be charted along several dimensions of communicative access and democratic opportunity. Discursive methods employed by Jackson and Lucas throughout the four procedural stages will be scrutinized for indications of whether the two producers are attempting to promote democratic opportunities for online fans within the processes of media culture, or are seeking to manipulate the Internet to consolidate prevailing hierarchies of economic power across the three fields of practice.

Pre-Production: Positioning the Players on the Field

During the early 1980s, as Lucas was being crowned the premiere Hollywood *auteur* for the *Star Wars* trilogy, and Jackson was entering the cinematic production field with his first 10-minute film, Pierre Bourdieu was gaining American recognition with the English language publication of *Distinction: A Social Critique of the Judgment of Taste* (1984). Although the three authors were at different stages in their careers—Bourdieu was 14 years older than Lucas and 26 years older than Jackson—each was attracting a cult following within his respective field of practice. In an interesting parallel between the pre-eminent cultural critic and the fledgling cultural producer, Jackson's first feature-length film—a grotesque horror comedy featuring alien cannibals—was entitled *Bad Taste* (1987). At that time, while Bourdieu was theorizing connections between social class distinctions and aesthetic tastes, he might not have realized that many of the same student intellectuals who were aligned with the "bourgeois aesthetic" inherent in the dominant cultures of higher education and material wealth, were simultaneously immersed in the "popular aesthetic" inherent in the dominated cultures of mass communication and working class entertainment. They might have read Tolkien, watched *Star Wars* or *Bad Taste*, and debated the difference between individual and structural identities—all in one day. Bourdieu did, however, accord a primacy to youth in the field of cultural production. As early as 1971, with the French publication of *The Production of Belief*, Bourdieu (1993b) recognized an alignment between intellectual artists and middle-class youth that had begun during the social movements of the 1960s. Bourdieu explains that both intellectual artists and middle-class youth belonged to subcultures that were refusing to adopt the bourgeois worldview of power, money, tradition and a "spirit of seriousness" (1993b, p. 105). Those subcultures, based in "the eternal present," established a tension between institutional, canonized structures and the introduction of new, youthful practices. Bourdieu then uses this dialectic to demonstrate that within the field of cultural production, the advent of an artistic work has the potential to out-mode or out-date a classic work, causing it to slip mechanically into the past:

On one side are the dominant figures, who want continuity, identity, reproduction; on the other, the newcomers, who seek discontinuity, rupture, difference, revolution. To "make one's name" [faire date] means making one's mark, achieving recognition (in both senses) of one's difference from other producers, especially the most consecrated of them; at the same time, it means creating a new position beyond the positions already occupied, ahead of them, in the *avant-garde*. (p. 106)

Bourdieu's statements can clearly be applied to Jackson's and Lucas's respective positions in the field of media production at the time Jackson began working on the cinematic adaptation of J.R.R. Tolkien's (1954/1986) *The Lord of the Rings* in 1997. Lucas was one of the most financially successful Hollywood filmmakers and was highly esteemed as a leader in digital production advances and global marketing strategies. After a 19-year hiatus from working with the *Star Wars* narrative—during which time he was a screenwriter-executive producer for the Indiana Jones adventure trilogy *Raiders of the Lost Ark* (1981), *Indiana Jones and the Temple of Doom* (1984), and *Indiana Jones and the Last Crusade* (1989)—Lucas was beginning to film the first of three prequel episodes, *The Phantom Menace* (1999). Conversely, Jackson's position was one of a Hollywood outsider, a youthful unknown who was aiming to achieve recognition and make his mark in the field. Thus, Lucas's main strategy would be to use his prestige and power to retain control of his dominant position, while Jackson's main strategy would be to create a new position as an *avant-garde* filmmaker. Similarly, Lucas's trajectory would be to adopt a holding pattern of practices designed to maintain the *status quo*, while Jackson's trajectory would be to gain a higher status through transformative practices that "succeed in overturning the hierarchy of the field without disturbing the principles upon which the field is based" (Bourdieu, 1993b, p. 83). Although both directors ultimately had the same goal—to produce critically and commercially successful films—the differing amounts of "symbolic capital" and "economic capital" (Bourdieu, 1998) each held would have a direct effect on the defensive and offensive strategies he would choose to employ.

[. . .]

Production: Using the Internet to Maximize Economic and Symbolic Profits

When Peter Jackson and partner Fran Walsh began adapting Tolkien's novels into a screenplay, they faced three main challenges, two of which were considered to be standard hurdles in the filmmaking process: to secure the approval and financial backing of a Hollywood studio, and to produce a filmic adaptation that could be critically and commercially successful. The third challenge was somewhat unusual: to connect with 100 million loyal Tolkien fans and avoid alienating as many as possible.

[. . .]

As Jackson was continuing to redraft the three scripts, formulate the hiring of cast and crew, and schedule the filming of the production, he made the first move to connect with Tolkien fans. Jackson asked media critic Harry Knowles, of Aint-it-Cool-News.com, to conduct an online interview that would be based on questions submitted to Knowles's Web site. Knowles agreed, and the first interview took place in August, 1998. Before answering the 20 questions that Knowles had compiled from over 14,000 submissions, Jackson thanked the fans, asserting, "A lot of the concerns you raise focus on the same areas that we are currently grappling with." The filmmaker emphasized the importance of his communication with the fans, pledging to conduct a second interview within a few months. He also acknowledged the Web as a communal meeting place: "Using Harry's site was the only way I could imagine reaching all of you in an efficient way" (Knowles, 1998).

The multi-layered questions, collated by Knowles, encompassed detailed aspects related to the ongoing decisions that were being made at that time by the screenwriting team. Jackson earnestly discussed the inadequacies of the fantasy film genre as a whole, the difficulty in the cinematic portrayal of Tolkien's intellectual vision, historical authority, and linguistic talents, the proposed departures of the filmic narrative from the literary texts, the literary depth and dramatic tension of the filmic texts, the extent to which the films would include Tolkien's songs, poetry, and lyrical style, the realistic scope of the battle scenes, and the actual titles of the three cinematic installments.

[. . .]

In fall of 2000, after the TolkienOnline.com fan site had collected 16,000 virtual signatures petitioning Jackson "not to violate the integrity of Tolkien's work," Jackson made an official announcement stating that the filmic text would adhere more closely to the novels than had originally been planned (Davis, 2001, p. 127). With this victory, the Purists were somewhat mollified with the results from their monitoring of the film production. Nevertheless, throughout the production and subsequent distribution of the three films, all deviations from the novels would continue to be deplored on fan Web sites.

From a critical viewpoint, Jackson's online interviews with Tolkien fans can be seen as a strategic move to co-opt the overall import of fan opinion. By presenting himself as a Tolkien fan who is ideologically attracted to casting fannish actors, Jackson is reassuring the fans that their opinions have the "inside track" and are being represented by the cast and crew. For example, actor Ian McKellen highlights his alliance with fans in a *Newsweek* interview: "Although it's not made exclusively for the fans, it's made by fans. We're all allies" (Giles, 2001, p. 4). Similarly, Jackson echoes this sentiment in an interview with Collura (2002a): "I really made the conscious attempt to make the film that I would like to see because, I mean, I read the book, I was a fan . . . So I was really making the film for myself." After declaring himself to be an admirer of the novels and expressing his solidarity with Tolkien fans, Jackson intends for his confession, that of making the film for himself, to carry a connotation of popular sovereignty and representative decision-making, rather than arrogant dismissal of fan opinion.

From a more utopian viewpoint, Jackson's discourse with online fans can be seen as a technologically-inspired antidote to traditional demarcations between the production and consumption of cultural artifacts. Authorship has characteristically been a solitary endeavor, enacted in an environment that is isolated from the intended audience. By using the Internet for social communication while he is drafting the scripts, Jackson is able to be a "filter," a "final arbiter for a lot of good ideas from a group of people" (Bauer, 2002, p. 8). Ideally, he draws inspiration from the fans' thoughtful perspectives and studied observations on the proposed cinematic adaptations while he simultaneously increases his credibility with the future audience of the films. Such a utopian viewpoint is obviously not the norm for present-day media entertainment culture. However, this essay argues that the precedents set by Jackson,

New Line Cinema, and online fans have provided an alternate model for envisioning future producer-consumer alliances in the field of media production.

Clearly, major changes in the processes of production and consumption must occur before the model could be applied widely. At the present time, Jenkins reports that the vast majority of cultural production by fans is occurring extemporaneously to, not collaboratively with, the "official" authorship of the narratives. Due to the nature of their sampling and appropriation practices, fans' involvement in a chosen textual universe is likely to remain more evident throughout the processes of circulation and consumption, rather than within the originating processes of narrative creation. Even if commercial practices were to be drastically transformed to streamline consumer input, some texts will never be amenable to fandom co-production. As one anonymous reviewer has pointed out, those fan bases that have experienced a lengthy shared legacy and sense of inheritance will be the most inclined to desire roles in the co-production of artifacts that contribute to their narrative universe. Both *Lord of the Rings* and *Star Wars* fans are vested with feelings of legacy and inheritance, while fans of *The Matrix* films (1999, 2003a, 2003b), for example, are not. Whether or not Jackson's discourse with online fans heralds the democratizing of media entertainment by Internet culture, it is a potentially useful exercise to document his strategies with fans, to compare them with Lucas's strategies, and to attempt to calculate how these strategies may be affecting their respective trajectories. To further characterize the participation of *Lord of the Rings* and *Star Wars* fans in the practices of circulation and consumption, two types of comparisons will now be made—between fandom perception of Lucas's and Jackson's symbolic capital, and between the Internet marketing strategies of Lucasfilm and New Line Cinema.

Circulation: Active Fans as "Agents of Consecration"

With the advent of participatory fandom, a new class of consecrating agents has been introduced into Bourdieu's "circle of belief" (1993b, p. 77). Due to their close textual readings, their enthusiastic critical analyses, their extreme dedication, and their growing numbers, active fans are beginning to be recognized as important contributors to the formation of collective belief. As Bourdieu explains in *The Field of Cultural Production* (1993a), every artistic field is characterized by opposing forces that are struggling to either transform or conserve the existing system's power to shape the larger social order. Cultural producers harness these forces by forming alliances with members of different social classes, or target audiences, in order to maximize their symbolic and economic profits. In the marketplace of symbolic goods, which Bourdieu situates within a larger field of power and a still larger field of class relations, the value of an artistic work is determined, in part, by the opinions of "agents of consecration" (1993c, p. 126). These agents—who may be critics, scholars, or professionals—possess special knowledge and are conversant in aesthetic codes that are endemic to a particular field of cultural production. Their pronouncements serve to form a respected consensus that, although based on "collective belief or, more precisely, collective misrecognition" (1993b, p. 81), preserves the consumers' faith in the game. Active fans form a hybrid class of consecrating agents—they may possess scholarly knowledge without being scholars, or they may possess a discriminating eye without being professional critics.

Jenkins (1992) has identified several levels of activity that are endemic to participatory fandom's engagement with the chosen narrative universes. The three practices that are most relevant to this discussion are: a tendency toward close textual readings that combine "emotional proximity and critical distance" (p. 277), the ongoing production of a "contemporary folk culture" through the sampling and appropriation of commercial texts, discourses, and images (p. 279), and the use of the Internet as a "base for consumer activism" such as speaking back to producers and media companies, or lobbying for alternative developments (p. 278). Each of these levels of activity, which range from highly individualized creative expressions to highly collectivized patterns of communication, provide opportunities for cultural producers to either "commodify" or "consecrate" fandom practices within the existing systems of circulation and consumption. Moreover, the strategies and trajectories adopted by each producer will depend upon both internal and external factors, including personal characteristics and ambitions, prior accumulation of economic and symbolic capital, and the respective positions of other producers within the field of practice. Therefore, how a relatively unknown director from New Zealand became a model for one of the most commercially successful American filmmakers can be explained by combining Bourdieu's and Jenkins's insights.

According to Bourdieu, consecrating agents not only contribute to the formation of collective belief surrounding the value of symbolic goods, but also to the evaluation of a cultural producer's symbolic capital. This evaluation is somewhat reliant on the "sincerity" of the producing agent, which is only achieved "when there is a perfect and immediate harmony between the expectations inscribed in the position occupied . . . and the dispositions of the occupant" (1993b, p. 95). Under Bourdieu's analysis, Jackson's disposition has been generally acknowledged to be sincere and in harmony with his position, while Lucas's disposition has often been attacked as insincere and in disharmony with his position. At least one contributing factor to this discrepancy is that Jackson is perceived as an encourager of participatory fan practices, while Lucas is perceived as an inhibiter of those practices.

Unlike Jackson's fairly straight trajectory, Lucas has had a series of ups and downs with both critics and fans. To be fair, Lucas has been a major player in Hollywood for almost three times as long as Jackson and, in many instances, Lucas's phenomenal amounts of economic and symbolic capital have insulated him from his attackers. However, at certain tumultuous points in his career, he has been forced to confront accusations of both personal arrogance and over-commercialization of the Star Wars saga. After the 1999 release of Episode I: The Phantom Menace, Brooker (2002, p. xvi) cites fans' grievances:

> Star Wars fans feel that they should be the custodians, but are faced with a situation where someone else still owns the story, is pitching to a far wider audience than their dedicated group, cares not at all for their interpretation of the saga, and will attempt to shut down their sites forcibly if they contradict his version of the characters and plot.

Brooker's explanation correlates a "harsh voice of criticism" against Lucas personally as a writer/director who callously disregards fans' creative interpretations of the narrative, with a corresponding "general sense of distrust" in Lucas professionally as the owner of a media empire that seeks commercial profit at the expense of human relationship (2002, p. 90).

The largest decline in Lucas's symbolic capital occurred as the result of fans' tremendous disappointment in the Phantom Menace production. Many Star Wars fans, especially the older ones who had invested their childhoods and sometimes their careers in their relationships with the Star Wars narrative, were harshly critical of Lucas and the direction his franchise had taken. Webmaster Kolnack of the CloneWars unofficial fan site complains in an open letter to Lucas:

> [M]uch of the movie was too influenced by marketing . . . The movie should have had us, (the die-hard fans), in mind more than it did and we all know that. George Lucas should have consulted with us, the fans, as to what we think and what we'd be most excited to see in this film . . . [We] hope he doesn't repeat the same mistakes twice. Make this one for us, George; after all, it's fans like us who've made you and your family millionaires many times over!
>
> (Kolnack, 2000, Section 8)

While Kolnack does not specifically contrast Lucas's conduct with Jackson's, other Star Wars fans have been more explicit in their comparisons. A 2001 online petition, signed by over 7,000 fans, requested:

> We, the undersigned, in the spirit of our raped childhoods, ask that George Lucas give over his reign as director and writer of Episode III to one Peter Jackson . . . In light of recent George Lucas movies, more specifically The Phantom Menace and the soon-to-be released Attack of the Clones, we beg thee of Star Wars creation to pass all creative rights to Peter Jackson.
>
> (Petition, 2001)

Realistically, there has been no indication that Lucas has considered a bequest of his artistic creation to Jackson, and very little indication that Lucas has been swayed by Jackson's alliance with Tolkien fans. However, partially as a result of Jackson's example, Lucas was urged by Fox Studios to become more responsive to Star Wars fans after they "mercilessly attacked" Lucas for The Phantom Menace's weak narrative and shallow characters (Blumberg, 2002). Furthermore, there is some evidence that Lucas has developed a new paternal fondness for fan filmmakers who have been circulating their Star Wars-based digital shorts on the Internet over the past decade; he even recruited some of those grass-roots filmmakers to work on Episode II (Brooker, 2002).

[. . .]

Based upon the personal experiences of Jackson and Lucas, it may be proposed that the nature of the relations that cultural producers choose to establish with any fan base that is attached to their particular artistic products will affect, to some extent, the accomplishment of the producers' desired outcomes. The scope of effect will be related to the longevity and intensity of the fans' engagement with a particular text or narrative, and will exist on a participatory continuum throughout the processes of production, circulation, and consumption. Logically, the types of fans who will seek the highest level of participation at all stages of those processes will be ones whose investments in the shared narratives have dramatically shaped their life worlds and life choices. In the case of both the Star Wars and Lord of the Rings film franchises, this type of fan is often the rule, rather than the exception. The differing manners in which the official Web sites for Star Wars and Lord of the Rings discursively interact with those fans along the participatory continuum can be revealed in a comparison of the corporate media marketing practices of Lucasfilm and New Line Cinema. According to Jenkins (2003), the "winners" in the "current media revolution" will be those cultural producers who attempt to offset polarizing issues over intellectual property rights by recognizing the economic and political imperative of collaboration with active fan consumers.

Consumption: Online Fans and Participatory Media Culture

Jenkins (2003) describes active fans as a specific type of audience that can be substantially distinguished from the majority of media consumers. For such fans, the act of watching a particular film or playing a certain video game can comprise an experiential unit that is interconnected to an expansive multi-textual environment—one which may encompass magazines, books, collectibles, interactive media, online clubs, conferences, and role-playing events. As active participants, fans often appropriate corporate-generated imagery, and then embellish or transform it with personal artistic expressions such as poetry, songs, paintings, scholarly essays, creative fiction, photographs, digital films, collages, or clothing. Due to their personal identification with the texts, fans may also adopt attitudes, language, or behaviors that are an outgrowth of their "immersion in a special lexicon" (Harris, 1998, p. 8). Thus, participatory fandom is marked by a sustained emotional and physical engagement with a particular narrative universe—an engagement that visualizes a non-commercial, shared ownership with the media company that holds the commercial, legal property rights.

Paradoxically, the nature of media marketing culture ensures that participatory fandom can be both the overt strength for, and the covert weakness against, its success. On the one hand, media companies could not survive without loyal fan participation. Jenkins (2003, p. 284) points to the commercial promotions of the *Star Wars* franchise as an illustration of this point: "This new 'franchise' system actively encourages viewers to pursue their interests in media content across various transmission channels, to be alert to the potential for new experiences offered by these various tie-ins." By definition, an active and loyal fan will constantly be on the alert for updated products and enhanced engagement with the lexicon. The size and dedication of a participatory fan base will affect both the perceived amount of commercial risk and the perceived likelihood of commercial success for a proposed franchise addition.

On the other hand, participatory fandom is the enemy of media companies. The battle-lines are drawn over the issues of copyright and intellectual property law (Lessig, 2001). Jenkins (2003, p. 289) proposes a fan manifesto that re-imagines an old media/mass culture as a new media/folk culture:

> Fans reject the idea of a definitive version produced, authorized, and regulated by some media conglomerate. Instead, fans envision a world where all of us can participate in the creation and circulation of central cultural myths . . . Fans also reject the studio's assumption that intellectual property is a "limited good," to be tightly controlled lest it dilute its value. Instead, they embrace an understanding of intellectual property as "shareware," something that accrues value as it moves across different contexts, gets retold in various ways, attracts multiple audiences, and opens itself up to a proliferation of alternative meanings.

Within the world of the Internet and online fan clubs, corporate products are easily treated as abstract digital bits of information, or more concretely, as raw material for fans' creative re-interpretation. A basic disagreement over the nature and ownership of cultural texts results in a constant re-negotiation of the relationship between media producers and active fans. At certain times, the media producers will court online fans as consumer affiliates; at other times, they will attack them as illegal pirates. This discursive tension is clearly exemplified in the differing, character-specific manners in which the official Web sites for the *Star Wars* and *Lord of the Rings* franchises have maintained a balance between promotional strategies and protection of copyrighted assets.

New Line Cinema's official Web site, LordoftheRings.net, was launched in 1999, two and a half years prior to the scheduled release of the first film of the trilogy. As director of interactive marketing, Gordon Paddison maintains the Web site, networks with other Tolkien fan sites, handles all Internet publicity, and deals with online issues that arise in connection with New Line's legal rights to the *Lord of the Rings* intellectual property. Engaging in dual insider-outsider roles, Paddison maintains a delicate balance between his two identities as a Tolkien Web host and a film studio's marketing director. In his insider role, Paddison knows the most current product information, answers over 100 emails each day, gives away a plethora of computer-related *Lord of the Rings* merchandise, and provides the premier Web access to online film clips. In his outsider role, Paddison seeks to protect his company's copyrighted assets by preventing pirated images and videos from being displayed on any of the Tolkien Web sites, and by monitoring *Lord of the Rings* chat rooms and discussion boards (Davis, 2001).

By all accounts, Paddison's relationship with fans and unofficial fan sites has been largely respectful and accommodating; the fans have generally reciprocated with cooperative attitudes. Flynn (2001) reports, for example, that one fan called the police when *Lord of the Rings* production footage was being offered for sale on the Internet, prior to the release of the first film in the trilogy. The fan's information led to the arrest of three crew members and the return of the stolen footage. In another instance, New Line's altercation with a New Zealand resident, who had been taking photographs of the production site and posting them on an unofficial fan site, led to a camera-less conciliatory tour of the facilities.

In a 2001 interview with *Entertainment Weekly*, New Line's executive producer Mark Ordesky exclaims, "Gordon is a genius! He's been brilliant at keeping an inclusionary vibe, and it's just such a contrast to other big-budget Hollywood movies where the fans and the Internet are seen as things to be kept away" (Flynn, 2001, p. 44). Interviewer Flynn retorts: "Paging Mr. Lucas!" Apparently, Lucas's reputation has suffered from a long history of legal disputes over participatory fan practices, dating back 20 years and continuing to the present time. Jenkins charges: "Through the years, Lucasfilm has been one of the most aggressive corporate groups in trying to halt fan cultural production" (2003, p. 290). Finally, in the late 1990s, the StarWars.com official Web site began granting free Web space to fans who desired to post their creations, but only if their submissions would become the studio's intellectual property (see Lucas Online, 2003b). While some fans were appreciative, others have been highly critical of the policy, complaining that their creative designs are being co-opted by a corporate decision that violates fair use laws and compromises their personal chances of profiting from their artistic practices.

[. . .]

As Jackson's and New Line Cinema's strategies have shown, the active fan audience offers cultural producers the opportunity to forge strategic alliances that can democratically influence the power hierarchies in the artistic field and the larger field of class relations. The formation and character of these alliances depend upon the expectations of the fan base attached to a specific textual universe, and upon the pre-dispositions of the cultural producers, both personally and corporately. While Lucas's and Lucasfilm's flagrant commodification of participatory fandom has not visibly eroded the general audience consumption of their franchise products, it has clearly resulted in a loss of symbolic prestige among media critics and *Star Wars* fans. If Bourdieu is correct when he identifies such agents of consecration as important contributors to the circle of belief, then Lucas's egregious attitude toward active fans will continue to erode his status in the artistic field of practice and in the overarching field of class relations. [. . .]

Online/Offline Communication between the Fields of Power and Media Production

With the recent advent of media entertainment conglomerates cultural producers are achieving dominant positions in both the economic and political aspects of the field of power. On the personal level, Hollywood actors are becoming prominent politicians; on the corporate level, the incomes of media companies are eclipsing the budgets of entire countries. This ascendancy of cultural producers in the field of power has intensified the corresponding "heteronomous" (Bourdieu, 1993a, p. 40) hierarchy in the artistic field—the dominating influence of "cultural legitimacy" on the production and marketing of media products. As Gripsrud (2002) points out, those agents with the most economic and political power are strengthening their positions in the artistic field and are continuing to impose those norms and sanctions that best serve the preservation of the dominant power hierarchy. Within the mass production of Hollywood middle-brow culture, Bourdieu's system of class distinctions is maintained by media marketing practices that classify audiences based upon their spending power and choice of spending categories. Thus, Lucas Online can justify its exclusionary subscription service as a marketing-research tool for targeting a preferred audience—loyal, wealthy fans. However, Gripsrud also emphasizes the existence of "dialectical relations" between the intellectual and commercial poles in any artistic field of production. Tensions between "freedom and constraints, the individual and the collective, tradition and renewal" are actualized as struggles between young and old, liberal and conservative, dominated and dominant (2002, p. 294). Thus, New Line Cinema's liberal online marketing policies can reflect the cultivation of a youthful communitarian persona that promotes democratic access to both official and unofficial *Lord of the Rings* sites of cultural production.

Arguably, one of the major influences contributing to the increasing structural inter-reliance among Bourdieu's three fields of practice is computer-mediated communication. True to Gripsrud's (2002) model of "dialectical relations," the Internet is a venue that epitomizes the political struggle between utopian visions of participatory democracy and prevailing hierarchies of economic power. The utopian viewpoint emphasizes the Internet's potential for positive social interaction and virtual community-building (Baym, 1995; Fernback, 1999; McLaughlin, Osborne, & Smith, 1995; Meeks, 1997; Rheingold, 2000; Watson, 1997); the critical viewpoint characterizes the Internet as a "contested frontier" fraught with socially problematic hierarchies of access and discourse (Gunkel & Gunkel, 1997; Healy, 1997; Jenkins, 1992; MacDonald, 1998; Poster, 1995, 1997; Turkle, 1995). This foundational dialectical tension has led scholars Harrison and Falvey (2001) to propose a thesis-counterthesis model for a theoretical discussion of democracy and computer-mediated communication.

Reasoning that "democracy" is a contested term, Harrison and Falvey organize an analysis of Internet practices in terms of five root theses and countertheses: power access, information access, interactional access, opportunities for liberal democracy, and opportunities for deliberative democracy. They then evaluate each of those five dimensions within four main sites of deployment: interpersonal, communitarian, organizational, and governmental. Table 1 summarizes the relevant dimensions applicable to mapping congruencies between the Internet and media entertainment culture. In reading the table, it can be discerned that each of the three dimensions—power access, information access, and deliberative democracy—are inherently malleable. Therefore, at any given site of deployment, dual potentials exist for computer-mediated communication to become centralized, with restricted access, or to become decentralized, with open access. Consequently, as exemplified in the differing personal and corporate strategies of the producers of the *Lord of the Rings* and *Star Wars* film franchises, democratic practices can become allied with, exploited by, or simply excluded from producers' chosen trajectories within the cultures of media entertainment and the Internet.

With both pro and con arguments being persuasively presented by scholars and political commentators, Harrison and Falvey (2001) decline to favor one articulation over another, stating that definitive answers will not be obtained during "this period of intense social experimentation" (p. 32). They conclude, however, that "computer-mediated communication will play an important role in the evolution of democracy as the world transitions to network society" (p. 33). In correlating the authors' thesis-counterthesis model with the Internet's impact on Bourdieu's three fields of practice, the most obvious conclusion is that the Internet can be used for either nefarious or noble purposes by agents in all three fields. If this conclusion is common knowledge, then forewarned is forearmed.

Table 1 Dual Potential for Computer Mediation of Media Entertainment

Dimensions	Pro	Con
Power access	The Internet decentralizes decision-making, taking it from the elite and giving it to the masses.	The Internet is used to perpetuate and consolidate centralized power hierarchies.
Information access	Information is widely disseminated and accessed on the Internet.	Information is manipulated and commodified on the Internet.
Deliberative democracy	The Internet is a new public sphere that promotes political dialogue, public good, and community life.	The Internet is a limited forum that mirrors, yet conceals, the perpetuation of society's existing norms.

The most chilling, and potentially the most damaging, argument to the Internet's impact on democratic practices, however, is that of Barber's (1997) "concealed totalism." He warns that "talk of diversity will come quickly to mask 'a new form of totalism all the more dangerous because it boasts of choice and is sold in the language of freedom'" (p. 216, quoted in Harrison & Flavey, 2001, p. 19). Barber's caveat originates in Marx's theory of production and consumption, which Gripsrud (2002) succinctly applies to media culture:

> The general point is, then, that *the audience can never choose something it has not been offered, and any specific programme or product offered is always one of several "imaginable" answers to a more general demand.* It is always producers or senders that decide what is offered, and how these offers are shaped; and these decisions are always made with a view to other factors than the demand of the audience—not least the desire for maximum profit. (p. 289)

Consumers may believe that they are operating with free choice when, in fact, they are generally unable to change any of the cultural products being offered—their only choices are acceptance or rejection.

While the concealed totalism argument propounded by Barber (1997), Bourdieu (1998), and Gripsrud (2002) is a powerful one, it is grounded in two contested theoretical perceptions—that media production is a structurally determined "system of domination" (Marcuse, 1989, p. 240) and that audience consumption operates as a form of "mass deception" (Adorno & Horkheimer, 1989, p. 179). On at least three levels, this viewpoint can be viewed as overly pessimistic. First, it cedes an excessive amount of authority to the faceless institution, while minimizing the potential forces of individual social agency and political awareness. Second, it posits a relatively stable economic structure that is locked into a coercive cycle, while negating the capacity of that structure for dislocation and rupture (Laclau, 1990). Third, by focusing on one possible trajectory, it oversimplifies the complexity of the competing strategies involved in the politics of media entertainment culture. As one of those competing strategies, elite cultural producers will undoubtedly attempt to use the Internet to maximize profits and practice symbolic violence. However, their relative degrees of success will be conditioned by a complicated, changeable interplay with other cultural producers and an array of consecrating agents, including online fans promoting consumer activism and/ or furthering communitarian ideals. At the very least, it should be acknowledged that the producer-consumer dialectic is not solely weighted toward one-sided manipulation, but presents a more nuanced set of interactions.

To predict the future extent of the Internet's democratizing influence across Bourdieu's three fields of practice is to expound upon the competing forces of symbolic, political, and economic capital that are openly and clandestinely struggling for legitimacy. What do Jackson's and New Line Cinema's strategies with online fans portend for the role of computer-mediated communication in cultural production processes? While it can be concluded that this particular combination of director, studio executives, and fans will never be duplicated in the future, it is clear that the *Lord of the Rings* phenomenon portends a paradigmatic shift in producer-consumer affiliations—one that is grounded in new technologies and new participatory practices by active audiences. Furthermore, the democratizing influence of computer-mediated communication on the production, circulation, and consumption of cultural artifacts has larger implications for the intersection of Internet practices with the economic and political fields of power. As an admittedly utopian vision that militates against countervailing forces of concealed manipulation, the alliance of cultural producers with online fans can be seen as mapping new articulations of participatory democracy within the fields of artistic production, power, and class relations.

References

Adorno, T., & Horkheimer, M. (1989). Dialectic of enlightenment. In R.S. Gottlieb (Ed.), *An anthology of western Marxism: From Lukacs and Gramsci to socialist-feminism* (pp. 179–193). Oxford: Oxford University Press.

Ankeny, J. (2003). Biography of George Lucas. *Yahoo All Movie Guide*. Retrieved 3 August 2003 from http://movies.yahoo.com/shop?d = hc&id = 1800017101&cf = biog&intl = us.

Barber, B. (1997). The new telecommunications technology: Endless frontier or the end of democracy? *Constellations*, 4, 208–228.

Bauer, E. (2002, January/February). Interview with Peter Jackson: It's just a movie. *Creative Screenwriting*, 9, 6–12.

Baym, N.K. (1995). The emergence of community in computer-mediated communication. In S.G. Jones (Ed.), *CyberSociety: Computer-mediated communication and community* (pp. 138–163). Thousand Oaks, CA: Sage.

Blumberg, A.T. (2002, May). Attack of the fans: George Lucas Speaks! Part One. *Cinescape* [electronic version]. Retrieved 25 July 2003 from http://cinescape.com/0/print_ed.asp? aff_id = 0&action = page&obj_id = 34659.

Bourdieu, P. (1984). *Distinction: A social critique of the judgment of taste* (R. Nice, Trans.). Cambridge, MA: Harvard University Press. (Original work published 1979.)

Bourdieu, P. (1993a). The field of cultural production, or: The economic world reversed. In R. Johnson (Ed.), *The field of cultural production: Essays on art and literature* (pp. 29–73). New York: Columbia University Press. (Original work published 1983.)

Bourdieu, P. (1993b). The production of belief: Contribution to an economy of symbolic goods. In R. Johnson (Ed.), *The field of cultural production: Essays on art and literature* (pp. 74–111). New York: Columbia University Press. (Original work published 1977.)

Bourdieu, P. (1993c). The market of symbolic goods. In R. Johnson (Ed.), *The field of cultural production: Essays on art and literature* (pp. 112–141). New York: Columbia University Press. (Original work published 1971.)

Bourdieu, P. (1998). *Practical reason: On the theory of action*. (R. Johnson, Trans.) Stanford, CA: Stanford University Press.

Brooker, W. (2002). *Using the Force: Creativity, community and Star Wars fans*. New York: Continuum International Publishing Group.

Collura, S. (2002a). Lord of the Cinematic Rings—Part Two. *Cinescape* [electronic version]. Retrieved 25 July 2003 from www.cinescape.com/0/print_ed.asp?aff_id = 0&action= page& obj_id = 32054.

Collura, S. (2002b). Peter Jackson straddles *The Two Towers*—Part Two. *Cinescape* [electronic version]. Retrieved 25 July 2003 from www.cinescape.com/0/print_ed.asp?aff_id = 0&action = page&obj_id = 37269.

Davis, E. (2001, October). The fellowship of the ring. *Wired Magazine*, pp. 120–132.

Fernback, J. (1999). There is a there there: Notes toward a definition of cybercommunity. In S.G. Jones (Ed.), *Doing Internet research* (pp. 203–220). Thousand Oaks, CA: Sage.

Flynn, G. (2001, November 16). *Lord of the Rings:* Ringmasters. *Entertainment Weekly*, pp. 36–46.

Friedman, R. (2003, January). George Lucas "All Set for Failure." *Fox News.* Retrieved 25 July 2003 from http://foxnews.com/printer_friendly_story/0,3566,75540,00.html.

Giles, J. (2001, December 17). *Lord of the Rings:* A movie made by fans. *Newsweek*, p. 4.

Gripsrud, J. (2002). *Understanding media culture.* New York: Oxford University Press.

Gunkel, D.J., & Gunkel, A.H. (1997). Virtual geographies: The new worlds of cyberspace. *Critical Studies in Mass Communication*, 14, 123–133.

Harris, C. (1998). Introduction. In C. Harris & A. Alexander (Eds.), *Theorizing fandom: Fans, subculture, and identity* (pp. 3–8). Cresskill, NJ: Hampton Press.

Harrison, T.M., & Falvey, L. (2001). Democracy and new communication technologies. *Communication Yearbook*, 25, 1–43.

Healy, D. (1997). Cyberspace and place: The Internet as middle landscape on the electronic frontier. In D. Porter (Ed.), *Internet culture* (pp. 55–68). New York: Routledge.

Jackson, P. (Producer & Director). (1987). *Bad Taste* [motion picture]. Newark, NJ: Anchor Bay Entertainment.

Jackson, P. (Producer & Director). (2001). *The Fellowship of the Ring* [motion picture]. Burbank, CA: Warner Brothers.

Jackson, P. (Producer & Director). (2002). *The Two Towers* [motion picture]. Burbank, CA: Warner Brothers.

Jackson, P. (Producer & Director). (2003). *The Return of the King* [motion picture]. Burbank, CA: Warner Brothers.

Jenkins, H. (1992). *Textual poachers: Television fans and participatory culture.* New York: Routledge, Chapman, and Hall.

Jenkins, H. (2003). Quentin Tarantino's *Star Wars?:* Digital cinema, media convergence, and participatory culture. In D. Thorburn & H. Jenkins (Eds.), *Rethinking media change: The aesthetics of transition* (pp. 281–312). Cambridge, MA: MIT Press.

Knowles, H.J. (1998, August). Interview with Peter Jackson. *Ain't-It-Cool-News.* Retrieved 10 January 2002 from http://www.aint-it-cool-news.com/lordoftherings.html.

Knowles, H.J. (1999, January). Interview with Peter Jackson. *Ain't-It-Cool-News.* Retrieved 10 January 2002 from http://www.aint-it-cool-newa.com/lordoftherings2.html.

Kolnack, E. (2000). *Dear Mr. Lucas.* Retrieved 25 July 2003 from http://clonewars.netsville.com/pm_pros.htm.

Kurtz, G. (Producer), & Lucas, C. (Director). (1977). *Star Wars* [motion picture]. Century City, CA: Twentieth Century Fox.

Kurtz, G., & Lucas, G. (Producers), & Kershner, I. (Director). (1980). *The Empire Strikes Back* [motion picture]. Century City, CA: Twentieth Century Fox.

Laclau, E. (1990). *New reflections on the revolution of our time.* London: Verso.

Landau, J. (Producer), & Cameron, I. (Producer & Director). (1997). *Titanic* [motion picture].

Lessig, L. (2001). *The future of ideas: The fate of the commons in a connected world.* NY: Random House.

Lucas, G., & Kazanjian, H.G. (Producers), & Marquand, R. (Director). (1983). *The Return of the Jedi* [motion picture]. Century City, CA: Twentieth Century Fox.

LucasOnline. (2003a). *Introducing starwars.com Hyperspace.* Retrieved from http://www.starwars.com/site/news/2003/05/news20030530.html.

LucasOnline. (2003b). *Terms of Use.* [On-line]. Retrieved 25 July 2003 from http://www.starwars.com/site/copyright.html.

MacDonald, A. (1998). Uncertain utopia: Science fiction media fandom and computer mediated communication. In C. Harris & A. Alexander (Eds.), *Theorizing fandom: Fans, subculture, and identity* (pp. 131–152). Cresskill, NJ: Hampton Press.

Marcuse, H. (1989). An essay on liberation. In R.S. Gottlieb (Ed.), *An anthology of western Marxism: From Lukacs and Gramsci to socialist-feminism* (pp. 234–247). Oxford: Oxford University Press.

Marshall, F. (Producer), & Spielberg, S. (Director). (1981). *Raiders of the Lost Ark* [motion picture]. Hollywood: Paramount Pictures.

Marshall, F. (Producer), & Spielberg, S. (Director). (1984). *Indiana Jones and the Temple of Doom* [motion picture]. Hollywood: Paramount Pictures.

Marshall, F. (Producer), & Spielberg, S. (Director). (1989). *Indiana Jones and the Last Crusade* [motion picture]. Hollywood: Paramount Pictures.

Mason, A., & Silver, J. (Producers), Wachowski, A., & Wachowski, L. (Directors). (1999). *The Matrix* [motion picture]. Burbank, CA: Warner Brothers.

McCallum, R. (Producer), & Lucas, C. (Producer & Director). (1999). *Star Wars: Episode I—The Phantom Menace* [motion picture]. Century City, CA: Twentieth Century Fox.

McCallum, R. (Producer), & Lucas, G. (Director). (2002). *Star Wars: Episode II—Attack of the Clones* [motion picture]. Century City, CA: Lucasfilm/Twentieth Century Fox.

McLaughlin, M. L., Osborne, K.K., & Smith, C.B. (1995). Standards of conduct on USENET. In S.G. Jones (Ed.), *Cybersociety: Computer-mediated communications and community* (pp. 90–111). Thousand Oaks, CA: Sage.

Meeks, B. (1997). Better democracy through technology. *Communications of the* ACM, 40, 75–78.

Petition. (2001). *Peter Jackson to Write and Direct Star Wars III.* Retrieved 30 July 2003 from http://www.petitiononline,.com/dgkomxpq/petition.html.

Poster, M. (1995). In *The second media age.* Cambridge, MA: Polity Press.

Poster, M. (1997). Cyberdemocracy: Internet and the public sphere. In D. Porter (Ed.), *Internet culture* (pp. 201–231). New York: Routledge.

TheOneRing.net. (2003, July). *Ringer reviews.* Retrieved 23 July 2003 from http://www. theonering.net/movie/reviews.html.

Rheingold, H. (2000). *The virtual community: Homesteading on the electronic frontier* (Rev. ed.). Cambridge, MA: MIT Press.

Silver, J. (Producer), Wachowski, A., & Wachowski, L. (Directors). (2003a). *The Matrix Reloaded* [motion picture]. Burbank, CA: Warner Brothers.

Silver, J. (Producer), Wachowski, A., & Wachowski, L. (Directors). (2003b). *The Matrix Revolutions* [motion picture]. Burbank, CA: Warner Brothers.

Tolkien, J.R.R. (1985). *The Silmarillion.* New York: Ballantine/. (Original work published 1977.)

Tolkien, J.R.R. (1986). *The Hobbit.* New York: Ballantine. (Original work published 1937.)

Tolkien, J.R.R. (1986). *The Lord of the Rings.* New York: Ballantine. (Original work published 1954.)

Turkle, S. (1995). *Life on the screen: Identity in the age of the Internet.* New York: Touchstone.

Watson, N. (1997). Why we argue about virtual community: A case study of the Phish.net fan community. In S.G. Jones (Ed.), *Virtual culture* (pp. 102–132). London: Sage.

Transnational Documentaries: A Manifesto

7

JOHN HESS AND PATRICIA R. ZIMMERMANN

I. Introduction

A new world (image) order is indeed emerging. But it differs greatly from the one then-President George Bush prophesied during the 1991 Gulf War and the one President Bill Clinton fantasized in his 1992 and 1996 State of the Union addresses. While Clinton argued for V-chips to control media violence in the home and Internet connections in every school to salvage public education, his speech—focusing exclusively on media content—symptomatically repressed his unwavering, unexamined support for a totally unregulated concentration of media transnationals that will inhibit diversity, public debate, access and democracy.

On February 1, 1996, Congress overwhelmingly passed a new telecommunications law that effectively eliminates all constraints upon both vertical integration and horizontal concentration across industries. It will accelerate media megamergers. Writing in The Washington Post, Jonathan Tasini, president of the National Writers Union, declared that this law ushers in a new era of media "Robber Barons": it advances unrestrained transnational communication oligopolies, effectively annihilating freedom of speech and democratic control over media content. Tasini says, "Before it's too late, the public must snatch back the reins."[1] The current corporate transnational media universe, for example, features the most intensive cross-media merger activity in history, which has, for all intents and purposes, rendered competition an obsolete practice and concept: Disney/ABC Capital Cities, Turner/Time-Warner, Westinghouse/CBS, Sony-Columbia. According to a recent issue of Variety that tracked globalization, once the mergers are completed, the Disney and Turner combines will become the two largest media companies on the globe, with operations and distribution spanning every continent and nearly every technology.

In the midst of this corporate struggle for worldwide domination, however, new media practices and new transnational media organizations have emerged to challenge and remake connections between people across borders: anti-copyright work that deconstructs corporate images, the Gulf War Paper Tiger project on satellite, media pirates interrupting signals with low-end technologies internationally, the Guerrilla Girls' World Wide Web sites, indigenous Fourth World broadcasting and international documentary co-productions and community samizdat video on the war in Bosnia.

We need to reimagine radical media for the twenty-first century, throwing out oppositions of dominant and alternative media formulated during a different period of late capitalism. In this vein, we propose a provisional construct of transnational documentaries as a strategic and political move in a period of rampant civil wars, unprecedented corporate transnational concentration and degradation of humanity across the globe. We want to reclaim the term transnational in order to radicalize it. We need new imaginings to navigate and investigate the relationships between progressive documentaries and the post-cold war world. Projects are currently being launched around the globe to combat the rapid diminishment of the public sphere through globalization. The MacBride Roundtable on Communication, instituted in the late 1980s as a global consortium of policy activists, non-governmental organizations (NGOs), scholars and creators, meets yearly in different locations around the globe to, as its founding statutes declare, "promote democratisation of mass media, telecommunications and electronic networks, in line with the Right to Communicate as a basic human right of individuals and communities." The 8th MacBride Roundtable in Seoul, South Korea, held from August 24–27, 1996, interrogated the "new authoritarian forms" emerging in new technologies, such as "privacy" of transmission, intellectual property rights and copyright, as well as censorship and life threatening situations for journalists in the Middle East, Latin America, Africa and Asia.

[. . .]

We consider this project a polemical intervention into the emerging transnationalization of the world. For example, during the 1996 Summer Olympics in Atlanta, AT&T featured commercials lauding their global communications and information networks with montages of international athletes dressed in costumes from various countries high jumping, throwing the javelin and running. We want to bring into the current discussions of the new global hegemony—primarily economic and technological to date—a focus on oppositional cultural practices, aesthetics and policies. These multiple, fluid and mobile interventions into global communication flows require not only new forms of theorization about radical media, but also bold and innovative artistic and policy strategies, as well as "raids" across borders. This new work—on video, film, the Internet—moves simultaneously between the local, the regional, the national and the global, defying repressive nationalist territorialization.

Not simply a scholarly effort to create new theoretical labyrinths, we see transnational documentaries as a crucial organizational effort to connect thinking about media from all over the globe in order to open up new conceptual territories for both the theory and practice of film and other media. Indeed, this project seeks to deterritorialize documentary history and theory from its location in the North and West in order to provisionally think through new ways of making connections across real and imaginary borders of immigration, race, class, gender, identity, diaspora and nation. We believe that media scholars and activists need to think through the shifting, multiple relationships between the South and East, North and West as fluid, intersecting categories that are never stable or fixed. For example, Guillermo Gomez-Pena's El Naftazteca: Pirate Cyber-TV for A.D. 2000 (1995) was a live satellite broadcast mixing together English and Spanish, phone-ins, MTV-inspired deconstructive clips from Hollywood and Mexican films, images of "Aztecs," a virtual reality piece of a Mexican crossing the border and a talk show host dressed in a pastiche of Aztec headdress, a mariachi suit and Native American garb presenting newscasts about the new world where Anglos are a minority. The piece combines the old technology of cable access and radio call-ins with the new technologies of cyberspace, virtual reality and satellites to destroy the border between new and old technologies, English and Spanish, Mexico and the U.S.

II. Transnational Theory

[. . .]

For corporatist transnationalism, racial, gender, ethnic and sexual identities are to be dematerialized, depoliticized, declawed and decorporalized into new, further segmented markets for the new accelerated capital growth. The conflicts that mark and define these racial, sexual, gender and ethnic differences are neutralized within commodity fetishism. This process of commodification can be observed in blue jean ads geared toward a gay audience, in MTV Raps, in the United Colors of Benetton campaign (a favorite topic for deconstruction in the new literature on transnationalism) and in Hollywood's courting of young black directors like John Singleton and Mario Van Peebles.

If, as Richard Barnett and James Cavanaugh have pointed out in *Global Dreams* (1994), capital is without a home and migrates in cyberspace from site to site, it is also, increasingly, without racialized, gendered, ethnicized or sexualized bodies and denies the specificities of any bodies at all, turning them all into sites and discourses of consumption. In the virtual, fluid world of the transnational corporate landscape, everything is smooth functioning as long as racial, gender and national difference is controlled by ignoring the bodies of maquiladora workers in Mexico; of Guatemalan and Cambodian women sewing in textile factories in Los Angeles; of AIDS patients without health insurance; of immigrants from Latin America and Asia; of victims of nationalist aggression in Bosnia, Rwanda and Myanmar; and of African American and Asian communities within the U.S.

An adversarial transnationalism, therefore, will need to reassert the racial, gender, ethnic, sexual and national differences of multiple bodies. Our argument for a construct of adversarial transnational documentaries displaces categories of "alternative", "oppositional" or "guerrilla" media, terms that suggest that one can easily define the opposition in the first place and that it can be located in some definite, fixed space. The concept of adversarial transnational documentaries wrenches the notion of the transnational away from its corporatist location, moving it instead into the disruptive realms of bodies, people, movements and representational practices that dislodge corporate influence by creating new places for social justice on a global scale.

We believe instead that retrieving and fighting for public space—on public television, satellites, the Internet, public libraries, pirate radio, through fair use appropriations, in public schools, in arts funding, in NGOs like the MacBride Roundtables, in non-profit institutions like colleges and universities, media centers and art museums—is an absolutely essential move, as nearly all of this space has been whittled away by the forces of privatization and commercialization. Thus, we reject the idea of an idealized public sphere, as defined by Habermas and those influenced by his work, as too amorphous and undefined for the present tumultuous moment. We also reject the notion of a reinvigorated civil society that some theorists and policy activists have invoked to fight the transnational. Both terms are anchored within the domain of the liberal welfare state that is systematically being disposed of around the globe. We are unwilling to accept any notion that argues that a place exists outside of economic and material relations, an underground world of talk, when all the material relations of media production are being dramatically reengineered and reorganized to limit public space and debate. In addition, these spaces, economies and cultural productions are in more flux and change than either the concept of the idealized public sphere or the civil society can account for. This is not an academic argument over theory, however. People within the U.S. and all over the globe are being destroyed physically, economically, politically and psychically, and these communities—Los Angeles, Rio de Janeiro, Sarajevo, Kigali, Port au Prince, Belfast—are not public spheres, but spaces of destruction, starvation and torture.

Adversarial transnationalism, then, as a reimaging of relations among media, politics and the economy suggests a constant shuttle between domination and resistance, between hegemonic power and multi-oppositional alliances, between repression and hope. Films, videos, Web sites and CD-ROMs are emerging that operate within this new epistemological nexus—work that refigures the relationship between the local, regional, national and global as one of endless mediation, integration and negotiation rather than separation. It deploys multiple languages, hybridities and strategies to deconstruct the smoothness of the transnational and to repack its sedimented layers with frissure and conflict, the very disturbances that the transnational is always attempting to recuperate and recycle as commodities and markets. *Love, Women and Flowers* (1988), a film by Colombian filmmaker Marta Rodriguez, documents the effects of carnation production on the bodies of women workers and traces the movement of capital across borders. The film travels through several countries—Colombia, Netherlands and the U.S.—but constantly figures the workers as agents of struggle and change who disrupt the smooth flow of capital.

Traditional constructs of national cinema and national identity are complicated by the economic, psychic and political realities of transnationalization. Nevertheless, we are unwilling to completely abandon the concept of the national and the regional for a universalist fantasy of global citizens who forfeit their identities for a Disney World representation of cultural difference. The political and cultural functions of the nation retain power, although the economic operations of the nation have been transnationalized-Chinese and Mexican immigrants are denied" entry to the U.S., Muslims are harassed in Paris, Turks are fire-bombed in Germany and Serb nationalism mercilessly destroys Sarajevo, once a symbol of multiculturalism. We would like, however, to begin an investigation into how the transnational functions within and around concepts of the national, the regional and the local.

III. Transnationalization and Culture

Most accounts of the relationship between transnationalization and culture expose two blind spots that animate our efforts to reimagine a radical, adversarial form of documentary. First, most of these approaches to transnationalization—whether the *Social Text* special issues on Edward Said and on Civil Society, or the many books emerging on transnationalism—discuss media and culture mainly in terms of its location within corporatist transnational systems, often referring to it as cultural capital, and using examples of the worldwide penetration of Disney, CNN and Hollywood productions.

While these cultural formations certainly form one layer of our media landscape, these writers have usually ignored the emerging adversarial fields and the interventions that have also multiplied across borders. These practices use both high- and low-end technologies in an attempt to rewire, reroute and find openings within the horizontal webs of transnational corporate control over new means of distribution from satellite, Web pages, CD-ROM, video, cable and telephone lines. Most of this writing, then, has focused on media practices and telecommunications that emanate from first world transnationals, rather than the truly pluralized, heterogeneous, decentralized work that connects across nations, races, genders and other identities to displace the horizontal webs of control. For example, in *Papapapa* (1996), New York video artist and animator Alex Rivera uses animation, live action and appropriated footage from multiple sources to raise questions about the complex relationships between Peru and the U.S., immigration, the Conquest, potato chips, racism and popular culture.

Media pirates and the anti-copyright movement within the cyber-sector provide an excellent example of how heterogeneous work connecting across identities can raid the transnationals and put dents in the horizontal webs. Mix tapes, produced by African American, Latino and Asian youth cultures across the globe, use old-fashioned turntables and digital sound recording equipment to remix music "owned" by large music companies. Bertelsmann (one of the largest media transnationals in the world), Sony-Columbia and Atlantic have launched campaigns to induce federal and state government officials to do sweeps of areas where these mix tapes are sold on the streets.

In film and video, stealth attacks on the monopoly ownership of images by the media transnationals have produced a new form of adversarial documentary operating within the cracks of the 1978 Copyright Law, which allows for "fair use" of images for purposes of parody, criticism or education. These works seek to liberate images from their corporate confines, affirming that image culture is part of public culture. Brian Springer's *Spin* (1995) is a tour-de-force compilation tape that appropriates satellite feeds. In one sequence, George Bush and Larry King discuss how to obtain nonprescription drugs in Israel. In another, a hospital administrator in Los Angeles reveals to a network morning talk show host that his hospital sees worse things than any facility in the third world. Craig Baldwin's *Sonic Outlaws* (1995) operates as a manifesto for media pirates, deploying all forms of media to steal images and conduct what the situationists terms detourne: satellite, police scanners, pixel vision, 16mm film, Hi-8 video, the Internet, sound recording, folk songs, video compilation, found footage and media pranks like the Barbie Liberation Organization. The film on one level traces the Irish rock band U2's lawsuit against media appropriators, specifically the cyber-group Negativland. But on a more complex political and aesthetic level, the aggressively and viscerally edited film is a salvo against copyright as a form of authoritarianism for corporate control and a call to action for media piracy.

[. . .]

The tension between the rapid corporate transnationalization of media within the last 10 years and an emerging adversarial transnationalism has constructed new social and aesthetic spaces that require astute and careful analysis. How are these new social and aesthetic spaces mapped visually in new global documentaries? What spaces within the emerging horizontal, cybernetworks of the new transnational economy provide openings for contestation and social change?

III.   Transnational Documentary Film

As transnational media corporations spread their tentacles around the world to homogenize cultures and consume differences, a new configuration of documentary arises to resist this process by focusing on the complexities of cultural, national and regional collisions. A plethora of exciting documentary work from all over the world has erupted in response to transnationalization and the massive displacements of people, urging an international rethinking of the relationships between politic(s) and media(s).

Historical work anticipating this modality of the transnational documentary has been produced across the globe—Chris Marker's *Sans Soleil* (1982, Great Britain), Johann Van Der Keuken's *The Way South* (1981, Netherlands), Kidlat Tahimik's *Perfumed Nightmare* (1977, Philippines), Andrei Zagdansky's *Interpretation of Dreams* (1989, Ukraine), Jean-Pierre Gorin's *Poto and Cabengo* (1979, France), Peter Kubelka's *Unsere Afrikareise* (1961–66, Austria), Dennis O'Rourke's *Cannibal Tours* (1987, Australia), Su Friedrich's *The Ties that Bind* (1984, U.S.), Peter Watkin's *The Journey* (1987, Great Britain) and Marcel Ophuls's *November Days* (1992, France).

This list is not intended as inclusive nor is it put forward as a claim to establish a new "genre" of international cinema. Rather, it suggests that while a construct of transnational documentary is emerging, it is not an entirely new paradigmatic shift in filmic discourse; instead, it is one that has transmuted out of the old for a new set of social and political conditions. Adversarial transnational documentaries reclaim and rehabilitate modes from these older films—tracing interactions between and around cultures; performing histories; imagining new subjectivities and alliances; mapping conflicts as multidimensional; traversing fantasies and material limits, cultures and political economies; formulating new analytics; and locating new emancipatory places. But it reworks them within the demands of the new world system in the post-cold war era.

In his book *The Geopolitical Aesthetic: Cinema and Space in the World System* (1992), Fredric Jameson analyses some films that provide a mapping of the world system—such as *The Parallax View* (1974, by Alan J. Pakula), *Perfumed Nightmare* (1977, by Kidlat Tahimik), *Videodrome* (1983, by David Cronenberg)—as allegories of unconscious, political effort. Noting the changes in the world system produced by the disappearance of the nation, he argues: "For it is ultimately always of the social totality itself that is a question in representation, and never more so than in the present age of a multinational global corporate network." In advocating a concept of adversarial transnational documentaries, we broaden this claim to ask where representation, artistic practice and policy can intercept and reroute transnational corporate networks consciously and pragmatically, rather than only allegorically and unconsciously.

Both globalization and the demise of a certain kind of nationhood have precipitated a decline in the availability of points of identification. Therefore, in the process of charting out this imaginary territory of the transnational documentary, we have discerned two political strategies that independent media has taken to deal with economic globalization and the death of nationhood. These two distinct strategies represent ways in which new modes of identification and community can be constructed: one local, the other a radical, communal transnational. The local strategy is epitomized by the use of small-format video by activist communities working for AIDS education, reproductive rights, indigenous rights, etc. This work on small format, which is distributed through alternative channels on the strength of the mail or word of mouth has grown exponentially because of the availability and affordability of the means of production. For example, Chris Hill, a Buffalo, New York-based video artist and curator, has been collecting and screening video samizdat work produced during the revolutions of Eastern Europe in Hungary, the former Czechoslovakia, the former East Germany, Poland and the former Yugoslavia. She is collaborating with community media makers in Eastern Europe to create a traveling program of these underground videos that were central in organizing democratic political groups during the revolutions of 1989. Slovenian scholar Marina Grzinic is also working to theorize the development of the new media spaces of the ex-Yugoslavia as zones of liberation and hope during the Bosnia war by looking at the underground video produced by youth subcultures that reject nationalism and exhibit in rock clubs.

This localism suggests a search for foundational identity. It can be understood as an inflection of the "imagined community" described by Benedict Anderson, one that secures its identity through communications technologies that create the fiction of unity. On the more emancipatory end, this localism helps to coalesce tenuous communities like those formed around reproductive rights and clinic defense, environmentalism and AIDS. On the more repressive level, localism reverts to warring ethnicities that reject community across difference, typified in Bosnia-Hercegovina. It, therefore, has congruencies with a whole range of socio-political practices arising in the 1980s, such as religious separatism, states rights and health care reform.

The other strategy is the transnational. In this sense, we are attempting to rescue the construct of the transnational from its multinational corporate environs to hypothesize its conceptual and political utility as a way to form alliances across a whole range of borders. We use the term transnational as both a description of documentary practice, and as a more utopian projection of the tact that political documentary might take within the new world orders. These transnational documentaries displace the economic and psychic nation and the national imaginary, rejecting a notion of the nation as an essentialist given. These films supersede the opposition between the first and third world, between the center and the periphery.

For example, in *Handsworth Songs* (1986, by John Akomfrah and Black Audio Collective), the third world is in the first world, and the nation is marked by Diaspora and ideological battle, constantly in conflict over definition, space, location and power. Daniel Reeves's masterpiece *Obsessive Becoming* (1995) combines an excavation of family psychological and physical abuse with an interrogation of war and technological iconography infusing the construction of masculinity in the twentieth century. Morphing family images to create a continuous stream of connections and relationships between fractured images and damaged psyches, *Obsessive Becoming* deploys digital layering techniques to cross borders between the personal and the political, between nations and between identities. Reeves's own voice-over, simultaneously an expurgation of his pain and a reconnection of words to images, is edited with a voice-over of the Buddhist peace activist Thich Nhat Hanh describing the horrors of the Vietnam War. Blending old technologies like family photos and home movies with new digital imaging systems, *Obsessive Becoming* refutes the borders between media, families, nations and identities, morphing them all into a continuous stream of history, memory, fantasy and political ethics.

This development of a new documentary practice is different from 1970s and 1980s political documentary strategies, particularly in countries of the North. These transnational documentaries, of course, do not simply break with 1970s modes that reconstitute submerged discourses, but incorporate, for example, talking heads or linear history, as one of many strategies of explanation of the transnational webs. Despite the aesthetic realities that these newer films intertwine with older strategies in their texts, it is worth noting some of the differences as a way to chart out some distinctions between these new works and previous documentary incarnations.

A whole array of revisionist, and somewhat realist documentaries of the 1970s and 1980s— for example *Word is Out* (1977, by Mariposa Film Group), *Times of Harvey Milk* (1984, by Robert Epstein), *Life and Times of Rosie the Riveter* (1980, by Connie Field), *The War at Home* (1980, by Glenn Silber and Barry Alexander Brown), *Eyes on the Prize Parts I and II* (1986–89, produced by Henry Hampton) reassume the nation as a unified entity. These films dive into a hidden area of repressed history, such as that of gays, women or labor, with the goal of widening and expanding the concept of nation.

The transnational documentary, on the other hand, subverts the notion of nation as well as identity politics that search for the self within the nation. The historiographic project of these films is to pluralize the concept of nation. In Gorin's *Poto and Cabengo*, for example, twin girls speak their own language, a mother speaks German and a California working class father hardly speaks at all, producing a veritable babel of languages and silences. Gorin has not simply rendered an ethnography on a pair of unusual girls, but has explored how language relates to nationality and location, and how it is never "pure." Such transnational documentaries, then, explore how cultures, nations and identities are constructed, how they evidence all sorts of contradictions, hybridities and combustions and how new social spaces are always in volatile, contentious development.

We can find another corollary to the assumption in 1970s and 1980s revisionist documentary that the nation might be reformed by repositioning spectatorship. These films support national reformation by implicitly working with the idea that identification with the text and the characters in the text is a good thing, that the spectator occupies a valuable position. These films create a mythology of community through emotional address bolstered by rational argument; spectators are lured into joining, for 90 or so minutes, a utopian community. Although we criticize this strategy as politically deficient for the transnational era, we very much want to retain the notion of community. We believe that political and cultural work must still have the goal of working within differences rather than evening them out. A plethora of visually challenging, even beautiful and compelling experimental work from the 1980s, however, seems to have inverted the old adage that "the personal is political" by mapping nearly everything as only personal, seeing the political as only an inflection or context upon which psychic investigation can be mobilized. The 1970s and 1980s documentaries extended the ideas of John Grierson, who saw the role of documentary as basically reforming the state to increase participation in community. The Grierson project presumes that the economic, civic and cultural nation is available to all, that it is unified and malleable without major structural interventions or changes. The Griersonian project, then, hinges on a concept of nation and identification with the text, a point brilliantly argued by Brian Winston in his recent book *Claiming the Real* (1995).

These documentaries produced over the last quarter of a century, as well as many television documentaries and international support films, for South Africa and Central America, for example, reveal the persistence of this tradition of a direct link between public culture, the public good and the survival of the nation. Information and community will bolster the national purpose, enfranchise more people, pluralize the nation and thereby strengthen it. This approach was extremely effective at various political moments and during various political struggles in the last 20 years. However, within the new transnational corporate webs and the restructurings of the world system after the fall of the Berlin Wall, Tiannamen Square and the Gulf War, new theorization and practice is necessary to confront the closing down of political alliances, the privatization of nearly all communication systems worldwide and the precipitous decline of access to communications production. What happens when the nation has moved to many different places and spaces within the transnational webs?

V. What Can Be Done

Old theoretical categories linking documentary practice to the nation have changed dramatically in the post-cold war and transnationalized cultural economy; they have been reorganized, reconceptualized, rearranged, remade, rewired. Borders of every kind—national, technological, theoretical and psychic—have been crossed and hybridized. Conventional categories have blurred. Nationalist "us vs. them" conflicts have erupted, demanding new political and aesthetic responses.

[. . .]

In this polemic on the transnational documentary, we seek to open up a terrain for imagining new world visual orders. A wide swathe of analytical methodologies—as multiple and fluid as possible so that they overlap and critique each other—are necessary: political economy, postcolonial theory, feminist theory, third cinema, queer theory and cultural studies. This new adversarial transnational work needs to utilize deconstructive methodologies to unpack visualities, and visualities to deconstruct policy. Policy is no longer only the domain of the policy wonks for NGOs—scholars and artists must enter the fray.

Adversarial documentaries have burgeoned in the last five years around the globe from a variety of producers and across a variety of nations and regions that offer critique of this new transnational world. These documentaries refuse the fragmentation, isolation and nationalism that is the corollary of corporatist transnationalism by looking for and imagining new social and aesthetic alliances. They occupy and create new imaginary spaces in the new world order. They are acts of refusal and hope.

[. . .]

References

Rabia Ali and Lawrence Lifschultz, 'Why Bosnia.' Writings on the Balkan War, (Stoney Creek, CT: Pamphleteer's Press 1993).

Benedict Anderson, Imagined Communities: Reflections on the Origin and Spread of Nationalism (London: Verso, 1983).

Ben H. Bagdikian, The Media Monopoly, third edition (Boston: Beacon Press, 1990).

Angelika Bammer, ed., Displacements: Cultural Identities in Question (Bloomington: Indiana University Press, 1994).

Richard J. Barnett and John Cavanaugh, Global Dreams: Imperial Corporations and the New World Order (New York: Simon and Schuster, 1994).

Phyllis Bennis and Michel Moushabeck, eds., *Altered States: a Reader in the New World Order* (Brooklyn: Olive Branch Press, 1993).

Michael Berube, *Public Access: Literary Theory and American Cultural Politics* (London: Verso, 1994).

Homi K. Bhabha, *The Location of Culture* (New York: Routledge, 1994).

Homi K. Bhabha, ed., *Nation and Narration* (New York: Routledge, 1990).

Joel Bleifuss, "The Death of Nations," *In These Times* July 24, 1994, p. 12.

James Brook and Iain A. Boal, eds., *Resisting the Virtual Life: The Culture and Politics of Information* (San Francisco: City Lights, 1995).

Frederick Buell, *National Culture and the New Global System* (Baltimore: The Johns Hopkins University Press, 1994).

Craig Calhoun, ed., *Habermas and the Public Sphere* (Cambridge: The MIT Press, 1994).

Gina Dent, ed., *Black Popular Culture: A Project by Michele Wallace* (Seattle: Bay Press, 1992).

Tony Dowmunt, ed., *Channels of Resistance: Global Television and Local Empowerment* (London: British Film Institute, 1993).

Slavenka Drakulic, *The Balkan Express: Fragments from the Other Side of War* (New York: Harper Perennial, 1993).

Alex Dupuy, "The New World Order and Social Change in the Americas": Ten Theses; *Radical America*, Vol. 25, no. 4, pp. 6–23.

Terry Eagleton, Fredric Jameson and Edward Said, *Nationalism, Colonialism, and Literature* (Minneapolis: University of Minnesota Press, 1990).

Earth Island Press, *The Case Against "Free Trade": GATT, NAFTA, and the Globalization of Corporate Power* (San Francisco: Earth Island Press, 1993).

8th MacBride Roundtable, Seoul, Korea, August 24–27, 1996, "Objectives, Program, Communication, and Culture": MacBride Roundtable on Communication: http://people.rfem.or.kr/macbride/.

Jack C. Ellis, *The Documentary Idea: A Critical History of English-Language Documentary Film and Video* (Englewood Cliffs, NJ: Prentice Hall, 1989).

Russell Ferguson, Martha Gever, Trinh T. Minh-ha and Cornel West, eds., *Out There: Marginalization and Contemporary Cultures* (Cambridge: The MIT Press, 1990).

Reebee Garofalo, "Whose World, What Beat? The Transnational Music Industry, Identity, and Cultural Imperialism," *Radical America*, Vol. 25, no. 4, pp. 24–39.

Guillermo Gomez-Pena, The New World Border, (San Francisco: City Lights Books, 1996).

Avery E. Gordon and Christopher Newfield, eds., *Mapping Multiculturalism* (Minneapolis: University of Minnesota Press, 1996).

John Hess and Patricia R. Zimmermann, "Global Village or Global Office? Notes Toward a Definition of Transnational Documentary," DOX, no. 5 (Spring 1995), pp. 12–16.

Fredric Jameson, *The Geopolitical Aesthetic: Cinema and Space in the World System* (Bloomington: Indiana University Press, 1992).

Elaine Katzenberger, ed., *First World, Ha Ha Ha! The Zapatista Challenge* (San Francisco: City Lights Books, 1995).

Peter Ludlow, ed., *High Noon on the Electronic Frontier: Conceptual Issues in Cyberspace* (Cambridge: The MIT Press, 1996).

John R. MacArthur, *The Second Front: Censorship and Propaganda in the Gulf War* (Berkeley: University of California Press, 1993).

Steven Henry Madoff, "Art in Cyberspace: Can It Live Without a Body?" *The New York Times*, January 26, 1996, section b, p. 1 and pp. 34–35.

Armand Mattelart, *Mapping World Communication: War, Progress, Culture* (Minneapolis: University of Minnesota Press, 1994).

——, *Transnationals and the Third World: The Struggle for Culture* (South Hadley, MA: Bergin and Garvey Publishers, 1983).

Richard Maxwell, "Caught in the Maelstrom: Globalization and Social Immobility" *Directions*, Vol. 7, nos. 1 and 2 (1993), pp. 1–9.

Robert W. McChesney, Ellen Meiksins Wood and John Bellamy Foster, guest eds., "Capitalism and the Information Age," special volume of *Monthly Review*, Vol. 48, no. 3 (July–August 1996).

Kobena Mercer, *Welcome to the Jungle: New Positions in Black Cultural Studies*, (New York: Routledge, 1994).

David Morley and Kevin Dobins, *Spaces of Identity: Global Media, Electronic Landscapes and Cultural Boundaries* (London: Routledge, 1995).

Chantal Mouffe, *The Return of the Political* (London: Verso, 1993).

Hamid Mowlana, George Gerbner and Herbert I. Schiller, eds., *Triumph of the Image: The Media's War in the Persian Gulf—A Global Perspective* (Boulder, CO: Westview Press, 1992).

Bill Nichols, *Blurred Boundaries: Questions of Meaning in Contemporary Culture* (Bloomington: Indiana University Press, 1995).

——, *Representing Reality: Issues and Concepts in Documentary* (Bloomington: Indiana University Press, 1991).

Kenneth B. Noble, "Defying Airwave Rules and Exporting the Way," *The New York Times*, January 24, 1996, section a, p. 10.

Andrew Parker, Mary Russo, Doris Sommer and Patricia Yeager, eds., *Nationalisms and Sexualities* (New York: Routledge, 1992).

Jim Pines and Paul Willemen, eds., *Questions of Third Cinema* (London: British Film Institute, 1989).

Mark Poster, *The Modes of Information: Poststructuralism and Social Context* (Chicago: University of Chicago Press, 1990).

Michael Renov and Erika Suderburg, eds., *Resolutions* (Minneapolis: University of Minnesota Press, 1996).

Bruce Robbins, ed., *The Phantom Public Sphere* (Minneapolis: University of Minnesota Press, 1993).

Salman Rushdie, *Imaginary Homelands: Essays and Criticism 1981–1991* (New York: Penguin Books, 1992).

Jonathon Rutherford, ed., *Identity: Community, Culture, Difference* (London: Lawrence and Wishart, 1990).

Edward Said, *Culture and Imperialism* (New York: Alfred A. Knopf, Inc, 1993).

Herbert I. Schiller, *Culture Inc.: The Corporate Takeover of Public Expression* (Oxford, England: Oxford University Press, 1989).

——, *Information Inequality* (New York: Routedge, 1996).

Cynthia Schneider and Brian Wallis, ads., *Global Television* (Cambridge: The MIT Press, 1988).

Michael Shapiro and Hayward R. Alker, eds., *Challenging Boundaries* (Minneapolis: University of Minnesota Press, 1996).

Ella Shohat and Robert Stam, *Unthinking Eurocentrism: Multiculturalism and the Media* (New York: Routledge, 1995).

Leslie Sklair, *Sociology of the Global System* (Baltimore: The Johns Hopkins University Press, 1991).

Michael Skovmand and Kim Christian Schroder, eds., *Media Cultures: Reappraising Transnational Media* (New York: Routledge, 1992).

Eric Smoodin, ed., *'Disney Discourse.' Producing the Magic Kingdom* (New York: Routledge, 1994).

Jonathan Tasini, "The Tele-Barons: Media Moguls Rewrite the Law and Rewire the Country," *The Washington Post*, February 4, 1996, section c, pp. 1 and 4.

John Tomlinson, *Cultural Imperialism* (Baltimore: The Johns Hopkins University Press, 1991).

Trinh T. Minh-ha, *Woman Native Other* (Bloomington: Indiana University Press, 1989).

Videazimut, A *newsletter of the International Coalition for Audiovisuals for Development and Democracy*, 3680, rue Jeanne-Mance, Bureau 430, Montreal, Quebec, Canada H2X 2K5. E-mail: videaz @web.apc.org.

"Declaration of Cajamar" in *Videazimut Clips Special on the Videazimut International Seminar and First General Assembly*, no. 11 (October 1996).

Paul Virilio, *The Vision Machine* (Bloomington: Indiana University Press, 1994).

Brian Wallis, ed., *Democracy: A Project by Group Material* (Seattle: Bay Press, 1990).

McKenzie Wark, *Virtual Geography: Living with Global Media Events* (Bloomington: Indiana University Press, 1994).

Janet Wasko, *Hollywood in the Information Age* (Austin: University of Texas Press, 1994).

Janet Wasko and Vincent Mosco, eds., *Democratic Communications in the Information Age* (Toronto: Garamond Press, 1992).

Rob Wilson and Wimal Dissanayake, eds., *Global/Local: Cultural Production and the Transnational Imaginary* (Durham, NC: Duke University Press, 1996).

Brian Winston, *Claiming the Real: The Documentary Film Revisited* (London: British Film Institute, 1995).

Slavoj Zizek, *The Sublime Object of Ideology* (London: Verso, 1989).

PART THREE

MOTION PICTURES: FILM, MIGRATION, AND DIASPORA

Introduction

The essays in this section explore the ways in which diasporic identification and the political and affective aspects of migration entail imaginative leaps beyond the particulars of an individual's historical experience and give rise to new aesthetic expressions of cultural identity. The essays consider the extent to which transnational cinema maintains, despite its ever-growing formal self-consciousness and sophistication, a representational politics inevitably tied to some awareness of the cultural specificity of the individual subject both behind and in front of the camera.

As Hamid Naficy has argued in his book *An Accented Cinema: Exilic and Diasporic Filmmaking*, which is excerpted in this section, migrants and other displaced people are now acquiring the means to insert themselves and their particular experiences of transnational consciousness and mobility into the spaces of cinematic representation and legitimation. As a result of this, appropriation, loss, deterritorialization, and cultural ambivalence are coming to be seen as more or less permanent conditions and not simply as transitional states on the transnational subject's path to either assimilation, homecoming, or tragedy. According to Naficy, "[t]he variations among the films are driven by many factors, while their similarities stem principally from what the filmmakers have in common: liminal subjectivity and interstitial location in society and the film industry." Naficy suggestively explores the extent to which, in what he calls their "exilic," "diasporic," and "ethnic" incarnations, filmmakers themselves can be read as exemplary figures for considering the particulars of transnational citizenship and subjectivity as markers of a new cultural paradigm.

In "Beur Cinema and the Politics of Location: French Immigration Politics and the Naming of a Film Movement," Peter Bloom explores the complex cultural and political dynamics of beur cinema's engagement with issues of cultural identity and assimilation. In a passage that resonates strongly with Naficy's notion of "interstitiality" and that is applicable to much transnational cinema, Bloom argues that "[b]eur cinema locates itself firmly within the cracks of French institutional structures," emerging out of "the intersection between contemporary French immigration politics and popular culture, giving expression to the effects of an uneasy integration into metropolitan culture." As Bloom's essay makes clear, in politically charged situations the dynamics of ethnic representation in cinema, now perhaps even more than in popular music (currently the most widely disseminated and actively appropriated art form), are subject to widely varying types of "official" recognition, reception, and support.

David Desser argues in his essay that, despite the interconnectedness of world film cultures and the interstitial positions of many filmmakers, constructions of national identity still inform transnational cinematic production and reception. Examining the representations of China in Hong Kong cinema, Desser notes that much of the nationalist coding that provides the political unconscious for even the most manifestly innocuous of popular films often takes place through a particularized politics of language, place, and ethnicity. Desser reveals the role that linguistic and corporeal specificity often play in the demarcation of national types and subsequently of emotional identification for domestic audiences, while those same differences can be subsumed under general categories of "Asianness" for outsiders. Desser reveals the extent to which linguistic differences and the ethnic legibility of various stars, most notably Bruce Lee and Jackie Chan, have and continue to be a regulatory force in both hindering and facilitating the emergence of a transnational cinematic landscape.

Ann Marie Stock's essay explores the extent to which filmmakers in Latin America lack the autonomy that could enable them to fashion cinematic production exclusively or even primarily as an expression of personal desire and ethno-cultural sensibility. Stock articulates the ways in which the exploitation of popular genres as a means of fostering transnational readability complicates the straightforward positioning of films as reflections of either directorial will or national culture. She considers the extent to which the multinational casting and financing of many "Latin American" films complicates their status as national documents and suggests that "what remains when film-makers and films constantly cross borders is, in fact, a critical nostalgia for cultural purity and authenticity" that should give way to a positive recognition of forms of "post-national cultural expression."

Situating Accented Cinema   8

HAMID NAFICY

Accented Filmmakers

The exilic and diasporic filmmakers discussed here are "situated but universal" figures who work in the interstices of social formations and cinematic practices. A majority are from Third World and postcolonial countries (or from the global South) who since the 1960s have relocated to northern cosmopolitan centers where they exist in a state of tension and dissension with both their original and their current homes. By and large, they operate independently, outside the studio system or the mainstream film industries, using interstitial and collective modes of production that critique those entities. As a result, they are presumed to be more prone to the tensions of marginality and difference. While they share these characteristics, the very existence of the tensions and differences helps prevent accented filmmakers from becoming a homogeneous group or a film movement. And while their films encode these tensions and differences, they are not neatly resolved by familiar narrative and generic schemas—hence, their grouping under accented style. The variations among the films are driven by many factors, while their similarities stem principally from what the filmmakers have in common: liminal subjectivity and interstitial location in society and the film industry. What constitutes the accented style is the combination and intersection of these variations and similarities.

Accented filmmakers came to live and make films in the West in two general groupings. The first group was displaced or lured to the West from the late 1950s to the mid-1970s by Third World decolonization, wars of national liberation, the Soviet Union's invasions of Poland and Czechoslovakia, Westernization, and a kind of "internal decolonization" in the West itself, involving various civil rights, counterculture, and antiwar movements. Indeed, as Fredric Jameson notes, the beginning of the period called "the sixties" must be located in the Third World decolonization that so profoundly influenced the First World sociopolitical movements (1984, 180). The second group emerged in the 1980s and 1990s as a result of the failure of nationalism, socialism, and communism; the ruptures caused by the emergence of post-industrial global economies, the rise of militant forms of Islam, the return of religious and ethnic wars, and the fragmentation of nation-states; the changes in the European, Australian, and American immigration policies encouraging non-Western immigration; and the unprecedented technological developments and consolidation in computers and media.

Accented filmmakers are the products of this dual postcolonial displacement and postmodern or late modern scattering. Because of their displacement from the margins to the centers, they have become subjects in world history. They have earned the right to speak and have dared to capture the means of representation. However marginalized they are within the center, their ability to access the means of *reproduction* may prove to be as empowering to the marginalia of the postindustrial era as the capturing of the means of *production* would have been to the subalterns of the industrial era.

It is helpful, when mapping the accented cinema, to differentiate three types of film that constitute it: exilic, diasporic, and ethnic. These distinctions are not hard-and-fast. A few films fall naturally within one of these classifications, while the majority share the characteristics of all three in different measures. Within each type, too, there are subdivisions. In addition, in the course of their careers, many filmmakers move not only from country to country but also from making one type of film to making another type, in tandem with the trajectory of their own travels of identity and those of their primary community.

Exilic Filmmakers

Traditionally, exile is taken to mean banishment for a particular offense, with a prohibition of return. Exile can be internal or external, depending on the location to which one is banished. The tremendous toll that internal exile, restrictions, deprivations, and censorship in totalitarian countries have taken on filmmakers has been widely publicized. What has been analyzed less is the way such constraints, by challenging the filmmakers, force them to develop an authorial style. Many filmmakers who could escape internal exile refuse to do so in order to fight the good fight at home—a fight that often defines not only their film style but also their identity as oppositional figures of some stature. By working under an internal regime of exile, they choose their "site of struggle" and their potential social transformation (Harlow 1991, 150). When they speak from this site at home, they have an impact, even if and often because, they are punished for it. In fact, interrogation, censorship, and jailing are all proof that they have been heard. But if they move out into external exile in the West, where they have the political freedom to speak, no one may hear them among the cacophony of voices competing for attention in the market. In that case, Gayatri Spivak's famous question "Can the subaltern speak?" will have to be reworded to ask, "Can the subaltern be heard?" Because of globalization, the internal and external exiles of one country are not sealed off from each other. In fact, there is much traffic and exchange between them.

In this study, the term "exile" refers principally to external exiles: individuals or groups who voluntarily or involuntarily have left their country of origin and who maintain an ambivalent relationship with their previous and current places and cultures. Although they do not return to their homelands, they maintain an intense desire to do so—a desire that is projected in potent return narratives in their films. In the meantime, they memorialize the homeland by fetishizing it in the form of cathected sounds, images, and chronotopes that are circulated intertextually in exilic popular culture, including in films and music videos. The exiles' primary relationship, in short, is with their countries and cultures of origin and with the sight, sound, taste, and feel of an originary experience, of an elsewhere at other times. Exiles, especially those filmmakers who have been forcibly driven away, tend to want to define, at least during the liminal period of displacement, all things in their lives not only in relationship to the homeland but also in strictly political terms. As a result, in their early films they tend to represent their homelands and people more than themselves.

The authority of the exiles as filmmaking authors is derived from their position as subjects inhabiting interstitial spaces and sites of struggle. Indeed, all great authorship is predicated on distance—banishment and exile of sorts—from the larger society. The resulting tensions and ambivalences produce the complexity and the intensity that are so characteristic of great works of art and literature. In the same way that sexual taboo permits procreation, exilic banishment encourages creativity.[1] Of course, not all exilic subjects produce great or lasting art, but many of the greatest and most enduring works of literature and cinema have been created by displaced writers and filmmakers. But exile can result in an agonistic form of liminality characterized by oscillation between the extremes. It is a slipzone of anxiety and imperfection, where life hovers between the heights of ecstasy and confidence and the depths of despondency and doubt.[2]

For external exiles the descent relations with the homeland and the consent relations with the host society are continually tested. Freed from old and new, they are "deterritorial-ized," yet they continue to be in the grip of both the old and the new, the before and the after. Located in such a slipzone, they can be suffused with hybrid excess, or they may feel deeply deprived and divided, even fragmented. Lithuanian filmmaker and poet Jonas Mekas, who spent some four years in European displaced persons camps before landing in the United States, explained his feelings of fragmentation in the following manner:

> Everything that I believed in shook to the foundations—all my idealism, and my faith in the goodness of man and progress of man—all was shattered. Somehow, I managed to keep myself together. But really, I wasn't one piece any longer; I was one thousand painful pieces. . . . And I wasn't surprised when, upon my arrival in New York, I found others who felt as I felt. There were poets, and film-makers, and painters—people who were also walking like one thousand painful pieces.
>
> (Quoted in O'Grady 1973, 229)

Neither the hybrid fusion nor the fragmentation is total, permanent, or painless. On the one hand, like Derridian "undecidables," the new exiles can be "both and neither": the pharma-con, meaning both poison and remedy; the hymen, meaning both membrane and its violation; and the supplement, meaning both addition and replacement (quoted in Bauman 1991, 145–46). On the other hand, they could aptly be called, in Salman Rushdie's words, "at once plural and partial" (1991, 15). As partial, fragmented, and multiple subjects, these filmmakers are capable of producing ambiguity and doubt about the taken-for-granted values of their home and host societies. They can also transcend and transform themselves to produce hybridized, syncretic, performed, or virtual identities. None of these constructed and impure identities are risk-free, however, as the Ayatollah Khomeini's death threat against Salman Rushdie glaringly pointed out.[3]

Not all transnational exiles, of course, savor fundamental doubt, strive toward hybridized and performative self-fashioning, or reach for utopian or virtual imaginings. However, for those who remain in the enduring and endearing crises and tensions of exilic migrancy, liminality and interstitiality may become passionate sources of creativity and dynamism that produce in literature and cinema the likes of James Joyce and Marguerite Duras, Joseph Conrad and Fernando Solanas, Ezra Pound and Trinh T. Minh-ha, Samuel Beckett and Sohrab Shahid

Saless, Salman Rushdie and Andrei Tarkovsky, Garcia Marquez and Atom Egoyan, Vladimir
Nabokov and Raúl Ruiz, Gertrude Stein and Michel Khleifi, Assia Djebar and Jonas Mekas.

Diasporic Filmmakers

Originally, "diaspora" referred to the dispersion of the Greeks after the destruction of the
city of Aegina, to the Jews after their Babylonian exile, and to the Armenians after Persian
and Turkish invasions and expulsion in the mid-sixteenth century. The classic paradigm of
diaspora has involved the Jews, but as Peters (1999), Cohen (1997), Tölölyan (1996), Clifford
(1997, 244–77), Naficy (1993a), and Safran (1991) have argued, the definition should no
longer be limited to the dispersion of the Jews, for myriad peoples have historically under-
gone sustained dispersions—a process that continues on a massive scale today. The term
has been taken up by other displaced peoples, among them African-Americans in the
United States and Afro-Caribbeans in England, to describe their abduction from their African
homes and their forced dispersion to the new world (Gilroy 1993, 1991, 1988; Mercer 1994a,
1994b, 1988; Hall 1988). In these and other recodings, the concept of diaspora has become
much closer to exile. Consequently, as Khachig Tölölyan notes, "diaspora" has lost some of
its former specificity and precision to become a "promiscuously capacious category that is
taken to include all the adjacent phenomena to which it is linked but from which it actually
differs in ways that are constitutive" (1996, 8).

   Here I will briefly point out the similarities and differences between exile and diaspora
that inform this work. Diaspora, like exile, often begins with trauma, rupture, and coercion,
and it involves the scattering of populations to places outside their homeland. Sometimes,
however, the scattering is caused by a desire for increased trade, for work, or for colonial
and imperial pursuits. Consequently, diasporic movements can be classified according to
their motivating factors. Robin Cohen (1997) suggested the following classifications and
examples: victim/refugee diasporas (exemplified by the Jews, Africans, and Armenians); labor/
service diasporas (Indians); trade/business diasporas (Chinese and Lebanese); imperial/
colonial diasporas (British, Russian); and cultural/hybrid diasporas (Caribbeans). Like the
exiles, people in diaspora have an identity in their homeland *before* their departure, and their
diasporic identity is constructed in resonance with this prior identity. However, unlike exile,
which may be individualistic or collective, diaspora is necessarily collective, in both its
origination and its destination. As a result, the nurturing of a collective memory, often of
an idealized homeland, is constitutive of the diasporic identity. This idealization may be
state-based, involving love for an existing homeland, or it may be stateless, based on a
desire for a homeland yet to come. The Armenian diaspora before and after the Soviet era has
been state-based, whereas the Palestinian diaspora since the 1948 creation of Israel has been
stateless, driven by the Palestinians' desire to create a sovereign state.

   People in diaspora, moreover, maintain a long-term sense of ethnic consciousness and
distinctiveness, which is consolidated by the periodic hostility of either the original home or
the host societies toward them. However, unlike the exiles whose identity entails a vertical
and primary relationship with their homeland, diasporic consciousness is horizontal and
multisited, involving not only the homeland but also the compatriot communities elsewhere.
As a result, plurality, multiplicity, and hybridity are structured in dominance among the
diasporans, while among the political exiles, binarism and duality rule.

These differences tend to shape exilic and diasporic films differently. Diasporized filmmakers tend to be centered less than the exiled filmmakers on a cathected relationship with a single homeland and on a claim that they represent it and its people. As a result, their works are expressed less in the narratives of retrospection, loss, and absence or in strictly partisanal political terms. Their films are accented more fully than those of the exiles by the plurality and performativity of identity. In short, while binarism and subtraction in particular accent exilic films, diasporic films are accented more by multiplicity and addition. Many diasporic filmmakers are discussed here individually, among them Armenians. Black and Asian British filmmakers are discussed collectively.

Postcolonial Ethnic and Identity Filmmakers

Although exilic, diasporic, and ethnic communities all patrol their real and symbolic boundaries to maintain a measure of collective identity that distinguishes them from the ruling strata and ideologies, they differ from one another principally by the relative strength of their attachment to compatriot communities. The postcolonial ethnic and identity filmmakers are both ethnic and diasporic; but they differ from the poststudio American ethnics, such as Woody Allen, Francis Ford Coppola, and Martin Scorsese, in that many of them are either immigrants themselves or have been born in the West since the 1960s to nonwhite, non-Western, postcolonial émigrés. They also differ from the diasporic filmmakers in their emphasis on their ethnic and racial identity within the host country.

The different emphasis on the relationship to place creates differently accented films. Thus, exilic cinema is dominated by its focus on there and then in the homeland, diasporic cinema by its vertical relationship to the homeland and by its lateral relationship to the diaspora communities and experiences, and postcolonial ethnic and identity cinema by the exigencies of life here and now in the country in which the filmmakers reside. As a result of their focus on the here and now ethnic identity films tend to deal with what Werner Sollors has characterized as "the central drama in American culture," which emerges from the conflict between descent relations, emphasizing bloodline and ethnicity, and consent relations, stressing self-made, contractual affiliations (1986, 6). In other words, while the former is concerned with being, the latter is concerned with becoming; while the former is conciliatory, the latter is contestatory. Although such a drama is also present to some extent in exilic and diasporic films, the hostland location of the drama makes the ethnic and identity films different from the other two categories, whose narratives are often centered elsewhere.

Some of the key problematics of the postcolonial ethnic and identity cinema are encoded in the "politics of the hyphen." Recognized as a crucial marker of ethnicity and authenticity in a multicultural America, group terms such as black, Chicano/a, Oriental, and people of color have gradually been replaced by hyphenated terms such as African-American, Latino-American, and Asian-American. Identity cinema's adoption of the hyphen is seen as a marker of resistance to the homogenizing and hegemonizing power of the American melting pot ideology. However, retaining the hyphen has a number of negative connotations, too. The hyphen may imply a lack, or the idea that hyphenated people are somehow subordinate to unhyphenated people, or that they are "equal but not quite," or that they will never be totally accepted or trusted as full citizens. In addition, it may suggest a divided allegiance, which is a painful reminder to certain groups of American citizens.[4] The hyphen may also suggest a divided mind, an irrevocably split identity, or a type of paralysis between two cultures or nations. Finally, the hyphen can feed into nativist discourses that assume authentic essences that lie outside ideology and predate, or stand apart from, the nation.

In its nativist adoption, the hyphen provides vertical links that emphasize descent relations, roots, depth, inheritance, continuity, homogeneity, and stability. These are allegorized in family sagas and mother-daughter and generational conflict narratives of Chinese-American films such as Wayne Wang's Eat a Bowl of Tea (1989) and The Joy Luck Club (1993). The filmmakers' task in this modality, in Stuart Hall's words, is "to discover, excavate, bring to light and express through cinematic representation" that inherited collective cultural identity, that "one true self" (1994, 393). In its contestatory adoption, the hyphen can operate horizontally, highlighting consent relations, disruption, heterogeneity, slippage, and mediation, as in Trinh T. Minh-ha's Surname Viet Given Name Nam (1985) and Srinivas Krishna's Masala (1990). In this modality, filmmakers do not recover an existing past or impose an imaginary and often fetishized coherence on their fragmented experiences and histories. Rather, by emphasizing discontinuity and specificity, they demonstrate that they are in the process of becoming, that they are "subject to the continuous 'play' of history, culture and power" (Hall 1994, 394). Christine Choy and Rene Tajima's award-winning film Who Killed Vincent Chin? (1988) is really a treatise on the problematic of the hyphen in the Asian-American context, as it centers on the murder of a Chinese-American by out-of-work white Detroit autoworkers who, resentful of Japanese car imports, mistook him for being Japanese.

Read as a sign of hybridized, multiple, or constructed identity, the hyphen can become liberating because it can be performed and signified upon. Each hyphen is in reality a nested hyphen, consisting of a number of other intersecting and overlapping hyphens that provide inter- and intraethnic and national links. This fragmentation and multiplication can work against essentialism, nationalism, and dyadism. Faced with too many options and meanings, however, some have suggested removing the hyphen, while others have proposed replacing it with a plus sign.[5] Martin Scorsese's ITALIANAMERICAN (1974) cleverly removes the hyphen and the space and instead joins the "Italian" with the "American" to suggest a fused third term. The film title by this most ethnic of New Hollywood cinema directors posits that there is no Italianness that precedes or stands apart from Americanness. In this book, I have retained the hyphen, since this is the most popular form of writing these compound ethnic designations.

The compound terms that bracket the hyphen also present problems, for at the same time that each term produces symbolic alliance among disparate members of a group, it tends to elide their diversity and specificity. "Asian-American," for example, encompasses people from such culturally and nationally diverse roots as the Philippines, Vietnam, Cambodia, Korea, Japan, Thailand, China, Laos, Taiwan, Indonesia, Malaysia, India, Bangladesh, and Pakistan. To calibrate the term, such unwieldy terms as "Southeast Asian diasporas" have also been created. Similar processes and politics of naming have been tried for the "black" British filmmakers.

Independent film distributors, such as Third World Newsreel, Icarus-First Run Films, and Women Make Movies, exploit the hyphen and the politics of the identity cinema by classifying these films thematically or by their hyphenated designation. Such classifications create targets of opportunity for those interested in such films, but they also narrow the marketing and critical discourses about these films by encouraging audiences to read them in terms of their ethnic content and identity politics more than their authorial vision and stylistic innovations. Several postcolonial ethnic and identity filmmakers are discussed individually and collectively.

Diaspora, exile, and ethnicity are not steady states; rather, they are fluid processes that under certain circumstances may transform into one another and beyond. There is also no direct and predetermined progression from exile to ethnicity, although dominant ideological and economic apparatuses tend to favor an assimilationist trajectory—from exile to diaspora to ethnic to citizen to consumer.

[. . .]

The Stylistic Approach

How films are conceived and received has a lot to do with how they are framed discursively. Sometimes the films of great transplanted directors, such as Alfred Hitchcock, Luis Buñuel, and Jean-Luc Godard, are framed within the "international" cinema category.[6] Most often, they are classified within either the national cinemas of their host countries or the established film genres and styles. Thus, the films of F. W. Murnau, Douglas Sirk, George Cukor, Vincent Minnelli, and Fritz Lang are usually considered as exemplars of the American cinema, the classical Hollywood style, or the melodrama and noir genres. Of course, the works of these and other established directors are also discussed under the rubric of "auteurism." Alternatively, many independent exiled filmmakers who make films about exile and their homelands' cultures and politics (such as Abid Med Hondo, Michel Khleifi, Mira Nair, and Ghasem Ebrahimian) or those minority filmmakers who make films about their ethnic communities (Rea Tajiri, Charles Burnett, Christine Choy, Gregory Nava, Haile Gerima, and Julie Dash) are often marginalized as merely national, Third World, Third Cinema, identity cinema, filmmakers, who are unable to fully speak to mainstream audiences. Through funding, festival programming, and marketing strategy, these filmmakers are often encouraged to engage in "salvage filmmaking," that is, making films that serve to preserve and recover cultural and ethnic heritage. Other exilic filmmakers, such as Jonas Mekas, Mona Hatoum, Chantal Akerman, Trinh T. Minh-ha, Isaac Julien, and Shirin Neshat, are placed within the avant-garde category, while some, such as Agnès Varda and Chris Marker, are considered unclassifiable.

Although these classificatory approaches are important for framing films to better understand them or better market them, they also serve to overdetermine and limit the films' potential meanings. Their undesirable consequences are particularly grave for the accented films because classification approaches are not neutral structures. They are "ideological constructs" masquerading as neutral categories (Altman 1989, 5). By forcing accented films into one of the established categories, the very cultural and political foundations that constitute them are bracketed, misread, or effaced altogether. Such traditional schemas also tend to lock the filmmakers into discursive ghettos that fail to reflect or account for their personal evolution and stylistic transformations over time. Once labeled "ethnic," "ethnographic," or "hyphenated," accented filmmakers remain discursively so even long after they have moved on. On the other hand, there are those, such as Gregory Nava, Spike Lee, Euzhan Palcy, and Mira Nair, who have made the move with varying degrees of success out of ethnic or Third World filmmaking and into mainstream cinema by telling their ethnic and national stories in more recognizable narrative forms.

[. . .]

Accented Style

If the classical cinema has generally required that components of style, such as mise-en-scène, filming, and editing, produce a realistic rendition of the world, the exilic accent must be sought in the manner in which realism is, if not subverted, at least inflected differently. Henry Louis Gates Jr. has characterized black texts as "mulatto" or "mulatta," containing a double voice and a two-toned heritage: "These texts speak in standard Romance and Germanic languages and literary structures, but almost always speak with a distinct and resonant accent, an accent that Signifies (upon) the various black vernacular literary traditions, which are still being written down" (1988, xxiii). Accented films are also mulatta texts. They are created with awareness of the vast histories of the prevailing cinematic modes. They are also created in a new mode that is constituted both by the structures of feeling of the filmmakers themselves as displaced subjects and by the traditions of exilic and diasporic cultural productions that preceded them. From the cinematic traditions they acquire one set of voices, and from the exilic and diasporic traditions they acquire a second. This double consciousness constitutes the accented style that not only signifies upon exile and other cinemas but also signifies the condition of exile itself. It signifies upon cinematic traditions by its artisanal and collective modes of production, which undermine the dominant production mode, and by narrative strategies, which subvert that mode's realistic treatment of time, space, and causality. It also signifies and signifies upon exile by expressing, allegorizing, commenting upon, and critiquing the conditions of its own production, and deterritorialization. Both of these acts of signifying and signification are constitutive of the accented style, whose key characteristics are elaborated upon in the following. What turns these into attributes of style is their repeated inscription in a single film, in the entire oeuvre of individual filmmakers, or in the works of various displaced filmmakers regardless of their place of origin or residence. Ultimately, the style demonstrates their dislocation at the same time that it serves to locate them as authors.

Language, Voice, Address

In linguistics, accent refers only to pronunciation, while dialect refers to grammar and vocabulary as well. More specifically, accent has two chief definitions: "The cumulative auditory effect of those features of pronunciation which identify where a person is from, regionally and socially" and "The emphasis which makes a particular word or syllable stand out in a stream of speech" (Crystal 1991, 2). While accents may be standardized (for example, as British, Scottish, Indian, Canadian, Australian, or American accents of English), it is impossible to speak without an accent. There are various reasons for differences in accent. In English, the majority of accents are regional. Speakers of English as a second language, too, have accents that stem from their regional and first-language characteristics. Differences in accent often correlate with other factors as well: social and class origin, religious affiliation, educational level, and political grouping (Asher 1994, 9). Even though from a linguistic point of view all accents are equally important, all accents are not of equal value socially and politically. People make use of accents to judge not only the social standing of the speakers but also their personality. Depending on their accents, some speakers may be considered regional, local yokel, vulgar, ugly, or comic, whereas others may be thought of as educated, upper-class, sophisticated, beautiful, and proper. As a result, accent is one of the most intimate and powerful markers of group identity and solidarity, as well as of individual difference and personality. The flagship newscasts of mainstream national television and radio networks have traditionally been delivered in the preferred "official" accent, that is, the accent that is considered to be standard, neutral, and value-free.

Applied to cinema, the standard, neutral, value-free accent maps onto the dominant cinema produced by the society's reigning mode of production. This typifies the classical and the new Hollywood cinemas, whose films are realistic and intended for entertainment only, and thus free from overt ideology or accent. By that definition, all alternative cinemas are accented, but each is accented in certain specific ways that distinguish it. The cinema discussed here derives its accent from its artisanal and collective production modes and from the filmmakers' and audiences' deterritorialized locations. Consequently, not all accented films are exilic and diasporic, but all exilic and diasporic films are accented. If in linguistics accent pertains only to pronunciation, leaving grammar and vocabulary intact, exilic and diasporic accent permeates the film's deep structure: its narrative, visual style, characters, subject matter, theme, and plot. In that sense, the accented style in film functions as both accent and dialect in linguistics. Discussions of accents and dialects are usually confined to oral literature and to spoken presentations. Little has been written—besides typographical accentuation of words—about what Taghi Modarressi has called "writing with an accent":

> The new language of any immigrant writer is obviously accented and, at least initially, inarticulate. I consider this "artifact" language expressive in its own right. Writing with an accented voice is organic to the mind of the immigrant writer. It is not something one can invent. It is frequently buried beneath personal inhibitions and doubts. The accented voice is loaded with hidden messages from our cultural heritage, messages that often reach beyond the capacity of the ordinary words of any language. . . . Perhaps it is their [immigrant and exile writers'] personal language that can build a bridge between what is familiar and what is strange. They may then find it possible to generate new and revealing paradoxes. Here we have our juxtapositions and our transformations—the graceful and the awkward, the beautiful and the ugly, sitting side by side in a perpetual metamorphosis of one into the other. It is like the Hunchback of Notre Dame trying to be Prince Charming for strangers.
>
> (1992, 9)

At its most rudimentary level, making films with an accent involves using on-camera and voice-over characters and actors who speak with a literal accent in their pronunciation. In the classical Hollywood cinema, the characters' accents were not a reliable indicator of the actors' ethnicity.[7] In accented cinema, however, the characters' accents are often ethnically coded, for in this cinema, more often than not, the actor's ethnicity, the character's ethnicity, and the ethnicity of the star's persona coincide. However, in some of these films the coincidence is problematized, as in the epistolary films of Chantal Akerman (*News from Home*, 1976) and Mona Hatoum (*Measures of Distance*, 1988). In each of these works, a filmmaking daughter reads in an accented English voice-over the letters she has received from her mother. The audience may assume that these are the voices of the mothers (complete coincidence among the three accents), but since neither of the films declares whose voice we are hearing, the coincidence is subverted and the spectators must speculate about the true relationship of the accent to the identity, ethnicity, and authenticity of the speaker or else rely on extratextual information.

One of the greatest deprivations of exile is the gradual deterioration in and potential loss of one's original language, for language serves to shape not only individual identity but also regional and national identities prior to displacement. Threatened by this catastrophic loss, many accented filmmakers doggedly insist on writing the dialogues in their original language—to the detriment of the films' wider distribution. However, most accented films are bilingual, even multilingual, multivocal, and multiaccented, like Egoyan's *Calendar* (1993), which contains a series of telephonic monologues in a dozen untranslated languages, or Raúl Ruiz's *On Top of the Whale* (1981), whose dialogue is spoken in more than a half dozen languages, one of them invented by Ruiz himself. If the dominant cinema is driven by the hegemony of synchronous sound and a strict alignment of speaker and voice, accented films are counterhegemonic insofar as many of them de-emphasize synchronous sound, insist on first-person and other voice-over narrations delivered in the accented pronunciation of the host country's language, create a slippage between voice and speaker, and inscribe everyday nondramatic pauses and long silences.

At the same time that accented films emphasize visual fetishes of homeland and the past (landscape, monuments, photographs, souvenirs, letters), as well as visual markers of difference and belonging (posture, look, style of dress and behavior), they equally stress the oral, the vocal, and the musical—that is, accents, intonations, voices, music, and songs, which also demarcate individual and collective identities. These voices may belong to real, empirical persons, like Mekas's voice narrating his diary films; or they may be fictitious voices, as in Marker's *Letter from Siberia* (1958) and *Sunless* (1982); or they may be accented voices whose identity is not firmly established, as in the aforementioned films by Akerman and Hatoum. Sergeï Paradjanov's four feature films are not only intensely visual in their tableau-like mise-en-scène and presentational filming but also deeply oral in the way they are structured like oral narratives that are told to the camera.

Stressing musical and oral accents redirects our attention from the hegemony of the visual and of modernity toward the acousticity of exile and the commingling of premodernity and postmodernity in the films. Polyphony and heteroglossia both localize and locate the films as texts of cultural and temporal difference.

Increasingly, accented films are using the film's frame as a writing tablet on which appear multiple texts in original languages and in translation in the form of titles, subtitles, intertitles, or blocks of text. The calligraphic display of these texts de-emphasizes visuality while highlighting the textuality and translational issues of intercultural art. Because they are multilingual, accented films require extensive titling just to translate the dialogues. Many of them go beyond that, however, by experimenting with on-screen typography as a supplementary mode of narration and expression. Mekas's *Lost, Lost, Lost*, Trinh's *Surname Viet Given Name Nam*, and Tajiri's *History and Memory* (1991) experiment with multiple typographical presentations of English texts on the screen linked in complicated ways to the dialogue and to the voice-overs, which are also accented in their pronunciation. In cases where the on-screen text is written in "foreign" languages, such as in Suleiman's *Homage by Assassination* (1991) and Hatoum's *Measures of Distance*, both of which display Arabic words, the vocal accent is complemented by a calligraphic accent. The inscription of these visual and vocal accents transforms the act of spectatorship, from just watching to watching *and* literally reading the screen.

By incorporating voice-over narration, direct address, multilinguality, and multivocality, accented films, particularly the epistolary variety, destabilize the omniscient narrator and narrative system of the mainstream cinema and journalism. Film letters often contain the characters' direct address (usually in first-person singular), the indirect discourse of the filmmaker (as the teller of the tale), and the free indirect discourse of the film in which the direct voice contaminates the indirect. Egoyan's *Calendar* combines all three of these discourses to create confusion as to what is happening, who is speaking, who is addressing whom, where the diegetic photographer and his on-screen wife (played by Egoyan and his real-life wife) leave off and where the historical persons Atom Egoyan and Arsinée Khanjian begin. The accented style is itself an example of free indirect discourse in the sense of forcing the dominant cinema to speak in a minoritarian dialect.

Embedded Criticism

As Dick Hebdige has noted, style—any style—is "a gesture of defiance or contempt, in a smile or a sneer. It signals a Refusal" (1979, 3). The accented film style is such a gesture, smile, or sneer of refusal and defiance. Although it does not conform to the classic Hollywood style, the national cinema style of any particular country, the style of any specific film movement or any film author, the accented style is influenced by them all, and it signifies upon them and criticizes them. By its artisanal and collective mode of production, its subversion of the conventions of storytelling and spectator positioning, its critical juxtaposition of different worlds, languages, and cultures, and its aesthetics of imperfection and smallness, it critiques the dominant cinema. It is also highly political because politics infuses it from inception to reception. For these reasons, accented cinema is not only a minority cinema but also a minor cinema, in the way that Deleuze and Guattari have defined the concept (1986).

However, this should not be construed to mean that the accented cinema is oppositional cinema, in the sense of defining itself primarily against an unaccented dominant cinema. Produced in a capitalist (if alternative) mode of production, the accented films are not necessarily radical, for they act as agents not only of expression and defiance but also of assimilation, even legitimization, of their makers and their audiences. As such, accented cinema is one of the dialects of our language of cinema.

Accented Structures of Feeling

Since the accented style is not a programmatic, already formed style, one may speak of it as an emergent "structure of feeling," which, according to Raymond Williams, is not a fixed institution, formation, position, or even a formal concept such as worldview or ideology. Rather, it is a set of undeniable personal and social experiences—with internal relations and tensions—that is

> still in process, often indeed not yet recognized as social but taken to be private, idiosyncratic, and even isolating, but which in analysis (though rarely otherwise) has its emergent, connecting, and dominant characteristics, indeed its specific hierarchies.

These are often more recognizable at a later stage, when they have been (as often happens) formalized, classified, and in many cases built into institutions and formations.

(1977, 132)

The accented style is one such emergent category—not yet fully recognized or formalized. Its structure of feeling is rooted in the filmmakers' profound experiences of deterritorialization, which oscillate between dysphoria and euphoria, celibacy and celebration. These dislocatory feeling structures are powerfully expressed in the accented films' chronotopical configurations of the homeland as utopian and open and of exile as dystopian and claustrophobic.

In some measure, what is being described here is similar to the feeling structures of postmodernism. In speaking about the formation of a new mass audience for post-modernist art, Fred Pfeil notes that experiencing such art is characterized by "a very unstable play between a primal delight and primal fear, between two simultaneous versions of the primary aggressive impulse, that which seeks to incorporate the world into itself and that which struggles to prevent its own engulfment. This dialectic is the postmodern 'structure of feeling' (1988, 386). To the extent that the accented and postmodernist cinemas both immerse us in these dystopic and euphoric moments of unresolved polarity, they are similar. However, not all postmodernist films are diasporically or exilically accented, while all accented films are to some extent postmodernist. Accented films differ from other post-modernist films because they usually posit the homeland as a grand and deeply rooted referent, which stops the postmodernist play of signification. Since exile (more than diaspora) is driven by the modernist concerns and tropes of nationalism and state formation, which posits the existence and realness of the earth, mountains, monuments, and seas as well as of the peoples, histories, politics, and cultures of the homeland, many exilically accented films are intensely place-bound, and their narratives are driven by a desire either to recapture the homeland or to return to it. As a result, during the liminal period of displacement, the postmodernist playfulness, indeterminacy, and intertextuality have little place in exilic politics and cinema. The referent homeland is too powerfully real, even sacred, to be played with and signified upon. It is this powerful hold of the homeland that imbues the accented structures of feeling with such sadness and sense of terminal loss as described by Edward Said:

Exile is strangely compelling to think about but terrible to experience. It is the unhealable rift forced between a human being and a native place, between the self and its true home: its essential sadness can never be surmounted. And while it is true that literature and history contain heroic, romantic, glorious, even triumphant episodes in an exile's life, these are no more than efforts meant to overcome the crippling sorrow of estrangement. The achievements of exile are permanently undermined by the loss of something left behind for ever.

(1990b, 357)

Sadness, loneliness, and alienation are frequent themes, and sad, lonely, and alienated people are favorite characters in the accented films.

Only when the grand return to the homeland is found to be impossible, illusory, or undesirable does the postmodernist semiosis set in. Then the nostalgia for the referent and the pain of separation from it may be transformed into a nostalgia for its synecdoches, fetishes, and signifieds—the frozen sounds and images of the homeland—which are then circulated in exilic media and pop culture (including wall calendars, as in Egoyan's *Calendar*).[8]

Multiple sites, cultures, and time zones inform the feeling structures of exile and diaspora, and they pose the representation of simultaneity and multisitedness as challenges for the accented films. Citing Sergei Eisenstein, George Marcus offered montage as a methodology that not only encodes multiple times and sites but also self-consciously problematizes the realist representation of the world. In the accented cinema, as in the multisited ethnography that Marcus describes, this is achieved by critical juxtapositions of multiple spaces, times, voices, narratives, and foci (1994).

[. . .]

Third Cinema Aesthetics

The genealogy of the accented style may be traced not only to the epochal shifts of post-colonialism and postmodernism but also to the transformation of cinematic structures, theories, and practices since the 1960s. Specifically, it begins with the emergence and theorization of a Latin-American cinema of liberation, dubbed "Third Cinema," and its later elaboration by Teshome H. Gabriel and others. Drawing upon the Cuban revolution of 1959, Italian neorealist film aesthetics, Griersonian social documentary style, and Marxist analysis, Brazilian filmmaker Glauber Rocha issued his passionate polemic, "The Aesthetics of Hunger," and Argentinean cinéastes Fernando Solanas and Spanish-born Octavio Getino, makers of the massive film *The Hour of the Furnaces* (*La Hora de los Hornos*, 1968), published their famous manifesto, "Towards a Third Cinema." These were followed by an avant-gardist manifesto, "For an Imperfect Cinema," written by the Cuban filmmaker Julio Garcia Espinosa.[9] Other "revolutionary" cinematic manifestos were issued in North Africa and the Middle East. In France, the SLON (later ISKRA) and Dziga Vertov groups, among others, and in the United States, Newsreel and other groups picked up the clarion call of these manifestos and issued their own summons for new radical cinematic practices. The Latin-American polemics and manifestos in particular, including *The Hour of the Furnaces*, critiqued the mainstream, capitalist, "first cinema" and the petit bourgeois, authorial "second cinema"; in their place they proposed a new research category of "Third Cinema"—a cinema that is not perfect, polished, or professional.[10] Indeed, in its formal practices, *The Hour of the Furnaces* is a clear progenitor of the accented style.

The accented cinema is one of the offshoots of the Third Cinema, with which it shares certain attributes and from which it is differentiated by certain sensibilities. As Gabriel elaborated, although Third Cinema films are made chiefly in the Third World, they may be made anywhere, by anyone, about any subject, and in a variety of styles and forms, as long as they are oppositional and liberationist (1982, 2–3). As a cinema of displacement, however, the accented cinema is much more situated than the Third Cinema, for it is necessarily made by (and often for) specific displaced subjects and diasporized communities. Less polemical than the Third Cinema, it is nonetheless a political cinema that stands opposed to authoritarianism and oppression. If Third Cinema films generally advocated class struggle and armed struggle, accented films favor discursive and semiotic struggles. Although not necessarily Marxist or even socialist like the Third Cinema, the accented cinema is an engagé cinema. However, its engagement is less with "the people" and "the masses," as was the case with the Third Cinema, than with specific individuals, ethnicities, nationalities, and identities, and with the experience of deterritorialization itself. In accented cinema, therefore, every story is both a private story of an individual and a social and public story of exile and diaspora. These engagements with collectivities and with deterritorialization turn accented films into allegories of exile and diaspora—not the totalizing "national allegories" that Jameson once characterized Third World literature and cinema to be (1986).

Third Cinema and accented cinema are alike in their attempts to define and create a nostalgic, even fetishized, authentic prior culture—before contamination by the West in the case of the Third Cinema, and before displacement and emigration in the case of the accented cinema. Like *The Hour of the Furnaces*, accented films are hybridized in their use of forms that cut across the national, typological, generic, and stylistic boundaries. Similarly, many of them are driven by the aesthetics of provisionality, experimentation, and imperfection—even amateurness—and they are made in the artisanal, low-cost mode of "cinema of hunger." In sum, despite some marked differences, both accented films and Third Cinema films are historically conscious, politically engaged, critically aware, generically hybridized, and artisanally produced. The affinity of the two cinemas and the impact of the one on the other are paralleled in the lives of some of the filmmakers, such as Fernando Solanas from Argentina and Miguel Littín from Chile, who moved from the Third Cinema in the 1960s to the accented cinema of the 1980s and beyond.

Border Effects, Border Writing

Border consciousness emerges from being situated at the border, where multiple determinants of race, class, gender, and membership in divergent, even antagonistic, historical and national identities intersect. As a result, border consciousness, like exilic liminality, is theoretically against binarism and duality and for a third optique, which is multiperspectival and tolerant of ambiguity, ambivalence and chaos.

The globalization of capital, labor, culture, and media is threatening to make borders obsolete and national sovereignty irrelevant. However, physical borders are real and extremely dangerous, particularly for those who have to cross them. In recent years no region in the world has borne deadlier sustained clashes over physical (and discursive) borders than the Middle East and the former Yugoslavia. The collisions over physical and literal lands, even over individual houses and their symbolic meanings, are also waged in the accented films. Since their widely received formulation by Anzaldúa (1987), borderland consciousness and theory have been romanticized, universalized, and co-opted by ignoring the specific dislocatory and conflictual historical and territorial grounds that produce them. However, borders are open, and infected wounds and the subjectivity they engender cannot be postnational or post-al, but interstitial. Unequal power relations and incompatible identities prevent the wound from healing.

Since border subjectivity is cross-cultural and intercultural, border filmmaking tends to be accented by the "strategy of translation rather than representation" (Hicks 1991, xxiii). Such a strategy undermines the distinction between autochthonous and alien cultures in the interest of promoting their interaction and intertextuality. As a result, the best of the border films are hybridized and experimental—characterized by multifocality, multi-linguality, asynchronicity, critical distance, fragmented or multiple subjectivity, and transborder amphibolic characters—characters who might best be called "shifters." Of these characteristics, the latter bears discussion at this point.

In linguistics, shifters are words, such as "I" and "you," whose reference can be understood only in the context of the utterance. More generally, a shifter is an "operator" in the sense of being dishonest, evasive, and expedient, or even being a "mimic," in the sense that Homi Bhabha formulated, as a producer of critical excess, irony, and sly civility (1994). In the context of border filmmaking, shifters are characters who exhibit some or all of these registers of understanding and performativity. As such, they occupy a powerful position in the political economy of both actual and diegetic border crossings. For example, in Nava's El Norte, a classic border film, the shifters consist of the following characters: the pollo (border-crossing brother and sister, Enrique and Rosa); the coyote (the Mexican middleman who for a fee brings the pollo across), the migra (the U.S. immigration officers who chase and arrest Enrique); the pocho (Americans of Mexican descent who speak Mexican Spanish imperfectly, the man in the film who turns Enrique in to the immigration authorities); the chola/cholo and pachuca/pachuco (young inhabitants of the border underworld who have their own dialect called caló); and the U.S.-based Mexican or Hispanic contractors who employ border crossers as day laborers (among them, Enrique).[11] The power of these border shifters comes from their situationist existence, their familiarity with the cultural and legal codes of interacting cultures, and the way in which they manipulate identity and the asymmetrical power situations in which they find themselves.

Accented films inscribe other amphibolic character types who are split, double, crossed, and hybridized and who perform their identities. As liminal subjects and interstitial artists, many accented filmmakers are themselves shifters, with multiple perspectives and conflicted or performed identities. They may own no passport or hold multiple passports, and they may be stranded between legality and illegality. Many are scarred by the harrowing experiences of their own border crossings. Some may be energized, while others may be paralyzed by their fear of partiality. Their films often draw upon these biographical crossing experiences.

Themes

Understandably, journeys, real or imaginary, form a major thematic thread in the accented films. Journeys have motivation, direction, and duration, each of which impacts the travel and the traveler. Depending on their directions, journeys are valued differently. In the accented cinema, westering journeys are particularly valued, partly because they reflect the filmmakers' own trajectory and the general flow of value worldwide. The westering journey is embedded, in its varied manifestations, in Xavier Koller's Journey of Hope (1990), Nizamettin Ariç's A Cry for Beko (1992), and Ghasem Ebrahimian's The Suitors (1989). In Nava's El Norte, a south–north journey lures the Mayan Indians from Guatemala to the United States.

There are many instances of empowering return journeys: to Morocco in Faridah Ben Lyazid's Door to the Sky (1989), to Africa in Raquel Gerber's Ori (1989), and to Ghana in Haile Gerima's Sankofa (1993). When neither escape nor return is possible, the desire for escape and the longing for return become highly cathected to certain icons of homeland's nature and to certain narratives. These narratives take the form of varied journeys: from the dystopic and irresolute journey of lostness in Tarkovsky's Stalker (1979) to the nostalgically celebratory homecoming journey in Mekas's Reminiscences of a Journey to Lithuania (1971–72) to the conflicting return journey to Japan and China in Ann Hui's Song of the Exile (1990).

Not all journeys involve physical travel. There also are metaphoric and philosophical journeys of identity and transformation that involve the films' characters and sometimes the filmmakers themselves, as in Mekas's films or in Ivens and Loridan's A *Tale of the Wind*.

[. . .]

The accented style is not a fully recognized and sanctioned film genre, and the exilic and diasporic filmmakers do not always make accented films. In fact, most of them would wish to be in Egoyan's place, to move out of marginal cinema niches into the world of art cinema or even popular cinema. Style permits the critics to track the evolution of the work of not only a single filmmaker but also a group of filmmakers. Asian Pacific American film-making has gradually evolved away from an ethnic focus toward diasporic and exilic concerns, while Iranian exilic filmmakers have evolved toward a diasporic sensibility. These evolutions signal the transformation of both filmmakers and their audiences. They also signal the appropriation of the filmmakers, their audiences, and certain features of the accented style by the mainstream cinema and by its independent offspring. Because it goes beyond connois-seurship to situate the cinéastes within their changing social formations, cultural locations, and cinematic practices, the accented style is nor hermetic, homogeneous, or autonomous. It meanders and evolves. It is an inalienable element of the social material process of exile and diaspora and of the exilic and diasporic mode of production.

Notes

1 I thank Bill Nichols for suggesting the parallel between exile and taboo. Also, see exile as "aesthetic gain" in Kaplan 1996, 33–41.

2 I have incorporated these and other attributes of exile and alterity to formulate a "paradigm of exile" (Naficy 1993a).

3 If Rushdie is an example of exilic hybridity, F. M. Esfandiary is an example of exilic virtuality. In the 1960s, Esfandiary wrote novels from exile about the horror of life in his homeland Iran (*The Identity Card* [1966]), but in the late 1980s he changed his name to FM-2030 and developed the concept of transhumanism, which dismissed all usual markers of continuity and identity. To be a transhuman is to be a universal "evolutionary being" (FM-2030 1989, 205).

4 This is particularly true for the Japanese-Americans whose loyalty to the United States was questioned during World War II and to the Muslim Americans whose loyalty is often questioned in contemporary times.

5 Peter Feng suggests removing the hyphen from "Asian-American," while Gustavo P. Firrnat recommends replacing it with a plus sign for "Cuban + American" (1994, 16). Some insert a forward slash between the two terms. On the politics of the hyphen, especially for Asian-Americans, see Feng 1995, 1996; Lowe 1991.

6 Although "international," even "transnational," these directors— whom Douglas Gomery (1991) labels "the individual as international film artist"—are not considered "exilic" or "diasporic" by the definition used here.

7 In the classical Hollywood cinema, the stars who retained their "foreign" accents fared differently. Some could not get parts because of their heavy accents. Scandinavian stars, particularly Greta Garbo, Sonja Henie, and Ingrid Bergman, were usually cast as European

and Soviet foreign characters. Some British-born stars, such as Cary Grant, acquired a "transatlantic accent," so named perhaps because it was both readily comprehensible and hard to place (Jarvie 1991, 93).

8   For more on the phenomenon of exilic nostalgia and fetishization, see Naficy 1993a, chap. 4.

9   These Latin-American and Third Cinema polemics and manifestos are collected in Martin 1997a.

10 There is disagreement over what constituted the first and second cinemas. Gabriel, for example, assigned First Cinema to the products of the mainstream film industry in capitalist market economies, while consigning Second Cinema to the products of the communist/socialist command economies (1982, chap. 1).

11 Other middlemen figures in the border drama include sanctuary movement advocates who assist potential refugees to gain asylum in the United States.

References

Altman, Rick (1989) *The American Film Musical* Bloomington: Indiana University Press.

Anzaldúa, Gloria (1987) *Borderlands/La Frontera: The New Mestiza* San Francisco: Spinsters.

Arasoughly, Alia (ed and trans) (1996) *Screens of Life: Critical Film Writing from the Arab World* Vol. 1. Quebec: World Heritage Press.

Armes, Roy (1996) *Dictionary of North African Film Makers* Paris: Editions ATM.

Asher, R.E. (ed) (1994) *The Encyclopedia of Language and Linguistics* Vol. 1. New York: Pergamon Press.

Bauman, Zygmunt (1991) "Modernity and Ambivalence" in *Global Culture: Nationalism, Globalization and Modernity*, Mike Featherstone (ed), 143–69, London: Sage.

Bhabha, Homi (1994) *The Location of Culture* London: Routledge.

Bloom, Peter (1995) "Locating Beur Cinema: Social Activism, Immigration Politics and the Naming of a Film Movement" paper presented at the Tenth Triennial Symposium on African Art, New York University, New York, April.

Bodman, Ellen-Fairbanks and Ronald L. Bartholomew (1992) *Middle East and Islamic World Filmography* Chapel Hill: University of North Carolina, Nonprint Materials Collection.

Brossard, Jean-Pierre (unknown) "Dictionnaire des principaux cinéastes" in L'*Algérie vue par son cinema*, 173–78. Locarno: Tisca Nova SA.

Clifford, James (1997) *Routes: Travel and Translation in the Late Twentieth Century* Cambridge, Mass: Harvard University Press.

Cohen, Robin (1997) *Global Diasporas: An Introduction*. London: UCL Press.

Crystal, David (1991) *A Dictionary of Linguistics and Phonetics* 3rd ed. New York: Blackwell.

Feng, Peter (1995) "In Search of an Asian American Cinema." *Cinéaste* 21, nos. 1–2:32–36.

Firmat, Gustavo Pérez (1994) *Life on the Hyphen: The Cuban-American Way* Austin: University of Texas Press.

FM-2030 (1989) *Are You a Transhuman?* New York: Warner Books.

Deleuze, Gilles and Félix Guattari (1986) *Kafka: Toward a Minor Literature*, Trans. Dana Polan. Minneapolis: University of Minnesota Press.

Diawara, Manthia (1993) *Black American Cinema* New York: Routledge.

Gabriel, Teshome H. (1982) *Third Cinema in the Third world: The Aesthetics of Liberation* Ann Arbor: Michigan: UMI Research Press.

Gates, Henry Louis Jr. (1998) *The Signifying Monkey: A Theory of African-American Literary Criticism* New York: Oxford University Press.

Gilroy, Paul (1993) *The Black Atlantic: Modernity and Double Consciousness* Cambridge: Harvard University Press.

Gomery, Douglas (1991) *Movie History: A Survey* Belmont, CA: Wadsworth.

Hall, Stuart (1994) "Cultural Identity and Diaspora" in *Colonial Discourse and Post-colonial Theory: A Reader*, Patrick Williams and Laura Chrisman (eds), 392–403, New York: Columbia University Press.

Hall, Stuart (1988) "New Ethnicities." ICA Documents, no. 7. 27–31, Special issue on Black film, British cinema.

Harlow, Barbara (1991) "Sites of Struggle: Immigration, Deportation, Prison, and Exile" in *Criticism in the Borderlands*, Héctor Caldrón and José David Saldivar (eds), 149–63, Durham, N.C.: Duke University Press.

Hebdige, Dick (1979) *Subculture: The Meaning of Style* London: Methuen.

Hicks, Emily D. (1991) *Border Writing: the Multidimensional Text* Minneapolis: University of Minnesota Press.

Iransk Film i Exil (1993) Festival catalog. Göteborg, Sweden, October 7–14.

Jameson, Fredric (1984) "Periodizing the 60s" in *The 60s without Apology*, Sohnya Sayers *et al.* (eds), 178–209, Minneapolis: University of Minnesota Press.

Jameson, Fredric (1986) "Third-World Literature in the Era of Multinational Capitalism" *Social Text* 15 (fall), 65–88.

Kaplan, Caren (1996) *Questions of Travel: Postmodern Discourses of Displacement* Durham, N.C.: Duke University Press.

Kaufman, Deborah, *et al.* (1991) *Independent Filmmakers: Looking at Ourselves* A Guide to Films Featured in the Jewish Film Festival, Berkeley: Jewish Film Festival.

Lowe, Lisa (1991) "Heterogeneity, Hybridity, Multiplicity: Making Asian American Difference" *Diaspora* 1, No. 1: 24–44.

Marcus, George E. (1994) "The Modernist Sensibility in Recent Ethnographic Writing and the Cinematic Metaphor of Montage" in *Visualizing Theory: Selected Essays from V.A.R., 1990–1994*, Lucien Taylor (ed), 37–53, New York: Routledge.

Marks, Laura (1994) "A Deleuzian Politics of Hybrid Cinema." *Screen* 35, no. 3: 244–64.

Mercer, Kobena (1994) *Welcome to the Jungle: New Positions in Black Cultural Studies* London: Routledge.

Modarressi, Taghi (1992) "Writing with an Accent." *Chanteh* 1, no. 1: 7–9.

Naficy, Hamid (1996a) "Identity Politics and Iranian Exile Music Videos" in *Middle Eastern Diaspora Communities in America*, Mehdi Bozorgmehr and Alison Feldman (eds), 104–23, New York: University, Hagop Kevorkian Center for Near Eastern Studies.

O'Grady, Gerald (1973) "Our Space in Our Time: The New American Cinema" in *The American Cinema*, Donald E. Staples (ed), 228–44, Washington, D.C.: U.S. Information Agency.

Omid, Jamal (1367/1988) *Farhang-e Sinema-ye Iran* Zendeginameh-ye Kargardanan, Tahiyehkonandegan, Filmnamehnevisan, Bazigaran, Filmbardaran, Tadvinkonandegan, ahangsazan, Tarrahan-e Sahneh, va [.] Tehran: Negah.

Palestinian Film Week (1992) *Jerusalem: Jerusalem Film Institute* (Film Catalog).

Peters, John (1999) "Exile, Nomadism, and Diaspora: The Stakes of Mobility in the Western Canon" in *Home, Exile, Homeland: Film, Media, and the Politics of Place*, Hamid Naficy (ed), 17–41, New York: Routledge.

Pfeil, Fred (1988) "Postmodernism as a 'Structure of Feeling'" in *Marxism and the Interpretation of Culture*, Cary Nelson and Lawrence Grossberg (eds), 381–403, Urbana: University of Illinois Press.

Pflaum, Hans Günther and Prinzler Hans Helmut (1993) *Cinema in the Federal Republic of Germany* Bonn: Inter Nationes.

Radvanyi, Jean (ed) (1993) *Le Cinéma Armenien* Paris: éditions du Centre Pompidou.

Rushdie, Salman (1991) *Imaginary Homelands: Essays and Criticisms*, 1981–1991 London: Granta.

Safran, William (1991) "Diasporas in Modern Societies: Myths of Homeland and Return" *Diaspora* 1 No. 1: 83–99.

Said, Edward (1990) "Reflections on Exile" in *Out There: Marginalization and Contemporary Cultures*, Russell Ferguson, Martha Gever, Trinh, Ti Minh-ha, and Cornel West (eds) 357–66, Cambridge, MS; MIT Press.

Salloum, Jayce (1996) *East of Here: (Re)Imagining the "Orient"* Catalogue of an exhibition held at YYZ Artists' Outlet, Toronto, November 20–December 14.

The Second Festival for Iranian Films in Exile (6–13 October, 1995) Göteborg: Sweden: Exile-Film Festival.

Sollors, Werner (1986) *Beyond Ethnicity: Consent and Descent in American Culture* New York: Oxford University Press.

Tavenas, Stéphane and Volard, François (1989) *Guide of European Cinema*, David Clougher (trans), Paris: éditions Ramsey/Eurocinéma.

Thomas, Nicholas (ed) (1990) *International Dictionary of Films and Filmmakers* 2nd ed., Chicago: St. James Press.

Tölöyan, Khachig (1996) "Rethinking Diaspora(s): Stateless Power in the Transnational Moment" *Diaspora* 5, no. 1: 3–36.

Williams, Raymond (1977) "Structure of Feeling" in *Marxism and Literature*, 128–35, London: Oxford University Press.

Beur Cinema and the Politics of Location: French Immigration Politics and the Naming of a Film Movement

9

PETER BLOOM

A 1991 compact disc entitled *de la Planète Mars*, released by the French rap group IAM, features the city of Mars . . . eilles as the planet Mars, and in a short glossary of terms in the liner notes calls the northern suburbs of Marseilles *Le côté obscur de Mars* – 'the dark side of Mars' that the French State refuses to see. Correspondingly, *beur* cinema stands as a significant metropolitan cultural reference for a resolutely fractured French identity. *Beur* cinema emerges out of the intersection between contemporary French immigration politics and popular culture, giving expression to the effects of an uneasy integration into metropolitan culture. As a loosely codified transnational film movement primarily based in France, *beur* cinema has explored the identity of a second generation of North African immigrants who have grown up in France. While related subjects have been depicted in feature-length films since the mid-1970s (Yves Boisset's *Dupont-la-Joie* (1974), for example), the term *beur* and its association with a generational consciousness in France is linked to recent political movements and uprisings in the housing projects throughout the 1980s and early 1990s.

The word *beur* is a back-slang derivation of *Arabe*, taken up by a second generation of North African immigrants, who, for the most part, grew up in housing projects on the peripheries of Paris, Marseilles, Grenoble, and Lyons. Terms such as *rhorhs*, (verlan for *frères*, meaning brothers), *cousins*, and *reub* (in yet another back-slang derivation of *beur*) were also used around the same time in different regions of France (Horvilleur, 1985). The popularisation of *beur* as an immediately comprehensible term for an outsider group also contained the more immediate connotation of Berber, the dominant ethnic group among the Algerian migrant population in France. *Beur*, the syllabic reversal of *Arabe*, also plays on the ignorance among French people concerning the diverse ethnic origins of North Africans in France. The Algerian village of Tlemcen, a still-remaining relic of the Roman Empire that was rebuilt by the French in 1842, was considered a rightful part of the early French medieval legacy during the colonial period. Tlemcen and the non-Muslim Berber and Kabyle population served as important territorial and spiritual justifications for the domination and assimilation of Algeria as part of the French colonial empire.

It is my intention here to trace the trajectory of the *beur* as a transitory sign of identification and protest during the 1980s and early 1990s. The resonance of the term *beur* as a transnational, hybrid identity can also be seen as the last hope for a French republican model of secular integration, and yet symptomatic of its breakdown, reviving age-old polarising battles between secular and clerical values. In the nineteenth century, the secular values of the State represented a renewed French republican ethos in opposition to the clerical values of the Catholic Church and the monarchy. In the late twentieth century, the fear of Islam in France, as associated with 'Islamic fundamentalism', has contributed to the reconsideration of citizenship rights for a second generation of Franco-Maghrebi citizens culminating in the 1993 Pasqua Laws. This has occurred in spite of the fact that less than half of Franco-Maghrebis in France are practising Muslims (Hargreaves, 1995, p. 119).

Emerging from social conflicts throughout the late 1970s and 1980s, *beur* identity is also tied to the postwar history of reconstruction, in which successive waves of North African immigrants were encouraged to come to France as part of a contractual manual labour force, transformed, as it were, from imperial subjects to immigrant workers. Overlapping histories of decolonisation and successive waves of economic migration adapted a surplus of decolonised subjects to the contingencies of the metropolitan workplace. Born into the break-up of a colonial order, the second generation found themselves slotted between a working-class French identity and an emerging multi-form immigrant population.

The national identity of the emerging *beur* youth population, who were born in France and largely of Algerian origin, has been continually contested by the State and resonates with the extensive media coverage of the 1989 Islamic headscarf controversy as well as rioting in Sartrouville (northwest of Paris), Vaulx-en-Velin (northeast of Lyon), and the northern sub-urbs of Marseilles. The Islamic headscarf controversy involved the suspension of three Muslim high-school girls, of Tunisian and Moroccan origin, from their school in Creil (30 miles north of Paris) for wearing an Islamic headscarf to class. The school headmaster, Ernest Chenière, claimed that the young women wearing the Islamic headscarf in school were engaged in a form of proselytism, which violated the secular nature of a State educational institution. Lest we forget, the French public educational system served as a bulwark for a secular social contract of *laïcité* dating from the beginning of the Third Republic, in the 1880s, under Jules Ferry.

On the grounds that Chenière's action discriminated against Muslim students and under pressure from anti-racist organisations such as MRAP,[1] the Movement against Racism and for Interracial Friendship, which had previously filed a complaint with the educational authorities in Creil, the then Minister of Education, Lionel Jospin, overturned Chenière's suspension order. The controversy in Creil stemmed, at least in part, from resentment among long-standing residents concerning the concentration of non-European immigrants in their communities, transformed from rural housing tracts in the late 1970s to State-financed middle- and low-income housing projects. In the aftermath of the controversy, Jean-Marie Le Pen's anti-immigrant National Front Party won the majority of seats in the December 1989 by-election held in Dreux (30 miles west of Paris). The political fallout of the events in Creil were also linked to the ongoing confrontations between *beur* youths and police in the Parisian suburbs of Sartrouville and Mantes-La-Jolie.

HLMs (H*abitations à Loyer Modéré*), which I have referred to as housing projects, are housing developments built primarily to accommodate tenants of limited means. Les Minguettes in Vénissieux (east of Lyon), with 28,000 residents was the largest of the HLMs, before being torn down in 1992. HLMs of various kinds exist throughout France and were primarily built as temporary dormitory-like lodging for low-income families to replace the inner-city *bidonvilles*.

The association between HLMs and North African immigrants has largely evolved from the legacy of SONACOTRAL[2] contractual labour dormitories, which were initially established in the 1950s as housing for Algerian workers in France (Diop and Michalak, 1996). The legacy of North Africans in France as a captive labour market and French soldiering force has contributed to a politics of separation and exclusion in the organisation of HLMs and the adjacent suburban *cités*. The large deteriorating HLMs have served as a symbol of regional and national disinterest in the emerging multi-ethnic working classes. Alec G. Hargreaves explains that as the facilities began to deteriorate during the 1970s, a hierarchy of HLMs emerged – the less well-maintained properties were allocated to immigrant families and the better-maintained properties, financed by a payroll tax, to French families (Hargreaves, 1995, p. 72). Consequently, the cyclical irruption of violence between Franco-Maghrebi youths and police in the deteriorating HLMs became tied to continued citizenship controversies. This very logic of containment and regulation has carried over to shifts in French immigration practices.

The pairing of claustrophobic HLM apartments with the accompanying tundra-like wide-open empty spaces underscores a state of emotional and geographical dislocation prevalent in some of the best known *beur* films, such as Medhi Charef's Le Thé au harem d'Archimède [Tea in the harem] (1985). This film came to represent an early sketch of community belonging, petty thievery, and social rejection in the housing projects. [. . .]

Produced by Michelle Ray-Gavras, this film received significant press coverage highlighting its themes of exclusion, life in the housing projects, and the problems facing the *beur* community. [. . .]

Le Thé au harem d'Archimède was released within the context of a number of short films, and associated with several other feature-length films depicting the social context of the second generation of North African immigrants. Such feature-length films as Roger Le Péron's Laisse béton [Forget About It] (1983), Abdelkrim Bahloul's Le Thé à la menthe [Mint Tea] (1984), and Rachid Bouchareb's Baton Rouge [Baton Rouge] (1985) established a fertile terrain for the reception of Charef's film. Furthermore, the swell of social movements throughout the early 1980s, climaxing with the 100,000-strong 'Marche pour l'Egalite (March for Equality) in 1983 created a broad base for the reception of films about the second generation.

As a film movement, *beur* cinema has been defined as a cinema of community identification. That is, images and scenes of life relating to this minority group are the central setting for a corpus of *beur* films. Since 1985, a substantial number of *beur* films have also received some form of State-sanctioned support through FAS, the Social Action Foundation for immigrant workers and their families.[3] As a francophone film movement and as a representation of community, *beur* cinema addresses problems of national identity in addition to more specific issues related to integration in French society. Thematisations of imposed exile, family tradition, life in the housing projects, and various forms of delinquency overlaid with the lingering history of French colonial involvement link a number of these films. Urban decay and the coming of age of the invariably young *beur*, with an incapacitated or simply absent father figure, mark the process of socialisation as a search for belonging beyond the suffering and indignities of the previous generation.

[. . .]

An expanding reservoir of short films, which followed in the tradition of immigrant documentary filmmaking of the 1970s, established a variety of themes related to the *beur* experience, such as mixed coupling, violence between French and immigrant youths, images of the American dream, visions of successful integration, victimisation by the police, and the double exclusion of immigrant young women (Dhoukar, 1990a). The rapid increase in short films about the *beur* experience was linked to the new accessibility of video technology, as well as an already well-developed short-film circuit of financing and festivals.

The notion of a *beur* filmmaking aesthetic draws on short-subject films that foreground the cultural divide between immigrant parents and their assimilated children in the inhospitable claustrophobic world of the housing projects (Fahdel, 1990). In the short film entitled *Le Vago* [The Drifters] (directed by Aïssa Djabri, 1983), the filmmaker follows two unemployed *beurs* from a housing project who buy a second-hand car to return to Algeria, their imagined homeland. Their dream of return dissolves into despairing violence in the concrete world of the French housing projects, decrepit mall-like commercial centres, and poverty. As Abbas Fahdel suggests, the beur filmmaking aesthetic is the stylistic representation of a compressed spatial economy of HLM apartment living and a nostalgia for return, manifested as potentially violent confrontations.

In several films about the second generation, the *banlieue* (low-income suburbs) as well as certain areas of Paris, such as Pigalle, La Goutte d'Or (a.k.a. Barbès), and Belleville, become coterminous with the protagonists in the film. Abdelkrim Bahloul's *Thé à menthe* was filmed almost exclusively in La Goutte d'Or, the daytime Arab and African capital of Paris (Vuddamalay, 1991), and depicts varying degrees of assimilation into French society through the protagonist Hamou, a young hustler, and his mother, from a traditional village in Algeria on her first trip to Paris. Bahloul's second feature film, *Le vampire au paradis* [The Vampire in Paradise] (1991), inverts this geography of Paris in which Nathalie, the daughter of a family that lives in the exclusive sixteenth *arrondisement*, is bitten by a *beur* vampire. The sixteen-year-old Nathalie becomes prone to outbursts in Arabic that terrorise her family and tutors, compelling her father to enter the Arab cafés of Clichy in order to find the vampire and a cure for his daughter.

Nathalie's transformation from the obedient bourgeois daughter to a natty-haired Berber woman renders her nearly unrecognisable to passport officials upon her departure from Paris to Algeria. Her arrival at a hotel for the cure is finally complemented by an amorous encounter with another teenager, an Algerian, who only speaks French and listens to classical music. The final scene of a shared psychotic political and cultural harmony between the two young lovers optimistically predicts the dawning of a new geopolitical psychology of return, where the vampire's bite establishes a psychological and cultural reversal – the cure can no longer be found in the metropolitan centre.

The marking and demarcation of a Parisian geography, long depicted as the jewel of emotional and sexual centralisation in a number of French poetic realist films from the 1930s, such as Julien Duvivier's *Pépé Le Moko* (1937) or in the numerous depictions of Pigalle as the tolerant locus of social and sexual transgression, is used as an essential *mise-en-scène* for many *beur* films. In Medhi Charef's *Miss Mona* (1987), for example, Pigalle stands as the transgressive atmosphere in which friendship is established between an aging transvestite and a young unemployed *beur* pickpocketer. The first feature film by young *beur* filmmaker Karim Dridi bears the title *Pigalle* (1995). It depicts the intrusion of a sadistic gangster figure who threatens to disrupt the workings of a sedate sex shop in Pigalle. Interestingly, the only *beur* figure in this film is a young orphan who befriends the leading male protagonist.

Other sections of Paris also serve as contested geographic spaces in which cultural and class-based differences are played out through the politics of assimilation. In Gérard Blain's

Pierre et Djemila (1986), a housing project in the nineteenth *arrondisement* near La Villette, serves as the backdrop for a tragic love affair between a young mixed couple. Djemila, from a traditional Algerian family, and Pierre, from an upwardly mobile French family on their way out of the housing complex, encounter one another at school and see each other secretly. Polarisations within the French Catholic community concerning the acceptability of Muslims and their religious practices provide a social context for the film and position Pierre's father as a voice of moderation. The film correlates assorted incidents of religious desecration, tyre slashing, and physical confrontations, culminating with the stabbing of Pierre. The murder of Pierre by Djemila's brother, Djaffar, goes beyond the manifest conflict within the housing complex and is tied to a broader confrontation over historical, cultural, and familial values.

The individuated behaviour of Pierre and Djemila is opposed to that of Djaffar, who represents 'traditional' values, but acts alone. Djaffar kills Pierre in order to destroy the very individuating forces of assimilation that threaten to take Djemila away from the family. While Blain's depiction of community difference lacks cultural precision by stereotyping Djemila as the well-adapted *beurette* in opposition to her brother Djaffar as righteous reborn Muslim, these terms correspond to a continued geographic and emotional breach. In spite of the particularly clichéd romantic denouement that features the stabbing of Pierre followed by Djemila's final act of suicide, the polarisation of community within the housing project suggests a site of incubation for the emergence of an avenging violence.

[. . .]

Despite its history of activism, *beur* cinema is thoroughly dependent on French filmmaking institutions, existing between a politicised Third-World filmmaking ethic and variations on a post-New Wave French filmmaking aesthetic. Teshome H. Gabriel's early articulation of three phases in Third World filmmaking politics and aesthetics is a useful starting point in elucidating this *in between* position of transnationalism (Gabriel, 1989a). Gabriel begins by describing the iterative practices of unqualified cinematic assimilation, in which Hollywood narratives are adapted. This phase is followed by a remembrance phase, or the return of the Third World exile. In the remembrance phase, the cinematic frame is a site of reflection, punctuated by thoughtful long takes and wide shots in which characters are dwarfed by the timeless expanse of the natural landscape. The third phase is combative, representing an aesthetic of political rupture, and a search for ideological alternatives.

While Gabriel addresses a dynamic associated with a dialectic of decolonisation in the cinema, the appearance and codification of *beur* cinema represents another kind of dynamic – where the terms of debate have permanently shifted. As a post-New Wave phenomenon, *beur* cinema in France does not pretend to offer a coherent array of stylistic innovations as it is primarily unified through its treatment of social exclusion in France and appeal for social change; though contiguous with a combative decolonised cinema of the 1960s and 1970s, *beur* cinema addresses multicultural metropolitan situations.

[. . .]

Gabriel's thematisation of third cinema (Gabriel, 1989b) and Hamid Naficy's notion of exilic cinema (Naficy, 1993; 1999) explore the ways in which transnational experiences translate as cinema, reaching beyond a monolithic conception of national identities. That is, a passage into a new political landscape which can no longer define itself in opposition to

Hollywood or a colonial dominant. Although the term *beur* might be understood as a combative position heralding a rupture or break with a dominant institutional order that advocates restrictive notions of French citizenship and identity, *beur* cinema locates itself firmly within the cracks of French institutional structures that are no longer considered a force to be vanquished, but to be negotiated. While both positions make a claim for French citizenship and cultural specificity, their difference resides in the tactics of potential outcomes of a 'battle of position', to invoke Antonio Gramsci's well-worn turn-of-phrase.

[. . .]

The second generation of Algerians in France, so often opposed to the 'good' hardworking Portuguese immigrants under Valéry Giscard d'Estaing's term in office during the late 1970s, or the Italians from an earlier generation, remain at the centre of citizenship controversies in France. With the unresolved legacy of the Algerian War, which is primarily understood as a war of independence, French, Algerian, and a panoply of formerly colonised peoples were pitted against one another – with alternating allegiances. As a profoundly significant political rupture within France, the Algerian War marked the decline and fracture of an imperial order, whose ruinous fragments still remain lethally present both in France and Algeria. In Algeria, a protracted civil war has claimed as many as 100,000 lives since 1992, in which the style of violence and terror tactics, involving throat-slitting or testicular torture methods, are reminiscent of the violence practised during the Algerian war. In France, questions of national belonging are still under consideration. In particular, the sons and daughters of *harkis*, Algerians who served as volunteers in the French Army between 1954 and 1962, remain politically and socially marked both in France and Algeria. In fact, the incapacitated *harki* father, who is either mentally unstable or simply unable to work due to injuries incurred during the war, is a common feature in a number of *beur* films, such as Malik Chibane's film, *La douce France* [Gentle France] (1995).

The naming of the film movement – the appellation *beur*, between Berber and butter (*beurre*) – contains difference and assimilation while facilitating a reversal. Serge Meynard's comedy, *L'oeil au beur(re) noir* [The Black Buttered Eye] (1987), featuring the well-known comedy team *Les Inconnus* [The Unknowns], focuses on one of its member's encounters, as a *beur* (Smaïn), searching for a moderately-priced Parisian apartment. The *beur* as hybrid, which activates a comedy of refusals and repartees in *L'oeil au beur(re) noir*, is inserted into an ever-present ambivalence concerning racial, sexual, and class-based difference. Smaïn plays the successful *beur*, with all the necessary documents for an apartment, overshadowing his two unemployed delinquent French cohorts, played by Didier Bourdon and Bernard Campan. Mireille Rosello has provocatively described *L'oeil au beur(re) noir* within the terms of the Rachid system of double and triple meanings, in which the redeployment of racial stereotypes by Rachid, as the *beur* and yet not like 'other' *beurs*, serves as an ultimately humorous and yet unstable foil (Rosello, 1998).

The *beur* as connected with a social movement, however, takes on a significantly different configuration when associated with a visual coding. *Beur* cinema suggests an identity politics of visible difference which highlights the second generation, who do not fit into a Universalist paradigm of difference. This particular tendency has developed with great force in the early 1990s, following the decline of the associative social movements so vocal during the mid-1980s. The cover of *Le Figaro Magazine* from September 1991 depicts the indecision as to whether the *beur* (transformed into a Muslim) is capable of being integrated into French society. The cover photograph foregrounds the fully exposed face and open neck of Marianne (symbol of the French republic) in opposition to an unknown woman in the Islamic headscarf, both of which are cast in white alabaster and titled, 'Immigration ou Invasion?'.

The magazine cover served as a lead-in to a polemic launched by Valéry Giscard d'Estaing, who called for a return to citizenship based on family tradition and blood (droit du sang) in opposition to citizenship based on territorial rights (droit du sol). A polemic grounded in a fear of invasion, it came to symbolise immigration as a threat to an essential French identity. Although Giscard favoured a notion of 'affirming and developing our French identity', rather than 'defending our [French] identity' (Giscard D'Estaing, 1991, p. 57), these two concepts seem remarkably similar rhetorically. Nonetheless, 'defending French identity' is a slogan and symbol frequently associated with Vichy, which remains dear to Jean-Marie Le Pen and the extreme-right National Front. 'Affirming and developing our French identity' is more related to the Universalism of Marianne and the French Revolution (as depicted in the cover photo) – a vision that keeps open the possibility for successful integration. In the cover photo, the unknown, veiled woman suggests the dark shadow of Marianne's Universalism. With the caption 'Immigration or Invasion?', the unseen face of the female subject, as pupil and child bearer, represents the refusal of French republican social and educational values. The transformation of the headscarf into a fear of unassimilated immigration, or 'invasion', hails a defensive strategy in the name of protecting Marianne's Universalism for all.

[. . .]

The exclusionary 1993 Pasqua laws, which created a new framework of immigration restrictions for Franco-Maghrebi residents in France, were part of a longer history of immigration legislation that focused on regulating a foreign work force – a work force historically tied to the rescue of French industry from a shortage of labour during the First World War (Mauco, 1933). The idea of zero immigration, however, dates from the mid-1970s, and is tied to a moratorium on immigration that Giscard d'Estaing enacted while serving as head of State during the late 1970s. As a response to an anticipated labour surplus precipitated by the 1973 oil-price-shocks, Giscard d'Estaing's government introduced repatriation assistance for Portuguese, Spanish, and North African contractual labourers. Algerian immigrants in particular were targeted for repatriation due to remaining animosity left by the Algerian War (Weil, 1988, pp. 56–57). Nonetheless, the economic repatriation of immigrant families only had a limited impact on foreign immigration. The immigration reforms proposed by Giscard d'Estaing were rejected by the French legislative assembly on the grounds that they were in conflict with the long-standing French policy that protected political asylum seekers.

[. . .]

The Pasqua laws of 1993 (June and July) limited French nationality for Franco-Maghrebis to: (1) children born in France after 1 January 1963 to parents born in Algeria before that date (i.e., prior to the dissolution of French Algeria), only if their parents had been living in France five years prior to their birth; (2) children of harkis and other Muslims repatriated to France since 1962 whose parents were French or had the right to apply for French citizenship until 1967; and (3) other foreigners (such as Tunisians and Moroccans), only if they were born in France and resided there from 13 to 18 years of age. As of June 1993, Franco-Maghrebis can only become French citizens if they willingly apply for French nationality before a magistrate between the ages of 16 and 21; however, citizenship may be denied if they have received prison sentences for more than six months (Wihtol de Wenden, 1994).

[. . .]

Immediately preceding the French presidential elections in 1995, the release of Matthieu Kassovitz's film La haine [Hate] demonstrated how a seemingly social activist film was neutralised by presidential sloganeering. Upon being elected to office, Jacques Chirac publicly ordered his cabinet to see La haine, in a dubious gesture reinforcing his successful campaign theme of mending the 'social rupture' in French society. In a recent article about La haine (Elstob, 1998) it has been noted that the Minister of Interior and the Prime Minister had watched the film three times in order to understand better the underlying causes for the July 1995 riots in the Parisian suburbs of Chanteloup-les-Vignes, in the Noé Concerted Development Zone (ZAC de la Noé) – where the film was shot. The visual immediacy of this film as part of a new New Wave of in-your-face, Tarrantino-influenced French film-making rather than an in-depth depiction of a long-standing history of social unrest puts into question the role and function of cinema as a voice of social activism. Clearly, watching La haine three times, while it might be gripping cinematically, does not substitute for sustained political engagement with immigration policy and the geographic exclusion of the HLMs located in low-income suburbs.

La haine is a uniquely stylised social activist film, featuring a slick steady-cam music-video look with box office appeal. The no-exit depiction of the friendship between three young men of Arab, West African, and Jewish backgrounds is staged in the concrete expanses of the ZAC de la Noé in the aftermath of an all night battle between youths and the French riot police, unleashed by the police beating of a local teenager. The inexorable clock, which appears intermittently, is counterpointed by the youths' discovery of a gun, lost by one of the French riot policemen, and leads to the final violent denouement of the film. The gun and the clock contribute to the action-packed, black-and-white fast-paced violence of La haine in which the carceral violence of the housing projects dips into the oblivious Parisian centre. Although this film resonates stylistically with a number of black American gangster films and Reebok sneaker commercials featuring black American athletes, the aesthetics of violence and a coded slang overcomes any possibility for negotiation with the forces of order. To its credit, the film did call popular attention to the psychological underpinnings of the deadly stand-off between police and youths in the HLMs. However, the promotion and reception of La haine was subject to the fickle sensationalism of the French domestic media marketplace that trivialised the historical roots and activism associated with this ongoing social crisis.

Finally, the term beur can no longer accurately characterise this second generation of naturalised immigrants. The ubiquity of the term, which was picked up by the media and even incorporated into the French dictionary by the Académie Française as early as 1984, has blunted its initially resistant edge. A four-page spread in the April 1984 issue of the woman's maga-zine Marie Claire even proclaimed the Look Beur, which is beau et beur à la fois – drawing in part on the 1970s American slogan, 'black is beautiful' (Battegay and Boubeker, 1993). Thus, the republican beur as a stylish ethnic look, an acculturated métissage, came to contain a new chain of oppositions.

Since the Islamic headscarf controversy in 1989 and the Gulf War in 1991, the term beur has become almost a misnomer. The blurring of the term Muslim with the fear of Islamic fundamentalism has led to the wide-scale abandonment of the HLMs by the regional authorities. Islamic youth associations like the Young Arabs from the Greater Lyons area, known as the JALB (Jeune Arabes de Lyon et sa Banlieue), have taken on the crucial community functions previously fulfilled by the publicly elected city councils, such as soup kitchens, basic health care, after-school recreation, and child care in several of the impoverished HLMs. The building of mosques and the proliferation of Muslim organisations have been tied to a resurgence in conversion to Islam among the second generation.

Islam is the second largest religion in France after Catholicism. In fact, a significant number of low-income French citizens of French ancestry who were born Catholic have also converted. Since Islam has become integral to the social fabric of the low-income *banlieues*, the term *beur* has also become more closely associated with a *beur-geoisie*, broken off from its former activist past. That is, a *beur-geoisie* who live in the urban centres and do not experience the same cultural exclusion associated with the HLMs, a lower standard of education, and high levels of unemployment. The label *beur*, as Battegay and Boubeker describe in their sociological study on media representations of immigrants in France, has also become a means of marking the success of a republican notion of integration, and thus the end of this 'immigrant' community as such (Battegay and Boubeker, 1993). This analysis of the successful *beur* as a fully integrated French citizen also implies that the remaining second and third generation Franco-Maghrebi citizens still residing in low-income, poorly-maintained HLMs with other multi-ethnic and French working-class people, exist on an exclusionary vanishing point of limited social, educational, and economic expectations.

[. . .]

As Battegay and Boubeker report, the terms used by the media to represent this population have shifted from 'immigrant workers' in the 1980s to a more recent set of terms in the 1990s: *beurs*, *illegals*, and *Muslims*. In this sense, a film movement might be initiated through a series of events reported in the media, but then establishes its own autonomy as a series of loosely amalgamated films which are produced, distributed, and promoted as popular spectacle in the theatres. In effect, a series of violent events and images of social contestation in the news creates a reservoir of social meaning which can be dipped into and presented as a relevant story, congruent with the naming and organisation of current events.

Classifying these events as *immigration*, *integration*, *beurs*, *marches*, and *banlieues* is closely tied to a process of staging and saturating public opinion. These terms come to act as vectors of a flow that serves a repetitive and hypnotic machine of media representations – a maligned media dreamwork of social reality. In fact, the accumulation of indexical imagery fails to distinguish between the building of a mosque in Lyon, rioting on the outskirts of Marseilles, and Islamic fundamentalism in Algeria. It is in this sense that the reception of *beur* cinema can be understood through a series of political and social conjunctures in the accretion of current events. These media representations, in turn, are transformed into 'handles' which exist on a continuum with the making and distribution of films. These terms act as indexical sites that facilitate the social interpenetration of cinema and establish it as a form of visual currency.

Media imagery establishes relationships of equivalence, creating an index in which related events are staged, interpreted, and continually repeated. The concrete phobic expanse of the housing projects, as well as an aesthetics of violence so well portrayed in so many beur films such as Le *Thé au harem d'Archimède*, *Cheb*, and La *haine* will continue to appear as part of a French political mediascape. Though subject to the tides of political patronage, the uneasy racial and ethnic integration of these peripheral housing communities, on the outskirts of Paris, Marseilles, Lyons, and Grenoble serve as advance guard experimental communities for an emerging multi-ethnic France.

Notes

1 MRAP is an acronym for Le Mouvement contre le Racisme et pour l'Amitié entre les Peuples, which translates as the Movement against Racism and for Interracial Friendship.
2 SONACOTRAL is an acronym for La Société nationale de Construction de logements pour les Travailleurs, which translates as the National Construction Company for Workers' Housing. Since 1963, 'Algerian' was dropped from the acronym and it is now called SONACOTRA. It remains one of the largest organisations for hotels and housing in France.
3 FAS is an acronym for Fonds d'Action Social pour les travailleurs immigrés et leurs familles, which translates as the Social Action Foundation for immigrant workers and their families. FAS was initially established in the late 1950s as a means of transferring the income of migrant workers back to their families in the country of origin; the FAS mandate was substantially expanded however, as they were charged with the housing and reintegration of the pieds noir community in France following the Algerian war.

References

Abdallah, M.H. (1993) 'Dix ans d'enquête en pays beur', M Scope: Revue Média, 4 (April): 93–98.

Battegay, A. and A. Boubeker (1993) Les images publiques de l'immigration, Paris: CIEMI L'Harmattan.

Bosséno, C. (1982) 'Du Collectif Mohammed: Le Garage, Zone immigré, La mort de Kader: des films provocateurs', CinémAction-Cinémas de l'émigration, 3 (24, January): 128–31.

— (1992) 'Immigrant Cinema: National Cinema, The case of beur film', in R. Dyer and G. Vincendeau (eds) Popular European Cinemas, London and New York: Routledge.

Dazat, O. (1985) 'Entretien avec Mahmoud Zemmouri', Cinématographe, July: 13–15.

Deleuze, G. (1992) 'Postscript on the Societies of Control', October, 59 (Winter): 3–7.

Dhoukar, H. (1990a) 'Les thèmes du cinéma beur', CinémAction, 56 (July): 152–60.

— (1990b) 'Mahmoud Zemmouri: Le mythe de l'Algérie, c'est fini', CinémAction: 56 (July): 182–85.

Diop, M. and L. Michalak (1996) 'Refuge and Prison: Islam, Ethnicity, and the Adaptation of Space in Workers's Housing in France', in B.D. Metcalf (ed.) Making Muslim Space, Berkeley: University of California Press.

Elstob, K. (1997–98) 'Reviews: Hate (La Haine)', Film Quarterly, 51 (2, Winter): 44–49.

Fahdel, A. (1990) 'Une esthétique beur?', CinémAction, 56 (July): 140–51.

Gabriel, T.H. (1989a) 'Towards a critical theory of Third World films', in J. Pines and P. Willeman (eds) Questions of Third Cinema, London: British Film Institute.

— (1989b) 'Third Cinema as a Guardian of Popular Memory: Towards a Third Aesthetics', in J. Pines and P. Willeman (eds) Questions of Third Cinema, London: British Film Institute.

Giscard D'Estaing, V. (1991) 'Immigration ou Immigration', Le Figaro Magazine, 14643 (21 September): 48–57.

Hargreaves, A.G. (1995) Immigration, 'Race' and Ethnicity in Contemporary France, London and New York: Routledge.

Hargreaves, A.G. and M. McKinney (1997) 'Introduction', in A.G. Hargreaves and M. McKinney (eds) Post-Colonial Cultures in France, London: Routledge.

Horvilleur, G. (1985) '[Interview with] Farida Belghoul', Cinématographe, 112 (July): 18–19.

Lopate, P. (1998) 'Grim, Shocking, Didactic, a New New Wave Rolls In', The New York Times, The Arts and Leisure Section, November 22: 15, 26.

Mauco, G. (1933) 'Immigration in France', International Labour Review, 27 (6, June): 781–82.

Mohammed [Collectif] (1981) 'Un outil d'enquête', CinémAction-Tumulte, 7: 86–88.

Naficy, H. (1993) 'Exile Discourse and Televisual Fetishization', in T.H. Gabriel and H. Naficy (eds) Otherness and the Media, Langhorne, PA: Harwood Academic Press.

— (1994) 'Phobic Spaces and Liminal Panics: Independent Transnational Film Genre', East-West Film Journal, 8 (2): 1–30.

— (1999) 'Between Rocks and Hard Places: The Interstitial Mode of Production in Exilic Cinema', in H. Naficy (ed.) Home, Exile, Homeland: Film Media, and the Politics of Place, New York and London: Routledge.

Ricoeur, P. (1991) 'Événement et Sens', Raisons Pratiques: L'événement en perspective, 2: 41–56.

Rosello, M. (1996) 'Third Cinema or Third Degree: the 'Rachid System' in S. Meynard's L'Oeil au beur(re) noire', in D. Sherzer (ed.) Cinema, Colonialism, Postcolonialism, Austin: University of Texas Press.

— (1998) Declining the Stereotype, Hanover and London: University Press of New England.

Tarr, C. (1993) 'Questions of Identity in Beur Cinema: from Tea in the Harem to Cheb', Screen, 34 (4, Winter): 321–42.

— (1995) 'Beurz N the Hood: the articulation of Beur and French identities in Le Thé au harem d'Archimède and Hexagone', Modern and Contemporary France, NS3, 40: 415–25.

— (1997) 'French Cinema and Post-Colonial Minorities', in A.G. Hargreaves and M. McKinney (eds) Post-Colonial Cultures in France, London: Routledge.

Vieillard-Baron, H. (1992) 'Deux Z.A.C. de banlieue en situation extrême: du grand ensemble stigmatisé de Chanteloup au 'village' de Chevry', Annales de Géographie, 564 (March–April): 188–213.

Vuddamalay, V., P. White, and D. Sporton (1991) 'The Evolution of the Goutte d'Or as an Ethnic Minority District of Paris', New Community, 17(2): 245–58.

Weil, P. (1988) 'La politique française d'immigration', Pouvoirs, 47 (November): 45–60.

White, P. (1997) 'Images of Race in Social Housing Estates in France', Immigrants and Minorities, 16 (3, November): 19–35.

Wihtol de Wenden, C. (1994) 'The French Debate: Legal and Political Instruments to Promote Integration', in H. Fassmann and R. Münz (eds) European Migration in the Late Twentieth Century, Laxenburg, Austria: IIASA.

Diaspora and National Identity: Exporting 'China' through the Hong Kong Cinema

10

DAVID DESSER

It has been clear for some time now in the English-language criticism of Hong Kong cinema, that something like a "Chinese nationalism" may be detected in a number of films emanating from the former British colony. For Stephen Teo, for instance:

> Bruce Lee stood for something that in the 90s is hardly deemed politically correct: Chinese nationalism as a way of feeling pride in one's identity . . . Lee's nationalism cannot be easily dismissed if one wishes to appreciate fully his appeal to Chinese audiences. . . . Kung fu films were particularly conducive to nationalism of the abstract kind . . . Lee is literally putting his bravest face (and body) forward in order to show that the Chinese need no longer be weaklings.[1]

Similarly, for Teo, Jacky [sic] Chan's movies of the 1980s "were practically alone in preserving Bruce Lee's tradition of kung fu as an instinctive but disciplined art linked to a cultural and national identity."[2] Steve Fore also relies on a kind of cultural nationalism to account for Chan's appeal in Asia:

> In East Asia, where Chan is already a major star, the "Chineseness" of his persona is, of course, more closely aligned with the cultural heritage and life experiences of the average moviegoer, whether at the primary level of cultural proximity (for audiences in Hong Kong, Taiwan, and the PRC), or at a secondary level (for non-Chinese audiences in Asian countries where Hong Kong movies are widely distributed).[3]

And it is certainly no stretch of the imagination to see how Tsui Hark's "Once Upon a Time in China" series, especially parts I, II and VI, play into nationalistic sentiments.[4]

But just when, exactly, do these nationalistic sentiments begin to occur and how? I would like to suggest that this nationalism, this "Chineseness," comes to be literally *embodied* on the *male body* of stars like Bruce Lee, Jackie Chan, and Jet Li; on a *body of knowledge* which we may call "Chinese learning," more specifically, the Chinese Martial Arts; on a *displaced body* in diaspora or in exile from a homeland, Hong Kong; on a *body of work*, specifically, the Hong Kong

Mandarin-language cinema and the return to Cantonese language productions thereafter. These bodies come to fruition in a particular historical moment which both enables and encourages this symbolic nationalistic body to appear, grow, develop and stabilize.

Clearly we can date this new Chinese symbolic nationalism to the middle-late 1960s. This was a period in which Hong Kong had achieved an economic strength while undergoing much internal turmoil and self-examination. In terms of cinematic culture, Hong Kong film could assume a new international space while asserting its own economic force: The cinema of the PRC was virtually inactive, thus removing much sense of a "Chinese cinema"; there was increasing competition from Taiwanese cinema, forcing both cinemas into a competitive mode, but also into transnational cooperation; and there was within Hong Kong an internal struggle between an almost strictly local cinema, a cinema of and for Cantonese speakers, and an emerging transnational cinema utilizing Mandarin dialect. Within this Mandarin cinema, most productively understood as the films of the Shaw Bros. studios, comes a new attitude not only in terms of global outreach but also within Hong Kong film genres, especially the martial arts film, Once the special province of Cantonese cinema, martial arts films made in Mandarin revolutionized the local cinema, created a global audience and, in so doing, highlighted an emerging (transnational) Chinese nationalism and identity. Through this body of work (the Mandarin-language cinema of Hong Kong) emerges the heroic male body, the nationalistic Chinese body of knowledge, which helps create this male body while displacing it across space and time.

There are a number of ways to demonstrate the emergence of the heroic, Chinese, masculinized male body and the interconnections this masculinized body has with the Chinese Martial Arts, with exilic or diasporic culture, and the body of work, the Mandarin cinema, in which these all occur. Space does not permit a full investigation of all the interconnections that feed into a resurgent cultural nationalism at the site of the male, Chinese body. Nevertheless it behooves us to see how Mandarin-language cinema becomes associated with a new form of masculinity; that this new masculinity is built on the body of a specifically Chinese knowledge; that these male figures are displaced from Hong Kong, the site of the films' production; but that the very site of this production creates a body of work that re-contains the exilic body. We will see that there is a cluster of images and motifs around which these bodies—male bodies, a body of knowledge, the body in diaspora—coalesce. Here I have in mind the image and significance of Japan and the Japanese and how the bodies of Chinese male stars, forged by a body of Chinese knowledge, interact with, defeat or otherwise highlight the ability of China to compete with Japan and, perhaps, with the West. In specific I have in mind the stardom of Bruce Lee, Jackie Chan and Jet Li and the concept of the *jingwu men*, the martial arts school as nationalist site. Lee, Chan and Li all made variations of the film, *Jingwu men*, as a means not only to assert their stardom, but to claim a kind of Chinese identity as well, an identity which comes to fruition in juxtaposition with the Japanese: Bruce Lee, *Jingwu men* (*Fist of Fury*, aka *The Chinese Connection*, 1972); Jackie Chan, *New Fist of Fury/Xin jingwu men* (1976); Jet Li, *Fist of Legend/Jingwu ying xiong* (1994).

Muscular Mandarin

If Bruce Lee was the biggest star in the history of Hong Kong cinema, is it ironic that in his films he is alienated from Hong Kong both by geographic locale and by dialect? That is, it has not been sufficiently theorized or even noted why all of Bruce Lee's Hong Kong films have been set outside of Hong Kong: *The Big Boss* in Thailand; *Fist of Fury* in pre-war Shanghai; *Way of the Dragon* in Italy, all released in the Mandarin dialect. Lee is, then, never in Hong Kong, never speaking Hong Kong Cantonese. He, as much as anyone, helped establish the reputation of Hong Kong cinema as a vital, action-oriented, masculine cinema without ever actually being in Hong Kong on screen, interacting with Hong Kong. A minor star of sorts in the Cantonese Hong Kong cinema of the early 1950s, Lee established another minor stardom in the U.S. in the 1960s. Fierce negotiations were undertaken upon his return to the territory in the early 1970s as if recognizing that he would be something new and special in the Hong Kong cinema. But Lee's cinema becomes less a "Hong Kong cinema" than a new symbol of "Chinese cinema" precisely by its diasporic relationship to Hong Kong and by its rejection of previous "Chinese cinema." The only way to understand Lee's image and its significance is to see how he brings to fruition a number of motifs bubbling up in the Hong Kong cinema immediately before his arrival.

The Hong Kong cinema achieved its international economic viability, along with a new aesthetic maturity, via the Mandarin-language martial arts films produced beginning in the middle of the 1960s. Now-familiar directorial names like King Hu and Zhang Che have become synonymous with the rise to prominence of the Hong Kong cinema, along with a roster of movie stars that only Hollywood in its hey-day could match. But why exactly did Mandarin-dialect films virtually displace Cantonese films in Cantonese-speaking Hong Kong by 1970? For the moment, let us equate the emerging dominance of Mandarin-language films with the output of the Shaw Brothers Studio. And let us recall that the vast majority of these films were martial arts films, *wuxia pian*. But even here we need recall that martial arts films were a commonality, indeed a staple, of Cantonese films and thus martial arts alone cannot explain the drastic, even shocking decline of Cantonese cinema, the special and unique province of the Hong Kong cinema since the 1930s.

At the time of this Mandarin-emergence in the Hong Kong cinema, there was a vital Cantonese language output, with first-class directors such as Chor Yuen and Lung Kong, and an impressive roster of stars, such as Josephine Siao and Chan Pochu. But as Sek Kei notes, "In the Cantonese cinema, a group of young female stars predominated, while in the Mandarin cinema, male action stars ruled the screens." Sek notes that both the Cantonese and Mandarin stars were young—a new generation of stars for a new generation of Hong Kong film-goers. But the female stars of the Cantonese cinema were, it seems, "comparatively gentle and conservative" whereas the male stars of the Mandarin cinema manifested "strong emotions more suited to the restlessness of the times." Sek goes on to claim that the new Mandarin cinema of Hong Kong marked a break from the Chinese tradition of the "weak male," a tradition taken up, with some exceptions, in the postwar Cantonese cinema with its emphasis on the female star.[5] This recognition of a female-centered Chinese cinema tradition is further seen in the recent Stanley Kwan film *Yin and Yang*, where the director claims that the figure of Bruce Lee brought a masculinist nationalist pride new to Chinese cinema. Tony Rayns also notes the particularly "masculinist" dimension of Lee's films, claiming that Lee became synonymous with "a very particular set of (male) dreams, concerning consummate physical prowess, Chinese racial identity, the status of the immigrant (especially the Chinese immigrant) and the relationship between China and other countries (especially western countries)."[6] But Lee was not alone in this "masculinization" of Hong Kong films. Critic Tian Yan notes the contributions of director Zhang Che, whose so-called "New Wuxia Pian" films were so popular that they "catalyzed the rise of the Mandarin cinema, which ultimately replaced Cantonese cinema." And central to Zhang's films was a "male-oriented/dominated ideology."[7] For Stephen Teo there is indeed a distinctly masculinist dimension to the Mandarin martial arts hero, one revolving around a newly economically assertive Hong Kong: "The *wuxia* or martial hero emerged in the mid-1960s, when China was asserting its newly acquired superpower status and Hong Kong was becoming 'an Asian tiger' while the Japanese economic expansion into East and Southeast Asia was at its most aggressive."[8] I'm not sure if Teo is implying that Japan's aggressive assertion in the Asian market led Hong Kong to a feeling of competition with their former colonizer and enemy, but Hong Kong's economic success unquestionably affected its self-image as a tiger, a fighter, a warrior, which was reflected in the newly emergent Mandarin-language cinema.

The masculinist dimension, then, seems to be the major factor behind the triumph of the Mandarin cinema, in conjunction with the economically assertive power of the Shaw Bros. studio. I will set that dimension aside and recommend, for instance, Poshek Fu's essay, "Going Global: The Transnational Cinema of the Shaw Brothers Studio, 1960–1970" for some of how the Shaws achieved an economic dominance of the Asian market.[9] Here I will simply note the total dominance of Mandarin martial arts films in the Hong Kong market beginning in 1970. From 1970–1972, for instance, as far as I can tell, virtually every film in the Top 10 highest grossing films list was a martial arts movie; in 1971 Bruce Lee's first HK film *The Big Boss* was number one and in 1972, *The Way of the Dragon* and *Fist of Fury* were 1 and 2 respectively. The "New Style" martial arts films, especially those of Zhang Che and his favorite star (later to turn director) Wang Yu are the major presences and influences in this early period. But this masculinist dimension of the Hong Kong cinema is not confined merely to the triumph of Mandarin cinema in the Zhang Che–King Hu-Wang Yu–Bruce Lee era, but returns later in the 70s. If martial arts films were no longer so thoroughly to dominate the Top Ten Highest Grossing lists in the middle of the decade (which marks the return to Cantonese production), they would do so again later in the decade with the emergence of Jackie Chan and the triumphs of director Lau Ka-leung (Liu Jialiang) and star Gordon Liu Chia-hui: films like *Drunken Master* and *Snake in the Eagle's Shadow*, along with *The 36th Chamber of Shaolin* and *Challenge of the Ninja* (aka *Heroes of the East*). That is to say, the emergence of new male stars later in the 1970s is very much in the tradition of Bruce Lee and they would return both martial arts and a resurgent nationalism to the fore. Though in the case of Jackie Chan and, later, Jet Li, it would be a Cantonese-inflected Chinese nationalism.

The Japanese Connection

The masculinist dimension to the Mandarin cinema, which involved something of a rejection of earlier Chinese cinema, including the Cantonese cinema, also involved an embrace of Japan. And I mean this in two ways: an embrace of certain Japanese genres and modes of production, and an embrace of Japan as on-screen foil for this newly masculinized Chinese male.

[. . .]

Imported Japanese Samurai movies came to dominate the popular imagination of overseas Chinese audiences from the middle of the 1960s, when the Chinese genre began with films like *The Jade Bow*, *Tiger Boy*, and *Come Drink With Me* (King Hu) until the early 1970s when swordfighting *wuxia* was replaced by kung fu fighting.[10]

The influence of Japanese cinema on the Hong Kong cinema was quite direct. While employed by the Shaw Bros. Xu Zhenghong (who directed the Chinese version of *Zatoichi Meets His Equal*, a joint venture between Katsu Productions and Golden Harvest, in 1971) led a delegation to Japan in 1966–1967, at the suggestion, interestingly, of Raymond Chow, then an executive at Shaw. They toured the Shochiku studios and watched location filming as well. The Shaw Bros. would rely almost exclusively on studio productions, and what they learned about set construction from Shochiku, the masters of the home drama, would stand them in good stead, even in their preferred mode of the action film. Xu specifically notes that the new style *wuxia* was indebted to Kurosawa's films and to the Zatoichi series. Similarly, screenwriter Qiu Gangjian notes that *Yojimbo* and *Sanjuro* were particularly influential for the way the films achieved their dramatic effects. It should be noted that by 1966, when the new-style *wuxia* appeared, several Japanese directors and cinematographers were employed at the Shaw studios. Most, however, would be unrecognizable by the credits, adapting their names to Chinese pronunciations according to screenwriter Qiu. One notable Japanese director who worked for the Shaws was Nakahiro Ko, under the name Yang Shuxi. Chinese directors, cinematographers and screenwriters actually saw a number of Japanese films at the Shaw studios, including and especially the Zatoichi series which was distributed in Hong Kong and Southeast Asia by the Shaw Bros. chain. Oftentimes the Shaw Bros. would acquire distribution rights to Japanese films, screen them for their production personnel, but not release them publicly so as to take away from the Hong Kong variations.[11]

As Japan provided personnel, production models and the opportunity for one of the great co-productions in film history in *Zatoichi Meets His Equal*, it also provided a kind of counter-model, the Japanese as enemy, which itself contributed to the continued growth and development of the Hong Kong cinema and the assertion of a pan-Chinese or transnational Chinese identity. Stephen Teo notes, as have many others, the significance of the war with Japan on Chinese cinema (though I would, along with many others, go farther and state the significance of the war with Japan on Chinese identity. [. . .] The national defense movie and the war with Japan would form one of the predominate tropes in the PRC cinema and thus it is no surprise to find the centrality of this theme in the early films of the Fifth Generation, such as *Yellow Earth* and *Red Sorghum*.

For the Hong Kong cinema and the new generation of wuxia films in the late 1960s–early 1970s, the Japanese on screen would be no less significant than they had been off screen. If *The One-Armed Swordsman* is the key text in the aesthetic maturity and hence economic triumph of the Mandarin-language *wuxia* sword film, star Wang Yu, directing himself, produced the key text in the *wuxia* kung fu genre: *The Chinese Boxer* (aka *Hammer of God*, 1970). Here he plays a kung fu student whose teacher is killed by Japanese karate fighters. After losing a battle with them, he vows to train even harder and masters the "Iron Palm" technique. Eventually he must combat a team of samurai swordsmen and karate fighters, defeating them all in climactic combat.[12] I want to claim that the very title, "The Chinese Boxer" (which is what kung fu is best called in English, i.e. Chinese boxing) indicates how the film sets off its Chinese-ness and does so in opposition to Japanese-ness, China/Japan, kung fu/karate. That *The Chinese Boxer* would set the tone for a whole genre is captured by a writer for the Hong Kong Movie List on the internet Hong Kong Movie database: "It has all the elements you would expect in a Wang Yu film—brutality, evil Japanese, training and secret styles."

Secret styles put to the service to defeat the Japanese appear again in *King Boxer*, (aka *Five Fingers of Death*, 1972), a fairly typical Shaw Bros. movie starring Lo Lieh, who had co-starred with Wang Yu in *The Chinese Boxer*. *Five Fingers of Death* is the film that started the whole Kung Fu Craze of 1973 in the U.S., along with Bruce Lee's first two Hong Kong films. In its vague outlines, *Five Fingers of Death* is quite similar to *Chinese Boxer*—a young kung fu fighter's mentor and friends are killed by the members of an evil kung fu school who have hired three Japanese fighters to do their evil bidding—a samurai swordsman, a judo fighter and a karate expert. This time the hero learns the "Iron Fist" technique (though it looks like the Iron Palm technique when his hands glow to the theme of the old *Ironside* TV series).

But it was Bruce Lee who truly internationalized Hong Kong cinema, and it was Bruce Lee's second film, *Jingwu men* (*Fist of Fury*, aka *The Chinese Connection*, 1972) which set the tone for the cultural nationalism of the Hong Kong kung fu film. Here, Lee plays Chen Zhen, whose master is betrayed by a Chinese lackey of the Japanese in pre-war Shanghai. The Japanese taunt him and his fellow classmates at their master's funeral, calling China, "the sick man of East Asia." Early in the film, Chen expresses his displeasure at anti-Chinese sentiments and at the racism of the Japanese, leaping into the air and tearing down a sign at the entrance to a public park which reads, "No Dogs or Chinese."

Throughout the rest of the film Lee goes out of his way to antagonize and fight with the Japanese, using unarmed combat and also the kung fu weapon, nunchuks, or nunchaku, which was to become a particular specialty of Lee's in his later films, especially *Enter the Dragon*. For critic Cheng Yu, it is kung fu which is of prime import to Lee and not simply or necessarily anti-Western or anti-Japanese sentiments:

> Instead, Lee's films are an attempt to "demote" karate and other foreign martial arts. . . . In the United States, the major obstacle to Lee's rise to stardom was Japanese karate and he was determined to prove that Chinese martial arts . . . were deadlier than the Japanese style. This concern resurfaces in various ways in Lee's films and when he later became an international legend, his name also became synonymous with Chinese kung fu.[13]

Lee's early demise had a great impact on the Hong Kong cinema in Hong Kong. Though stars like Wang Yu, Lo Lieh, along with Ti Lung and David Chiang, among others continued to produce, direct and star in films at a healthy rate, no one could quite replace Bruce Lee, especially and including the likes of Bruce Li and Bruce Le. But for those who know their Hong Kong film history a new star would indeed arise to the kind of acclaim and love that even, perhaps, Lee never achieved: Jackie Chan.

I want to claim that Hong Kong filmmakers were incredibly aware of the connection between anti-Japanese sentiments and the assertion of a pan-Chinese nationalism when it came to the star-making early roles of Chan. Though he had appeared in a handful of films by 1976, including an uncredited bit part in *Enter the Dragon* (1973), it was *New Fist of Fury/Xin jingwu men* (1976), directed by Luo Wei, who had directed Bruce Lee in *The Big Boss* and *Fist of Fury*, which helped make him a star. The film is something of a sequel to the Lee film. This time, the students of the kung fu school in Shanghai in which Lee was a student have already been killed off by film's start and the surviving remnants leave for Taiwan, which we will remember was under direct Japanese occupation before WW II. The direct link between the two films, besides director Luo Wei, is co-star Nora Miao, involved with Lee's character in the first film and then with Chan's in the sequel. (Miao, by the way, starred in all three of Lee's Hong Kong films—*The Big Boss*, *Fist of Fury* and *Way/Return of the Dragon*, thus she is herself an icon connecting Lee and Chan.)

We note that in this film Chan is not yet skilled in kung fu, but at the start is instead a petty thief who steals from his fellow Chinese. As he says shortly after his introductory scene, it's all the same to him whether the Japanese or the Chinese hit him. However, he soon learns the difference between the Chinese and the Japanese and becomes more Chinese precisely when he becomes anti-Japanese and when, at the same time, he learns kung fu. Like Lee, in his embracing of the Chinese *Jingwu men*, Chan, too, dies at the end of the film, though the same could not be said of his career, which was just beginning.

Chan's star would ascend permanently just two years later with *Snake in the Eagle's Claw* and *Drunken Master*. Both are period films revolving around the protagonist's mastery of kung fu, that paradigmatic sign of Chinese nationalism of the abstract kind. In the latter film, Chan plays the young Wong Fei-hung. And here is where the anti-Japanese competition intersects with the idea I have been developing of "a body of Chinese knowledge" that enables the hero to defeat the Japanese—Lee's kung fu and all those earlier Iron Palm/Fist Techniques; Chan's kung fu by the end of *New Fist of Fury*. For it is exactly "kung fu" or Chinese boxing that enables all those Japanese villains to bite the dust.

Wong Fei-hung and/as Chinese Knowledge

Jackie Chan carried on the nationalistic, masculinist legacy of Bruce Lee through the on-screen mastery of kung fu put to service in the anti-Japanese cause. Chan also extended the legacy of Bruce Lee's kung fu through his spectacular stuntwork, while connecting kung fu itself back to the earlier Cantonese cinema by his incarnation of Wong Fei-hung. In a perhaps tangential sense, Bruce Lee acknowledged his own debt to Wong Fei-hung as a marker of Chineseness in the use of actor Shi Jian in *Enter the Dragon*. As Tony Rayns notes, "Shi, the perennial villain of the Huang Feihong series, evokes the vanished Cantonese cinema of the 1950s [while] linking the conservative traditions of *wuxia pian* of the 1950s with the world-conquering ambitions of the *wuxia pian* of the 1970s."[14] Chan's Wong Fei-hung becomes an even clearer marker of a new, globalized Hong Kong which is the transmitter of this new (since the late 1960s) transnational Chinese nationalism. Though made in Cantonese, the filmic resurrection of Wong Fei-hung by Jackie Chan in *Drunken Master*, and the later apotheosis of the character by Jet Li in Tsui Hark's internationally popular "Once Upon a Time in China" films, are a far cry from the localized Wong Fei-hung of Kwan Tak-hing, the Cantonese cinema's most durable and popular star of the 1950s. Chan's stardom of the late 1970s and Li's of the early 1990s allowed Hong Kong and diasporic Chinese audiences to revel in their greatest stars since Bruce Lee. But even on the local level, Wong Fei-hung's Chinese kung fu and its ability to defeat Japanese enemies filtered through the local industry. Coincident to the rise to stardom of Jackie Chan, we may also find Lau Ka-leung (Liu Jialiang) directing Gordon Liu Chia-hui in *Challenge of the Masters* (1976), in which Gordon Liu plays Wong Fei-hung and *Challenge of the Ninja* (1979) in which Liu stars opposite Japanese actor Kurata Yasuaki in a film revolving around the superiority of kung fu over ninjitsu. One might claim that the combination of Bruce Lee tributes revolving around on-screen anti-Japanese combat and an incarnation of Wong Fei-hung seems a particular strategy in the star-making machinery revolving around Jackie Chan, Gordon Liu and Jet Li. This is to say that the muscular masculinity they all incarnated (Gordon Liu had the best physique since Bruce Lee, but both Chan and Jet Li are clearly skilled, like Lee, in martial arts) was expressed through anti-Japanese violence abetted by the mastery of the body of Chinese knowledge revolving around kung fu.

In this respect we must note Jet Li's version of the *jingwu men* archetype: *Fist of Legend/Jingwu ying xiong*. Though *Fist of Legend/Jingwu ying xiong*, a close variation on the Chinese title as well as the English title of the Lee and Chan films was certainly not Li's star-making role, as it had been for Lee and to a lesser extent for Chan, it solidified his status as Hong Kong's successor to both Lee and Chan. Of course there are differences in the status and image of Japan by the time of Li's film. Closer in spirit to Liu's *Challenge of the Ninja* (including the recurrence of Japanese actor Kurata Yasuaki) there is much less overt anti-Japanese rhetoric and most interestingly, Li speaks Japanese and, like Liu in the earlier film, has a Japanese girlfriend. This lessening of anti-Japanese rhetoric stems, no doubt, from the solid place the Hong Kong cinema occupies in the world film market, Hong Kong's success in the arena of global capitalism, and a few more decades worth of direct interchange between Hong Kong and Japan. By this point in time, for instance, two major stars of the Hong Kong cinema are Japanese: Takeshi Kaneshiro (a favorite of director Wong Kar-wei) and Yukari Oshima, action heroine extraordinaire. Japanese comic books, called manga, are as ubiquitous (though in Chinese translation) in Hong Kong as they are in Tokyo. Anime fills the TV and home video screens there as elsewhere. And a number of direct adaptations from Japanese anime and manga (not to mention literature) have made their way to HK screens, including Jackie Chan's *City Hunter* and Tsui Hark/Peter Mak's *Wicked City*. Japan and the Japanese, then, are much more normalized by this time. The anti-Japanese element of *Fist of Legend* helps solidify Li's participation in a stream of masculinist Chinese imagery that connects him to Bruce Lee and Jackie Chan even if that anti-Japanese dimension is toned down. For, in fact, it may have been less *Fist of Legend* that made Li a star and more his legacy of kung fu that more clearly situates Li within the masculinist Chinese nationalist imaginary.

If it wasn't *Fist of Legend* which made Jet Li a star, it surely was *Once Upon a Time In China*, known in Chinese as *Wong Fei-hung*. And in Tsui's brilliant epic *Wong Fei-hung* takes on a specifically nationalistic character, a far cry from Kwan Tak-hing's days where Wong was the marker of "Cantonese Chinese" (e.g., his Southern style kung fu and his Canton locale). For Tsui it is precisely Wong's kung fu and another body of Chinese knowledge, Chinese herbal medicine, that makes the character a model of anti-Western anti-Imperialism, a model of Chinese masculinity created by a body of Chinese knowledge.

Of course this idea of a body of Chinese knowledge has other expressions in the Hong Kong cinema. Another important manner in which Chinese knowledge is acknowledged is through the recurring use of the motif of secret scrolls, scrolls upon which are written a body of secret learning or knowledge. Iron Palm or Iron Fist techniques are often passed on from teacher to student via a scroll or a manual, as in *Five Fingers of Death*. Wang Yu's one-armed swordsman learns his craft from a manual of one-armed swordsmanship. Perhaps this is related to the traditional Chinese valuation of scholarship and the recurring figure of the scholar in Hong Kong cinema. In this manner two Chinese traditions—martial arts and scholarship—come together to create the newly masculinized Chinese hero. Thus there is something quite wicked in Tsui Hark's *Swordsman* trilogy which begins with the theft of a secret scroll, the object of attention throughout the remaining entries in the series. Mastery of the learning contained within the scroll necessitates castration, the demasculinization of the hero who is transformed thusly into a woman, specifically Brigitte Lin Ching-hsia who, by part III, becomes Invincible Asia!

The Chinese respect for learning not only translates into the recurring figure of the scholar and the recurring use of secret scrolls, but even more importantly into the figure of the priest, specifically the Shaolin priest. As much as Wong Fei-hung or Fong Sai Yuk or other folk heroes of the Chinese past, it is the Shaolin Temple which stands in as the ultimate repository of Chinese learning and, thus, of a specifically Chinese identity. The number of recurrences of the Shaolin Temple would be almost impossible to figure, but the Shaolin Temple is no less central to the masculinization of the Chinese cinematic hero than Wong Fei-hung himself. The films of Lau Ka-leung, for instance, *Executioners of Shaolin*, *The 36th Chamber of Shaolin*, *Shaolin Mantis*, *Shaolin Challenges Ninja*, *Shaolin and Wu-Tang*, *Martial Arts of Shaolin*, indicate the centrality of the Shaolin Temple to the New Style masculinized martial arts hero. Similarly, the association of Jet Li with the Shaolin Temple, as in *Abbot Hai Teng of Shaolin*, *Shaolin Kung Fu*, *New Legend of Shaolin*, and *Tai Chi Master*, conflates Li's image of master of Chinese martial arts with the image that he carries over from his Wong Fei-hung and Fong Sai Yuk films.

The clear association of Lee, Chan and Li with Chinese martial arts and anti-Japanese or other anti-imperialist causes is a major reason, I suggest, for their stardom, but clearly not the only reason. Nor would I suggest that lacking muscular masculinity or a particular association with Chinese knowledge prevents stardom: Chow Yun-fat, Andy Lau, Gordon Chan, Lau Ching-wan, etc., may have no such associations. Alternately, I would say that in the 70s, such associations were crucial to the star images not only of Bruce Lee and Jackie Chan, but also Wang Yu, Ti Lung, Alexander Fu Sheng and Gordon Liu. And I will insist that on the body of stars upon which Chinese knowledge has left its mark rests a major reason for the global impact of Hong Kong cinema and the manner in which Hong Kong cinema stands in for "Chineseness" in the Chinese diaspora.

Exile or Diaspora?

I pointed out above the irony of Bruce Lee's exilic or diasporic locations in all three of his Hong Kong films, the geographic distance of Thailand for *The Big Boss*, the spatio-temporal shift to pre-war Shanghai in *Fist of Fury*, and the setting in Italy in *Way of the Dragon*. One might even mention the Hollywood setting of *Game of Death*. This may mirror both the situation of those in Hong Kong who feel alienated from "China" and a large portion of the audience, which is, precisely, Chinese in the diaspora. Though Western audiences have been able to experience the significant pleasures of the Bruce Lee (and, later Jackie Chan and Jet Li) films, we must recall that these films were consumed by Chinese audiences in specialized, ethnic-oriented theatres, for many years exactly in "Chinatown." Watching Bruce Lee portray the immigrant, the innocent, in *The Big Boss* and *Way of the Dragon* clearly mirrored an immigrant's experience in the diaspora, while Lee's triumph, precisely through Chinese knowledge and culture (kung fu) is a happy wish-fulfillment of the immigrant's dream of acceptance and success. Moreover, Lee's substantial physical beauty and martial prowess themselves provide a source of pan-Chinese pride: Kwai-cheung Lo notes that "The characters Lee played were . . . generically 'Chinese' . . . He was broadly held as a 'Chinese hero' who used the power and philosophy of kung fu to defeat the Westerner and the Japanese, arousing a Chinese nationalistic fantasy in the Hong Kong audience more strongly than any particular local identification."[15]

While Lee's *Big Boss* and *Way of the Dragon* mirrored the contemporary diaspora of Hong Kong Chinese throughout the world—Southeast Asia, Europe, North America—the Shaw Bros.' Mandarin-language films mirrored the notion of exile that reflected the situation of all Hong Kong Chinese, in Hong Kong and across the globe: all were alienated from the mainland. The lack of Cantonese dialect in the Hong Kong cinema of the early 1970s, in Hong Kong and certainly across the diaspora, is among the most striking features of the era. But equally striking is the manner in which virtually every Shaw Bros. *wuxia* film is set in the past. Censorship laws in the territory made the production of politicized films problematic, while a continued focus on local social problems (a feature of 1960s Cantonese cinema) might itself have worked against the solidification of the transnational Chinese audience which the Shaw Bros. achieved through their domination of the Mandarin-language movie circuit. But the setting in the past and the use of Mandarin dialect situates the films, geographically and linguistically, in China and while the Shaw Bros. films use only the vague outlines of Chinese history for their settings, they specifically use Chinese knowledge for their themes. Ming vs. Qing conflicts, Manchu vs. Han, corrupt Emperors vs. the Shaolin Temple, only vaguely relate to the political history of China but clearly relate to the formation of a modern pan-Chinese identity, especially at a time when the Chinese Cinema (the PRC) is moribund.

The return of Cantonese dialect to the Hong Kong cinema in the 1970s marked an increased focus on contemporary settings within Hong Kong itself. Certainly this was perhaps the major feature of the Hong Kong New Wave. Hong Kong cinema through the films of Michael Hui and, later, the New Wave, could create for itself a local focus, a local identity. Pride in Hong Kong's accomplishments as a global economic power, including the Hong Kong cinema itself, certainly lent pride to a specifically Hong Kong identity. Yet this very specificity—of dialect, of issues—may be one reason that the global impact of Hong Kong cinema, achieved through the release of dubbed Mandarin-language films in the early and middle 1970s, declined. But in the 1980s we see something like the globalization of Hong Kong itself, not only as an established economic power, but as a globalized cinema, seen by a marked increase in the use of overseas locales in contemporary settings, where Cantonese language and culture comes to occupy the space within the frame; where Cantonese is spoken by all the characters, much the way that Hollywood cinema uses global locales while forcing every screen character to speak English. No other cinema save the Hollywood cinema, has so colonized global space for its own use. Jackie Chan broke the boundaries of Hong Kong filmmaking not only by becoming an international star, as, after all, Bruce Lee before him had, but also by situating his films globally: Mainland China in *Police Story 3: Supercop*; Russia and Australia in *First Strike*; *Mr. Nice Guy*, set entirely in Australia; *Armor of God* in Europe and *Armor of God II: Operation Condor*, set in Europe and Africa; and *Who Am I?* with its lengthy African sequence; finally reaching an apotheosis in *Rumble in the Bronx*, set in New York, shot in Vancouver. Not coincidentally, then, the final installment of the *Once Upon a Time in China* series takes place in the U.S., the end-point, as it were, of Hong Kong's globalized cinema and culture, Jet Li following Chan as an international star and an up-and-coming Hollywood icon.

It would be the work of stars like Chow Yun-fat, Danny Lee, Simon Yam, Gordon Chan, Lau Ching-wan, to create a local Hong Kong masculinized imaginary. Jet Li, too, could participate in the contemporary action drama (*Bodyguard from Beijing*, *High Risk*, *Hit Man*) and recoup for contemporary Hong Kong some of the masculinized nationalism typically and previously displaced onto the past or onto the global. But even here it is worth noting that only Chow Yun-fat has achieved an international stardom while being strictly associated with Hong Kong's contemporary era and setting (and mostly through the films of John Woo and Ringo Lam, who work in the globalized genre of the action film). This is to say that to assert a national identity on the part of the Hong Kong Chinese it still behooves them to work in the international arena, to create a transnational image, to become global sometimes at the expense of the local.

Export/Import/China

It is well-known by now that the Hong Kong cinema attained its first international presence in the early 1970s through the importation by U.S. and European distributors of Shaw Bros. and Golden Harvest films in dubbed versions. Previous to what was termed the "kung fu craze," Shaw Bros. had a profitable, if modest, circuit of overseas theatres which they owned and operated including a handful in the U.S.: in New York, San Francisco, Los Angeles, Honolulu. Their bread-and-butter was their Southeast Asian circuit and they benefitted, also, from Taiwan. This initial importation of martial arts films in the U.S. has been the subject of my previous research and there I noted that a substantial box-office impact was realized by these Hong Kong imports. Moreover, this marked the first time that Hong Kong cinema impacted U.S. genres, intersecting with Blaxploitation, for instance, and eventually leading to the creation of U.S. martial arts films and film-stars.[16] Yet Hong Kong had been producing martial arts films for over twenty years before *Five Fingers of Death* and *Fist of Fury* punched their way to the top of the US box-office charts in 1973. What accounts not for the successful importation of these films, but, rather, their successful exportation? That is, it is easy to see why these films were popular in the U.S., but why those films and not earlier ones? Most previous scholarship has focused on how Hong Kong films were received (and co-opted) by overseas film industries, but few have noted the manner in which this overseas importation coincides with the assertion of a Hong Kong/Chinese identity. Specifically, the beginnings of Hong Kong's assertion of its export potential is realized via the masculinization of the newly emergent domination of the male star through the imaging of Japan and the Japanese and the forceful foregrounding of Chinese martial arts in the Mandarin-language film productions of the Shaw Bros. Once, that is, the Hong Kong cinema had joined in what was essentially a masculinist domination of the world-wide action cinema (including Spaghetti Westerns, Black Action films, British Horror movies, etc.) it created a space for itself not only at the box-office at home, but also abroad.

By avoiding contemporary political issues, by rarely setting their films in Hong Kong itself, by utilizing muscular masculinity within specifically Chinese cultural dimensions (martial arts especially), the Shaw Bros. created and exported an image of China that came to replace earlier cinematic constructions, especially in an era (1966–76) when Chinese (i.e. Mainland) cinema itself had disappeared. And while it is the case that Taiwanese cinema had a powerful industrial impact on Hong Kong and throughout Southeast Asia (also through martial arts films, to be sure) it did not have the clout of the Shaw Bros. both in the European and American "Chinatown Circuit" and in the international arena of co-productions and sales to

Euro-American distributors. Thus it was that the Shaw Bros., and, later, Golden Harvest, came to be associated with Hong Kong cinema, which, in turn, became the premier creator and distributor of "China."

For the later generation of Hong Kong cinema, the ascension of Jackie Chan to super-stardom amid the routine production of Cantonese-dialect films, Hong Kong came to mean not just "China" but "Asia," enabling Chinese nationalism to become pan-Asian cultural nationalism.

[. . .]

There is thus a kind of imperialism taking place, but also a kind of pan-Asian identifica-tion. Jackie Chan's films, noted above, which take place outside of Hong Kong, represent a kind of "Asianization"—"a fusion or synthesis of different Asian cultures into one Asian culture . . . In other words, what Jackie Chan stands for is Asia, not Hong Kong. This creation of an Asian identity is the most important message that Chan's works have conveyed."[17] Thus if Bruce Lee's and the Shaw Bros.' films substituted Hong Kong for China, Chan's substitute Asia for Hong Kong. In the attempts to make Jackie Chan, Chow Yun-fat and Jet Li stars in the U.S. (as was the case with Bruce Lee earlier), we might even see the Asianization of Hollywood, an interesting and significant outcome of the masculinization of the Chinese man.

This newly (or recently) masculinized Chinese man accounts for the manner in which "the Asianization of Hollywood" as I have just termed it, precisely comes about. Certainly, it was an influx of Chinese directors who began this process, directors like John Woo, Tsui Hark and Ringo Lam who had been associated with "new wave" martial arts and gangster (hero) films that reintroduced Hong Kong cinema to world audiences in the late 1980s. Surely there is no need to rehearse the impact of John Woo on the action cinema, of Ringo Lam on the enormously influential Quentin Tarantino, etc. The point is that these Hong Kong directors came to Hollywood precisely to continue the masculinist practices which gained them their international fame, each director, perhaps oddly enough, making his U.S. film debut by directing Jean-Claude van Damme, himself a direct descendent of the Bruce-Lee influenced American martial arts film. But following the legacy of Bruce Lee and the action-oriented cinema of the Hong Kong directors, Hong Kong action stars could be slotted into the sorts of roles previously reserved for Caucasian or black actors.

Though Chow Yun-fat was relatively chaste with Mira Sorvino in The Replacement Killers (1998), by the time of the non-action oriented Anna and the King (1999) he could at least maintain a sexual presence. This is a far, cry from the original film version of Anna and the King of Siam (1946) and the more famous musical remake, The King and I (1956), when non-Asian actors had to play the role despite the chaste relationship between the eponymous leads. That there has been a particularly interesting pairing with black stars, male and female (Jackie Chan and Chris Tucker in Rush Hour [1998], Samo Hung and Arsenio Hall in the now-cancelled American TV show Martial Law, Jet Li and Aaliyah in Romeo Must Die [2000], etc.), should not disguise the significant fact of the Asian male action star in Hollywood cinema today. Strangely enough, in another phenomenon little noted, it is often the case that, for instance, the characters portrayed by Samo Hung and Jet Li are associated not with Hong Kong, but with the Mainland. Although it is the case that these stars, are, in fact, Mainlanders by birth, their cinematic association is with Hong Kong, yet their on-screen characters belie their Hong Kong associations. This disavowal of Hong Kong and the substitution of "China" continues the deja-disparu identified so memorably by Ackbar Abbas—here not the disappearance of

Hong Kong's culture within Hong Kong, but the disappearance of Hong Kong itself via the very directors and stars who called attention to Hong Kong in the first place.

Notes

1 Stephen Teo, *Hong Kong Cinema: The Extra Dimension* (London: BFI, 1997) 110–11.
2 Ibid., 122.
3 Steve Fore, "Jackie Chan and the Cultural Dynamics of Global Entertainment" in *Transnational Chinese Cinemas: Identity, Nationhood, Gender*, ed. Sheldon Hsiao-peng Lu (Honolulu: U of Hawaii P. 1997) 247.
4 Teo 169.
5 Sek Kei, "The War Between the Cantonese and the Mandarin Cinemas in the Sixties or How the Beautiful Women Lost to the Action Men" in *The Restless Breed: Cantonese Stars of the Sixties*. The 20th Hong Kong International Film Festival Catalogue (Hong Kong: Urban Council, 1996) 30.
6 Tony Rayns, "Bruce Lee and Other Stories," *A Study of Hong Kong Cinema in the Seventies*. The Eighth Hong Kong International Film Festival Catalogue (Hong Kong: Urban Council, 1984) 26.
7 Tian Yan, "The Fallen Idol—Zhang Che in Retrospect," *A Study of Hong Kong Cinema in the Seventies* 45.
8 Teo 97–98.
9 Poshek Fu, "Going Global: The Transnational Cinema of the Shaw Brothers Studio, 1960–1970," in *Border Crossings in Hong Kong Cinema*, The 24th Hong Kong International Film Festival (Hong Kong, 2000).
10 Teo 98.
11 Lau Shing-hon, "Three Interviews," *A Study of the Hong Kong Swordplay Film (1945–1980)*. The Fifth Hong Kong International Film Festival (Hong Kong: Urban Council, 1981).
12 Ibid, 103–04.
13 Cheng Yu, "Anatomy of a Legend," *A Study of Hong Kong Cinema in the Seventies* 24.
14 Rayns 29.
15 Kwai-cheung Lo, "Muscles and Subjectivity: A Short History of the Masculine Body in Hong Kong Popular Culture," *Camera Obscura* 39 (Sept. 1996): 110.
16 David Desser, "The Kung Fu Craze," *The Cinema of Hong Kong: History, Arts, Identity*, ed. Poshek Fu and David Desser (New York: Cambridge UP, 2000).
17 Ibid., 134.

Migrancy and the Latin American Cinemascape: Towards a Post-National Critical Praxis

11

ANN MARIE STOCK

[. . .]

"What remains of national identities in a time of globalization and interculturalism, of multinational coproduction?" asks cultural critic Néstor García Canclini. "What remains when information, artists, and capital constantly cross borders?" (1993, 28). These questions, posed from within the context of post-NAFTA Mexico, resonate throughout Latin America where film production has become increasingly transnational. Reduced budgets, devalued currencies, and soaring production costs mean that even established directors like Tomás Gutiérrez Alea, supported for decades from within Cuba's strong state-sponsored industry, must now seek collaborative financing. Alea's most recent film *Fresa y chocolate* (*Strawberry and Chocolate*, 1993) is a coproduction with Mexico; his next film, *Guantanamera*, will be financed by the Cuban and Spanish governments. The prevalence of coproduction can be appreciated by considering the production credits for just a few of the films showcased during the 1994 International Festival of New Latin American Cinema in Havana, which also illustrates the range of cross-cultural collaboration and the number of countries involved: *El acto en cuestión* (Argentina, Holland), *Angelito* (Chile, Australia), *Crucero/Crossroads* (Colombia, Canada), *Me faz volar* (Brazil, Cuba), *Miss Ameriguá* (Paraguay, Sweden), *El silencio de neto* (Guatemala, U.S.), *Simeon* (Martinique, France), *Sin compasión* (Peru, Mexico, France), and *De amor y sombras* (Argentina, U.S.).

Despite the multicultural collaboration driving film-making in the region, critical discourse continues to privilege cultural authenticity. Films recognizable as "Latin American" are embraced; those "tainted" by extra-national elements and influences are dismissed. *Un lugar en el mundo* (*A Place in the World*, 1992), a contender for an Academy Award for best foreign-language film of 1993, was disqualified when the national identity of the film was called into question. The Academy suggested that the film, submitted as Uruguay's entry, may actually be more Argentine than Uruguayan. After all, *Un lugar* had competed in Havana and in San Sebastian festivals as an Argentine entry and was registered in the same way for the Golden Globes. Moreover, Argentine collaborators far outnumbered the Uruguayan ones. Director Adolfo Aristarain's dual Argentine-Uruguayan citizenship only complicated matters. *Un lugar*, lacking a singular national passport, clearly did not find a place in the world of

Hollywood's Academy. To return to García Canclini's question, then, it seems that what remains when film-makers and films constantly cross borders is, in fact, a critical nostalgia for cultural authenticity.[1]

Contemporary critical discourse is driven by a nostalgia for what has been lost; changing cultural practices in the region are ignored altogether or perceived as threatening. This nostalgic discourse – lamenting loss rather than making sense of changing cultural practices – was already evident a century ago, when early moving pictures were accused of robbing the circus of its public: "No longer does the crowd queue up to see the mustachioed lion-tamer or Lovely Geraldine, sheathed in sequins" (Galeano 23). Rather than engage with the ways in which the new spectacle reshaped and rejuvenated the existing ones, critics lamented the perceived loss. Today this nostalgia prevails among critics who privilege "pure" national films and cinemas, such as the Argentine, Mexican and Cuban ones, while effectively marginalizing those films, film-makers and spectators bisecting geopolitical boundaries. Critical discourse remains fixed within national and regional paradigms, while globalization increasingly impacts that body of work known as Latin American Cinema.

I locate my study in this gap between film criticism and praxis: the desire for authenticity on the one hand and the transnational production and circulation of films on the other. More productive than lamenting a perceived loss, I argue, is developing a method capable of accommodating those films and film-makers who challenge the binary classification of authentic vs. inauthentic. I propose to reframe Latin American Cinema in terms of presence rather than absence, insisting that only by embracing the border crossings of film-makers, images and sounds, and audiences, will we as critics be positioned to move beyond "the genealogical rhetoric of blood, property and frontiers" (Carter 7–8) and to make sense of post-national cultural expression.

Critical Obsessions with Origin and Authenticity

García Canclini contends that transnational migration and communication have led us to abandon "obsessions with the immaculate conception of authentic national . . . cultures" (1992, 11–12). Indeed, the collaboration of producers, film-makers, actors and actresses from diverse cultural contexts attests to this cross fertilization. So, too, do the films themselves in combining and juxtaposing elements associated with various traditions. Consider the ways in which Guillermo del Toro draws our attention to multiple border crossings. The twenty-nine-year-old film-maker works both in his native Mexico and in the U.S. He distinguishes himself from other Mexican film-makers who have relocated to southern California, stressing that he will always be a "round-trip ticket" film-maker. "I am interested in making movies here in Los Angeles," he says, "but, of course, that's what airplanes are for. I always want to return home . . ." (De Palma). His first feature-length film *Cronos* (1992) further underlines the connection of diverse territories. Produced by Mexico's Iguana Productions and Los Angeles-based Ventana Films, *Cronos* counts with the participation of Argentina's Federico Luppi, Hollywood's Ron Perlman, and Mexico's Tamara Shanath and Margarita Isabel.

Cronos draws conventions from diverse traditions as well: vampire movies, love stories, family dramas, and black comedies.[2] The film-maker describes his creation as "a cross between a classic horror film and a melodrama" and anticipates the confusion this will cause for audiences. "People are going to say it's a Mexican, Catholic, vampire movie with *mariachis*, but it's not," he said. "I think of it more as a sick but really very tender love story" (De Palma). In defying categorization as a strict genre film, *Cronos* also eludes quick definition as either art or entertainment. Del Toro has noted that some critics have seen the film as "confrontational" and wonder why he made "a horror movie as an art movie." By way of explanation, the film-maker notes: "I've always had a pretty strong handle on what I was trying to do with the film . . . for me *Cronos* is a 'B' picture premise shot in the style of an 'A' picture . . . Mixing these things together gives me a strange taste that I like" (Johnston 1). Del Toro and his film defy binary classification within "either/or" categories.

The innovative use of language in *Cronos* challenges yet another binary – English vs. Spanish – and further foregrounds hybridity in the film. Spanish dialogues are interrupted by English and even "Spanglish." In one scene, for example, antique shop proprietor Jesús Gris (Federico Luppi) greets an entering customer with, "¿En qué le puedo servir?" A gum-chewing Ángel de la Guardia (Ron Perlman) responds in English. The conversation continues with seller speaking Spanish and buyer speaking English until the transaction is complete. Jesús rings up the sale and reaches into the cash register; Ángel dismisses him with "Keep the change." Both the English and the Spanish utterances are subtitled in the film, a clever marketing strategy on the part of the film-maker. "I know how lazy American audiences are to read subtitles," del Toro has commented, "and this blending makes 'Cronos' almost an unsubtitled movie" (Harrington G5). Del Toro is pleased with this dual-language version. Jury members echoed the sentiment; in 1993 *Cronos* garnered the Critic's Week Grand Prize at Cannes, nine *Ariel de Oro* awards in Mexico, and the opportunity to represent Mexico at the Academy Awards in Hollywood. An all-Spanish version of *Cronos* exists as well, in which the voice of the film-maker himself replaces that of Perlman. This version is targeted primarily for Spanish-speaking audiences in the U.S. (Toumarkine 8).

Del Toro and *Cronos* are clearly not "obsessed" with authentic national culture. In fact, they flaunt their migrancy and hybridity. Yet, García Canclini's claim that we have abandoned our "obsession" with "authentic national . . . cultures appears overly optimistic in terms of critical responses, for even works like *Cronos*, which conjoin territories, languages, genres and traditions, are evaluated in terms of authenticity. In an otherwise favourable review, Paul Lenti found the script to have "a few loose ends," namely that "some characters speak Spanish and others English, yet they all understand each other" (42). While the elusive identity of *Cronos* indeed confounds critics, they tend to agree on one adjective: "Mexican." "Guillermo Del Toro Brings a *Mexican* Perspective to Horror Films" reads the headline for Adriana S. Pardo's article in the *Los Angeles Times*; Anthony De Palma finds in *Cronos* the "very *Mexicanness* of connecting decay and salvation – crossing horror with hope"; and David Overbey states that Del Toro "gets to the heart of the eternal myth in *Mexican* style" (my emphasis). In the case of *Cronos*, it becomes clear that Del Toro's "origin" overrides the combination of distinct production currencies, the hybridity of the text, the employment of multiple languages, and the marketing to diverse audiences. In spite of the multiple borders crossed, then, the "genealogical rhetoric of blood" prevails.

The privileging of authenticity extends, in fact, to multicultural productions which cannot be traced to a Latin American director and/or producer and which make no pretence for cultural specificity. *The House of the Spirits* (1993), for example, would not appear to be "Latin American" in terms of its production. Directed by Danish film-maker Bille August, featuring notable U.S., British and Spanish stars, filmed in Portugal and Denmark, and financed by German and Danish producers, *House* is generally characterized as either a

"European coproduction" or a German-Danish-Portuguese-U.S. production (McCarthy 6). Despite the marked international collaboration, however, critics fault the film for its cultural inauthenticity. "One never feels the rhythms or smells the scents of a particular culture," complained David Ansen. "This German-produced movie, shot in Portugal and Copenhagen by a Danish director with an English-speaking cast, aims for universality. What it achieves, too much of the time, is inauthenticity" ("Esperanto Epic"). John Powers criticizes *House* for its location in "that eerie limbo known as "international cinema," with its deracinated settings" and actors "from everyplace but where the story is set." He remarks that "it seems clueless to populate a Latin American romance with northern European actors . . . By the time Antonio Banderas turns up . . . you can only laugh: With his olive skin, black hair and thick Spanish accent, the poor guy seems to have stumbled into the wrong movie" (56). Clearly the critical desire for a "Chilean" or "Latin American" film is thwarted; *The House of the Spirits* is not authentic enough to please.[3]

Why, one asks, must this multicultural collaboration exude "the scent" of a particular culture in the first place? The reference to *House* as a "Latin American romance explains, I think, the critical expectation for authenticity. Director Bille August adapted the film-script from Isabel Allende's 1982 novel *La casa de los espíritus*. Allende's novel is clearly tied to a specific cultural context; set in Chile, it draws upon the writer's own experiences including the assassination of her uncle, President Salvador Allende. This "true" story develops within a framework of Magical Realism, a style inextricably linked with the Latin American cultural tradition. Director August, however, opted for a generalized Latin American cinemascape rather than a specific Chilean context, and a style more literal than literary. This deviation from the "original" text, this loss of cultural authenticity in the translation from page to screen, has disappointed reviewers. In the case of *The House of the Spirits*, it is not the mixed blood of the cast nor the combination of production currency which have rendered the film inauthentic. Rather, it is its perceived unfaithfulness to an original, a text saturated with "Latin American-ness," a tale of political upheaval and social turmoil within a framework of Magical Realism.

I do not intend to suggest that cultural specificity has no place in critical discourse nor that claims for cultural authenticity be ignored. What I suggest, however, is a reframing of the critical question, since "Is the text or film-maker or element or language authentic?" provides for an answer of either presence or absence rather than for any engagement with issues of identity construction. That Ariel Dorfman chose to set *Widows*, his novel about the Dirty War, in Greece, for example, invites a series of questions about the role of the exile and the intersections of art and politics, rather than an assertion as to the novel's geopolitical and historical inauthenticity. Similarly, Luis Valdez's casting of an Italian-American actress in the role of Frida in his film about the Mexican artist, the ensuing protest by Latinos, and Valdez's decision to halt production provides a site from which to consider the power of claims to authenticity.[4] To insist upon viewing cultural phenomena through a singular authentic-inauthentic binary lens, is to employ "a language that is always shadowed by loss, an elsewhere, a ghost: the unconscious, an 'other' text, an 'other' voice, an 'other' world" (Chambers 3).[5] Such a language obliterates any space for engaging with the ways in which identities are constructed and negotiated.

Critical discourse must move beyond the binary classification of authentic-inauthentic and permit new questions: how does post-national culture promote a way of thinking that, in the words of Iain Chambers, "is neither fixed nor stable, but . . . open to the prospect of a continual return to events, to their re-elaboration and revision"? (3). To live "between worlds" is to have unique potential: "To come from elsewhere, from 'there' and not 'here', and hence to be simultaneously 'inside' and 'outside' the situation at hand, is to live at the intersections of histories and memories." Like Chambers' stranger, post-national culture is "cut off from the homelands of tradition" and therefore experiences "a constantly challenged identity . . . the stranger is perpetually required to make herself at home in an interminable discussion between a scattered historical inheritance and a heterogeneous present" (6–7).

Post-national practices of making and viewing films demand a critical strategy which does not privilege origins, which does not insist upon purity, and which is not intent on closure.[6] Fernando Pérez effectively develops such a strategy in *Madagascar* (1994). While *Madagascar* has the requisites to be deemed a national film,[7] Pérez jettisons historical chronology and territorial location. In doing so he challenges notions of identity as fixed, of cultures as authentic or inauthentic, and underlines instead the post-national state of migrancy.[8] To reappropriate Chambers' formulation of migrant culture, Pérez's film manages to inhabit "time and space not as though they were fixed and closed structures, but as providing the critical provocation of an opening whose questioning presence reverberates in the movement of the languages that constitute our sense of identity, place and belonging" (4).

From Origins and Destinations to Migrancy in Madagascar

It is migrancy, rather than point of origin or destination, which drives *Madagascar*. The narrative concerns the lives of three generations of women: Laura (Zaida Castellanos), her daughter Larita (Laura de la Uz), and her mother (Elena Bolaños). It resists the predictable formula of family saga, however, in which a history is traced through the generations. There is no direct correlation between past-present-future and wise elder-transitional intermediary-hopeful youth. The grandmother, for example, is clearly not the repository of tradition. Although a minor figure, she appears repeatedly playing Monopoly, posing for a mod portrait, and sporting hip sunglasses. The past cannot be contained as a single point on a linear trajectory. In one scene, Laura sits down with her scrapbook and moves a magnifying glass over a news clipping. A faded photo reveals a gathering of tens of thousands of people, presumably at the most optimistic point of the Revolution in Cuba. The image – even magnified – reveals nothing more than a grey mass. An extreme close-up obliterates the image completely, as an agitated Laura ponders aloud, "Where am I, *Dios mío*, where am I?" Indeed, her indeterminate location in the photo corresponds to the elusiveness of that moment. It is impossible to isolate the past. What remains of the young woman in that public square in the 1960s are memories inextricable from her yearnings of today and her hopes for the future. Thus, narrations of the past – or histories – create rather than capture beginnings and endings.

Madagascar defies treatment as a linear work. What structures the film is the constant of migrancy, of transition and transformation. The three women continually pack up, make their way to another home, and unpack. Piled boxes, crated furniture, squeaking pulleys, and empty rooms underline this perpetual state of transition. So, too, do the sequences revealing the faces and bodies of bicyclists which frame the film. The camera focuses first on close-ups of numerous faces, all sharing a look of determination. It cuts to rolling bicycle tires and feet pushing pedals and then to a shot which transforms the individual cyclists into a single moving mass. What stands out is not where the cyclists have come from nor where they are going but only their concerted efforts to keep moving. Once again it is not a point of origin or destination – a fixed point in time and space – which is foregrounded but the process of migrancy.

Madagascar draws attention to the transformations of both daughter and mother, thereby highlighting identity as permutable. Laura becomes impatient with her daughter, who seems to change as easily as her music shifts from rock beats to opera arias to religious hymns. Early in the film Larita is rebellious. She becomes consumed by art and then by religion. By the end of the film she has become the model daughter, returning to school, passing her exams and communicating with her mother. Laura experiences a transformation comparable in degree but different in direction. Initially confident and satisfied, she remarks: "If I'm not married, it's because I prefer to be single." This self assurance wanes, however, as Laura becomes increasingly concerned about her daughter and dissatisfied with her professional environment. Even as she is accepting an award for teaching in one of the final scenes, Laura ponders not going to work. Her words – "perhaps tomorrow I'll stay home" – are reminiscent of Larita's earlier refusal to go to school. Larita and Laura both change in the film, eventually adopting one another's attitudes and habits. By the end of the film, Laura echoes her daughter's earlier words in saying – "Do you have your bags packed? We're going to Madagascar."

The film's final sequences reaffirm the constant state of migrancy, the impossibility of locating oneself in place and time. Larita and Laura enter the tunnel walking their bicycles as do thousands of *Habaneros* each day. Their voices carry through the darkness which engulfs them. Rejecting the facile closure which would have been produced by the light at the end of the tunnel, Pérez leaves them pushing their bicycles along in the middle, somewhere between the entrance and the exit. The credits then roll over a lengthy take of a train clacking along the tracks past dilapidated buildings in a stark industrial zone. This is not the hopeful train of Fernando de Fuentes in ¡*Vámonos con Pancho Villa!* which chugs into post-revolutionary Mexico. Nor is it the train of Luis Gamboa in *La máquina negra* whose demise purportedly marks the end of the unique Costa Rican culture along the railway. Not heralding beginnings or signalling endings, not pulling out of one station or braking into another, this train is in motion. The image of the moving train is accompanied by the recognizable lyrics of *Quiéreme mucho* sung by the legendary Omara Portuondo: "Cuando se quiera de verdad, como yo te quiero a ti, es imposible tan separados vivir."[9] The song evokes nostalgia for the past and hope for the future, poignantly attesting to migrancy. The merging of spaces – where one has been and where one is going – becomes conjoined with time in this final sequence which resists closure. As Pérez says: "In my films there will always be a nearly inexpressible sentiment that human beings – and the values that define them – will invariably have another opportunity" (Borter).

What is Madagascar and why Madagascar? The most obvious answer to both questions is that like Cuba, Madagascar is an island physically isolated from a nearby continent. In the film, however, geographical and geopolitical definitions are not the focus. Madagascar, even for the characters, cannot be defined or determined in concrete terms; only in the negative can it be approximated. Larita describes Madagascar as "lo que no conozco" or "that which I don't know." Her desire to know, to simultaneously occupy the "here" and the "elsewhere," drives her repeatedly to invoke its name. In one scene, she stands atop a multistory building in Havana's colonial sector, arms outstretched, body forming a cross, and chants "Madagascar, Madagascar, Madagascar." The camera moves back to reveal similar figures across the city, T-shaped forms interrupting the uniform urban skyline. Like television antennae these receivers await distant signals, each one acting as a medium which both receives and transmits, each one a fluctuating point on an infinite matrix. The single voice blends with multiple voices, all chanting in unison, "Madagascar." Madagascar is more state of mind than a place, internal rather than external, intangible rather than concrete, emotional and spiritual rather than intellectual. Larita and the multitudes invoking Madagascar with her conjoin "home" and "the world."

As *Madagascar* shows, migrancy inevitably encompasses culturally-specific experiences. Shown at the 1994 International Festival of New Latin American Cinema, only months after the *balsero* crisis, the film resonated as a product of a specific place and time.[10] The question of who would stay and who would leave loomed large, and the film, like many viewers, exhibited an overwhelming preoccupation with those floating somewhere in-between. This attention is focused not on origin or destination but on the migrancy characterizing post-national culture. In this time of increasing migrancy, Iain Chambers encourages us to alter our critical praxis, acknowledging that critical thought "is not a permanent mansion but is rather a provocation: a platform, a raft, from which we scan the horizon for signs while afloat in the agitated currents of the world" (7).

A critical activity intent on policing the borders of Latin American Cinema is destined to dwell in the past and to marginalize current film-making practices. To insist on authenticity is to jettison a plethora of issues germane to present-day and future film production and distribution practices related to Latin America: the experience of exile as articulated through cinema (e.g. Raul Ruíz and Fernando Solanas);[11] the long tradition of exchange between Hollywood and Mexico City (e.g. Dolores del Río, Luis Buñuel, Orson Welles); the connection between Latin American and U.S. Latino audiences via Spanish-language news broadcasts and *telenovelas*; the role of transnational promotion channels such as the International Festival of New Latin American Cinema, Robert Redford's Sundance Festival and Karen Ranucci's International Media Resource Exchange; the recent international popularity of "Latin American flavour" (e.g. *Como agua para chocolate* and *Fresa y chocolate*), the extent to which "co"-production replicates or challenges extant relations of power, and so on.[12] To continue to define Latin American Cinema narrowly, insisting upon the criterion of authenticity, may very well bring about the demise of the critical object. As Latin American Cinema begins its second hundred years, the time is right for a post-national criticism, one intent on accommodating current practices and modes of expression rather than merely lamenting the disappearance of the Lovely Geraldine and the mustachioed lion tamer.

Notes

* I am grateful to David Campagna. Teresa Longo, Fernando Pérez and Robert Schirmer for their assistance in the preparation of this article. Research for this project was made possible in part by a College of William and Mary Faculty Research Summer Grant.

1 I have described the implications of this "national nostalgia" more fully in "La nostalgia nacional y la crítica cinematográfica: construyendo el cine latinoamericano," forthcoming in *Marges*, edited by Gastón Lillo,

2 *Cronos* reflects Guillermo del Toro's range of film-related experience: he has studied and written a book on the work of Alfred Hitchcock; he has designed special effects and makeup for several feature films; and he has directed three films for television (Overby).

3 The film did, however, meet with success among some audiences. At the 1994 International Festival of New Latin American Cinema in Havana, *House* was awarded the prize for best film about Latin America by a non-Latin American director. In Germany, the film grossed the equivalent of $20 million in its first two months of exhibition.

4 For specific details regarding the controversy, refer to essays by the following critics: Judith Green, Andy Marx and Daniel S. Moore, among others. Valdez's comments have been reprinted in *Variety* and in the Teatro Campesino newsletter.

5 Paul Rotha's 1952 words reflect the critical process of creating a binary classification and marginalizing cultural production: "The key to the position of the documentary in Latin America . . . is simply a catalog of lacks. Where there exists a will to use the film for public enlightenment, total absence of adequate sponsorship, equipment and skill makes impossible the development of any concerted programme equivalent to the documentary movements of Europe or North America" (341–43). The Latin American documentary movement is posited as Europe and North America's Other, thereby creating a perceived absence.

6 Chambers makes a useful distinction between migrancy and travel; whereas travel implies movement between fixed positions, a site of departure, a point of arrival, the knowledge of an itinerary," migrancy "involves a movement in which neither the points of departure nor those of arrival are immutable or certain" (5). Migrancy, then, implies the impossibility of returning to an originary place or moment, the impossibility of a homecoming.

7 Director Fernando Pérez has worked for two decades in ICAIC (Instituto Cubano de Arte e Industria Cinematográficos), Cuba's state-sponsored film institute, his *mediometraje* was financed solely with Cuban currency, the film stars three well-known Cuban actresses; and Havana and the surrounding countryside provide all the locations.

8 The film has met with critical success. At its premiere in Havana in December 1994 during the International Festival of New Latin American Cinema, *Madagascar* earned three prizes: a Coral award in the category of Jury's Special Prize, the Italian ARCI NOVA (Unión de Círculos Cinematográficos) prize, and the Cuban Critic's Prize (shared with *Amnesia*, directed by Chile's Gonzalo Justiano). Pérez's film then went on to win awards in Berlin and Freiburg.

9 Pérez's admiration for the singer is apparent in the documentary he made about her life and work entitled *Omara*.

10 Two other films which premiered at the Festival, *Rey y Reina* (Julio García Espinoza) and *El elefante y la bicicleta* (Juan Carlos Tabío), draw upon and allude to the current *periódo especial* in Cuba. *Rey y Reina* is a moving tale of an elderly woman, Reina, and her dog, Rey. When she can no longer find food scraps for the dog in this time of scarcity, he leaves her side to make his own way in the streets. *El elefante* takes as its subject matter the arrival of a *cine móvil* to a small island village. Viewers familiar with the political and cinematographic discourse in present-day Cuba will respond to Tabío's witty use of contemporary slogans.

11 Kathleen Newman has analysed the effect of exile on national redefinition, examining Fernando Solanas' *Sur* and *Tangos: El Exilio de Gardel*.

12 Whereas this article focuses on authenticity in terms of the "Latin American" part of the equation, the critical tendency manifests itself in terms of "Cinema," too. Critics continue

to define the term narrowly despite the significant increase in video production and circulation and the prominence of television, and the intersection of film with other forms of cultural expression like music, drama and painting. Again, the limited definition marginalizes numerous works and their makers, and ignores provocative intersections: the move of individuals trained in the state-sponsored film industry into television production, tourist promotion and advertising; the collaboration of film-makers like Fernando Pérez and writers like Gabriel García Márquez on video and television projects; the production of big-screen pilots for television mini-series as with Ramón Coll in Costa Rica; and so on.

Works Cited

Ansen, David. "Esperanto Epic." Newsweek 11 April 1994: n.p.

Borter, Beat. "Moving to Thought: The Inspired Reflective Cinema of Fernando Pérez." In Framing Latin American Cinema. Ed. Ann Marie Stock. Manuscript submitted to University of Minnesota Press, 1995.

Carter, Paul. Living in a New County: History, Travelling, Language. London: Faber and Faber, 1992.

Chambers, Iain. Migrancy, Culture, Identity. London and New York Routledge, 1994.

De Palma, Anthony. "From a Mexican Grave Comes Cronos." New York Times 20 May 1994: n.p.

Galeano, Eduardo. "The Cinema: Havana 1910." Century of the Wind. Trans. Cedric Belfrage. New York Random House, 1988.

García Canclini, Néstor. Culturas híbridas: estrategias para entrar y salir de la modernidad. Buenos Aires: Sudamericana, 1992.

——. "¿Habrá cine latinoamericano en el año 2000? La cultura visual en la época del postnacionalismo." Nueva Época 21 Feb. 1993, La jornada: 27–33.

Green, Judith. "'Frida and Diego' Director Caught in Culture Clash." L.B. Press-Telegram 26 Aug. 1992.

Harrington, Richard. "A Monster Hit That's Not Out To Scare You." Washington Post 22 May 1994: G5.

Johnston, Trevor. "Day of the Dead." Time Out (London), 30 Nov. 1994: 1.

Lenti, Paul. "Guadalajara Fest." Variety 3 May 1993: 41–42.

McCarthy, Todd. Review of House of the Spirits. Variety 27 Dec. 1993: 2, 6.

Marx, Andy. "Kahlo Biopic Gets New Wakeup Call." Variety 17 May 1993: 1, 6.

Moore, Daniel S. "'95 A Watershed for Latinos in H'wood." Variety 27 March 1995: 52.

Newman, Kathleen. "National Cinema after Globalization: Fernando Solanas's Sur and the Exiled Nation. Mediating Two Worlds: Cinematic Encounters in the Americas. Ed. John King. Ana M. López and Manuel Alvarado. London: British Film Institute. 1993. 242–57.

Overbey, David. "Latin American Panorama." Toronto Festival of Films, 1993: n.p.

Pardo, Adrianna S. "True to His Frightful Visions: Guillermo Del Toro Brings a Mexican Perspective to Horror films." Los Angeles Times 19 April 1994: F1, F8.

Powers, John. "Like Water for Decaf." New York 11 April 1994: n.p.

Rotha, Paul. Documentary Film. New York: Hastings House, 1952.

Toumarkine, Doris. "October Strikes Deal for Cronos." Hollywood Reporter 13 July 1993: 1, 8.

Valdez, Luis. "Luis Valdez Speaks Out on 'Frida' Controversy." Variety 21 Aug. 1992.

——. "A Statement on Artistic Freedom." El Teatro Dates Sept.–Oct. 1992: 2–3.

PART FOUR

TOURISTS AND TERRORISTS

Introduction

This last section traces the development of cinematic representations of "the foreigner" from its antecedents in travel narratives and representations of tourism to the figure of the terrorist in contemporary thrillers and works of film noir. When read in juxtaposition, these essays demonstrate that now more than ever throughout world cinema, the significance of crossing borders varies according to the identity of the traveler, most often along the lines of gender, "race," ethnicity, and religion. As the writers in this section suggest, the crossing of some borders, as happened most explicitly with 9/11, generates fundamental shifts in both the ethics and aesthetics of cinema as a representational art.

In "Romance and/as tourism: Heritage whiteness and the (inter)national imaginary in the new woman's film," Diane Negra considers "the ways in which romance in recent American cinema is implicated with the fantasy transcendence of US borders" (p. 169). Negra's essay focuses on the most limited and commercialized vision of transnational encounter, that which fetishizes an idealized image of Europe as the site for white American female self-fashioning. Such a vision must deploy essentially traditional notions of gender in order to forestall the possible legitimation of types of cultural difference specific to the complex realities of modern Europe. For many Americans, Europe is a fantasy space that offers the potential for personal renewal and the resolution of complex social problems. According to Negra, "[i]n the tourist romances, a false opposition is posited between a US social environment in which women are bombarded with "tough choices" about work and coupling as binarized categories and a Europe in which those categories are brought into a close alignment and rendered no longer problematic" (p. 174).

Complementing Negra's generic focus, John S. Nelson examines the generic conventions most commonly used to provide a framework for the cinematic articulation of discourses on terrorism. Nelson reveals how popular genres have served to represent the terrorist in various ideologically complex political guises, arguing that "[a]s conventional networks of figures, popular genres of cinema have been shaping our senses of terrorist ends and means" (p. 184). Yet ultimately, this ideological work is bound up in the aesthetic particulars of the genres themselves.

Finally, in a short piece that functions as a coda for both this section and this reader as a whole, Homi Bhabha places Hollywood cinema in the context of media culture in general and the rise of a global discourse of terrorism and socio-political interconnectedness and responsibility.

Bhabha uses the U.S. media's response to 9/11 to ruminate on the ethical consequences of transnationalism when it is enacted as an extralegal attempt to effect political change. Bhabha's final "[h]ope, that we might be able to establish a vision of a global society, informed by civil liberties and human rights, that carries with it the shared obligations and responsibilities of common, collaborative citizenship" may be, from the many perspectives presented by the writers whose work we have included in this reader, the possibility that makes the work of "transnational" thinking ultimately worth doing.

Romance and/as Tourism

12

Heritage Whiteness and the (Inter)National Imaginary in the New Woman's Film

DIANE NEGRA

In this chapter I devote attention to one of the ways in which romance in recent American cinema is implicated with the fantasy transcendence of US borders. Attending to the emergence of a set of films that centralize a narrative of Europeanization, I argue that these texts constituted an important new permutation of the woman's film in the 1990s. Films such as *Only You* (1994), *Four Weddings and a Funeral* (1994), *French Kiss* (1995), *The Matchmaker* (1997), and *Notting Hill* (1999) are bound together by a codified set of narrative protocols which include, for instance, the reluctant or accidental arrival of the protagonist in a nation in Western Europe, the discovery within that national setting of new possibilities for coupling and family formation, and the narrow averting of a return to the US by the heroine, who is instead inscribed within a "happy ending" achievable because of her symbolic acquisition of a foreign nationality.

[. . .]

In devoting attention to these films' presentation of imaginary European homelands, I will shed light on the complex interrelations between popular film and tourism as an experiential mode set up to resolve identity problems in late-twentieth-century US culture, and investigate the rescripting of romance to reflect perceptions of American national identity (and American whiteness) in crisis. Analyzing the contiguity of romance and expatriation, I will argue that these narratives rely on a formula in which tourism serves as the antidote for a variety of overtly or tacitly diagnosed social problems. When romance is correlated with the symbolic acquisition of alternate ethnic/national identity, it takes on a powerful new charge.

The tourist romance

Tourism, it is clear, is an ever more important social and economic phenomenon in contemporary life. If, in earlier phases of modern life, tourism was most often constructed as a tranquil, therapeutic respite from one's everyday cares, tourist experience is now most frequently positioned as an opportunity for integration and stimulation that will make up (implicitly or explicitly) for the deficiencies of daily life. Thrill-seeking tourism of all kinds boomed in the 1990s, with a particular emphasis on conquering nature through extreme sports. Climbing Mount Everest became increasingly popular (in some cases with disastrous results) throughout a decade which closed with the deaths of a number of adventure-seeking tourists in 1999 on a canyoneering tour in Interlaken, Switzerland. As Barbara Kirshenblatt-Gimblett has observed, the rewriting of tourist experience around higher grades of stimulation has produced a crisis for traditional sites of tourist interest: "Museums are experiencing a crisis of identity as they compete with other attractions within a tourist economy that privileges experience, immediacy, and what the industry calls adventure" (Kirshenblatt-Gimblett 1998: 7).

A key development in the recent history of tourism is the recognition on the part of tourist industries that tourists want to feel they know the place they are visiting. Thus, new modes of tourism attach value to those experiences that reflect the closest connection to the place being visited. Stress is increasingly placed on fully immersive modes of tourism predicated on integration in a new environment/culture. At the close of the twentieth century, particular emphasis has been placed on tourism that is personally enriching, with a fuller experience of local culture being demanded by a larger percentage of travelers. Recent tourist practice has been defined by the ascendance of the "authenticity"-driven "special interest," "active," or "adventure" tourism model, which presupposes the desire to integrate as fully as possible into local culture. As the authors of *Tourism: A Gender Analysis* have noted, "Tourism therefore involves the purchase of the particular social relations and characteristics of the host" (Kinnaird and Hall 1994: 13). In a climate emphasizing the postmodern play of identity, touristic pleasure is now more likely to be linked to the performance of those characteristics and the reproduction of those social relations. In *Staging Tourism: Bodies on Display from Waikiki to Sea World*, Jane Desmond trenchantly observes that "The natural, represented by this essential culture . . . emerges as something lost by white, middle-class tourists and briefly rediscovered through invigorating contact with representatives of that culture" (Desmond 1999: 255). As I will show in my discussion of the tourist romances, the desire to experience somatic stimulation and environmental encounters marked out as "authentic" pervades those fictions just as it increasingly factors as part of the appeal of vacation packages.

[. . .]

The dynamics of tourism have long implicated the male tourist in the consumption of indigenous femininity, whether overtly designated as sex tourism, or at a more implicit level. When women travel, romance is often presented as a natural outgrowth of immersive tourism. In a recent feature article a female journalist wrote, "While I wouldn't say that the possibility of meeting someone motivated my wanderings, it's always floated in the back of my mind like moonlight on the Taj Mahal" (Spano 1998: E7). The quest for romance is thus discursively figured as equivalent to the destination itself.

The desire to identify with indigenous populations and feel a sense of inclusion within local culture is a key feature of the recent tourist romances which assume that the national/cultural location visited is more "real" than the (inevitably American) culture the protagonists leave behind. *The Matchmaker* posits this distinction by equating American culture with the ersatz world of political "spin" and contrasting it to the comical "authenticity" of rural Ireland. Its heroine Marcy Tizard (Janeane Garafalo) is presented as a woman whose energies are fruitlessly expended in the service of a corrupt American politician. In Ireland, she meets

Sean, an Irishman who has abandoned a career in public relations because he perceives it to be morally bankrupt, and has resettled near his family in the West of Ireland. Marcy acquires the ability to critique slick, American-style political showmanship as she gains "insider" knowledge of Irish culture.

Tourism has traditionally operated as a mode of ideological reinforcement—we experience another place in order to return, rejuvenated, to our customary environment.[1] Yet in the tourist romances of recent film, this last link in the traditional social contract of tourism is emphatically severed—the films decisively emphasize the non-return of the native—Kate in *French Kiss* and Faith in *Only You* are narrowly prevented from returning to the US, while at the close of *Notting Hill* the heroine Anna Scott answers the question "How long are you intending to stay in Britain?" with a jubilant "Indefinitely." In all three films, satisfactory narrative closure strikingly hinges on the spectator's agreement that the greatest prospect for a happy future life for the heroine lies in expatriation.[2]

The tourist romance and the burdens of citizenship

Few critics have addressed the flourishing category of cinematic romance in the 1990s. Yet as Catherine Preston (2000) has shown, the romance has played an important role in the cinema of the 1990s and particularly in the filmographies of major female stars such as Julia Roberts, Meg Ryan, and Sandra Bullock. Preston argues that the generic status of the romance is somewhat blurred, and its prominence as a successful film formula is frequently obscured by the fact that it is often grouped with many other kinds of films. Nevertheless there has indeed been what she terms "a steady rise" in the production of film romances since the late 1980s and, further, those films have been among the most successful at the box office. Surveying the box office results for 1990–99, for instance, reveals that at least one film romance was among the top highest-grossing American films worldwide in every year except 1995 and 1998. In key respects, some of the most successful film romances of the late 1980s established precedents that are still being adhered to. From *Moonstruck* (1987) and *When Harry Met Sally* (1989) forward, a large number of cinematic romances have promoted regionalism as an accessory to romantic fusion through camerawork that is highly attentive to the local landscape. Such films would seem to serve as the domestic correlatives to the films I discuss here. I turn now, however, in more specificity to themes of internationalism in the romance.

Certainly Hollywood films have long treated themes of international romance. Postwar American film was particularly adept at thematizing the encounter between Americans and European culture, in films such as *The Quiet Man* (1952), *Gentlemen Prefer Blondes* (1953), and *Roman Holiday* (1953). Taking *Now Voyager* (1942) as another representative case, it is possible to see how earlier films display an altogether different conception of the relation between travel and female identity. In the melodrama, Bette Davis' Charlotte Vale is able to escape her mother's stifling, repressive influence by affiliating herself with the exoticism of travel (in this case to Brazil). Although Charlotte's mother has reproached her in the past, saying "You have all the vigor of a typical American tourist," this film figures tourism slightly differently than in the newer romances. Here, tourism is likewise emancipating, but it confers an identity that is sustainable upon a return trip home. Charlotte's romance on a cruise to Rio de Janeiro with Jerry (a married man also trapped in an unhappy domesticity) will live on after the two have returned to the US. Charlotte's new sense of herself enables her to transform her grim home life, and she is ultimately able to generate an alternative model of maternal behavior from the negative example set by her mother. She continues to wear a camellia corsage as a sign of her newly tropicalized identity, and at the close of the film, Charlotte and Jerry fondly recall their time together in Brazil and pledge to protect "that little strip of territory that's ours," as the film celebrates their reterritorialization of their sphere of the American social landscape. Now Voyager imagines its heroine spending time overseas to enrich her identity for a more empowered homecoming, in which she reshapes her domesticity to reflect what she has learned. Such returns are largely ruled out in the newer romances.

What I propose is that more recent American films cover much the same terrain, but they do so now under the terms of a new ideological agenda. A crucial shift involves the assumption of dysfunctional gender relations in the American context, and the proposition that US affiliation has become burdensome. Dissatisfaction with the prospects for romance in the US has been provocatively addressed even in romances that (strictly speaking) depart from the model I investigate here. Set in the US, such films nevertheless propose correction for the social problems that impede coupling through an invocation of Europe. In While You Were Sleeping (1995), heroine Lucy's (Sandra Bullock) quest to produce a home for herself (the real romance here is with the hero's family and the domestic security they represent) is associated with her fantasy of travel to Italy. An employee of the Chicago Transit Authority whose days consist of a series of anonymous urban encounters in a tollbooth, Lucy is obsessed with Florence, and carries an unstamped passport around as the film's sign of her emotional and geographic confinement. The unspoken mutual feeling between Lucy and Jack (Bill Pullman) appears to be cemented as he gives her a snow globe of Florence, and at the close of the film, Lucy proudly recounts, "Jack gave me the perfect gift—a stamp in my passport. He took me to Florence for our honeymoon."[3] The remake of Sabrina (1995) proceeds from the assumption that the titular heroine has found herself through Europeanization, becoming visible as a candidate for romantic attention only after a transformative stay in Paris. Other films, such as Next Stop, Wonderland (1998), centralize a heroine paralyzed by a kind of free-floating nostalgia that the film briefly anchors to her reminiscences of a childhood vacation in Ireland.

Up to this point, I have alluded only in rather vague ways to a widely shared perception in contemporary American romances that "social problems" impede coupling, noting that often the resolution of those problems involves the transference of the heroine from the US context to a setting in Western Europe. These social problems remain vague in narrative context because it is the nature of Hollywood film to showcase trajectories of transcendence/ resolution rather than to perform sustained social diagnosis. Yet, the tourist romances are bound together by their (muted) critique of a number of dominant features of contemporary US experience—social isolation, gender disempowerment, class difference, body anxiety, and conditions of environmental oppression. These features are brought together as the implicit catalysts for the heroine's identity crisis which is subject to adequate resolution only in a European context. By analyzing these dynamics I will begin to develop a response to the main question which this essay seeks to address: what function is Europe currently made to serve in the American romantic imaginary?

[. . .]

In a discussion of work re-engineering and its implications for family life in the 1990s, Sarah Ryan observes that many post-baby-boom Americans feel that the "social contract" that seemed to structure white American life in the post-World War II period has been increasingly violated. Ryan writes that:

> An almost constant sense of insecurity haunts American families in the 1990s. Nearly half the population worries that someone in their household will be out of work in the next year. Parents no longer expect their children to have a higher standard of living than themselves. Most expect large-scale layoffs to be a permanent feature of the modern economy; meanwhile, they experience more stress while at work and are contributing more and more hours to the job. No wonder nostalgia for more prosperous and predictable times is a recurring theme in politics and the arts, even among young people who have embraced the technology and values of the 1990s.
>
> (Ryan 1999: 332–333)

The widely held view that Americans now operate in a "postfeminist" environment in which the concerns of feminism are taken to be irrelevant and/or archaic has largely led to the stigmatization of a feminist vocabulary that might serve as a productive outlet for responding to this state of affairs and its impact on women. The disappearance of mainstream feminist discourse was chronicled in an editorial in USA *Today* in which founder Al Neuharth announced that Ms. magazine would soon cease publication. "Reason: Women's libbers are fewer and far less fanatical than 30 years ago" (Neuharth 2000: 12). The decreasing availability of feminism as a responsive mode to the continued disenfranchisement of women means that dominant Hollywood fictions (as well as self-help discourses and the new domestic regimes propounded by figures like Martha Stewart) faced little competition in their characterization of women's lives, interests, and concerns in 1990s US culture.

The expatriate romances restore quality of life for American women on terms now viewed as impossible in the US, for any notion of US citizenship is thus implicated with these competitive, precarious, social and economic conditions. In addition, definitions of American identity are increasingly bound up with anxieties over the loss of community, and the destruction of a viable definition of place.

[. . .]

In surprising ways, the tourist romances register the anxieties produced by these new forms of rootlessness and economic competitiveness. For the reasons I've indicated, their perceptions of US social problems are never presented in depth, and they are thus best understood by examining the strenuous efforts made toward their correction. For instance, the films demonstrate that the social isolation of heroines who are imprisoned by fame (*Notting Hill*) or confined by an all-encompassing job (*The Matchmaker*) will be corrected by their incorporation into a warm and enveloping community of friends and relatives when they resettle outside the US.

In some instances the films rely on the most clichéd of strategies to exposit their heroines' isolation, presenting them as real or implied orphans. This is the case in both *French Kiss* and *Only You*, which showcase heroines who have virtually no family and look ahead to the families they will gain by marriage. Both protagonists are schoolteachers "marrying up" to professional men (an oncologist and a podiatrist) in arrangements that are implicitly understood to connote their economic/class advancement. In the case of films like *The Matchmaker* and *Notting Hill* a stark incompatibility is shown between work and personal life; if the heroines of *French Kiss* and *Only You* will advance themselves economically through marriage, the protagonists of these films indicate an inverse case in which successful working women must forgo a rewarding personal life. It should be clear that this set of films thus maps out both dimensions of what 1990s popular cultural discourse defined as women's dominant lifestyle choice—to look to marriage for economic providence or, if choosing a professional path, to expect to be unable to sustain any other type of reward. In the fantasy structure provided in the tourist romance, all such problems of economics/class/social integration are made to dissolve in the European context. Kirshenblatt-Gimblett has written that "Tourists travel to actual destinations to experience virtual places" (Kirshenblatt-Gimblett 1998: 9), and this insight certainly enables us to understand better why the mechanics of tourism are so compatible with Hollywood narrative. In the tourist romances, a false opposition is posited between a US social environment in which women are bombarded with "tough choices" about work and coupling as binarized categories and a Europe in which those categories are brought into a close alignment and rendered no longer problematic.

[. . .]

Europe has become an ideal staging ground for nostalgic fantasies of American whiteness. In essence, these films really reflect a displaced nostalgia. Unlike the US-based ethnic romances, which often exhibit an anachronistic character despite their present-day setting, the tourist romances maintain a contemporary flavor by seeming to reveal to us that the vibrant family and community relations of the past still exist, awaiting our discovery, in Europe. In this way, the surface quest plot of the films facilitates an underlying travelogue which strongly thematizes a European past as a consumable good. American whiteness is now understood as an evacuated category, and the rootlessness of the heroines in the tourist romances reflects this. The single most important gesture of resolution in the tourist films is that they stabilize their migratory heroines.

If in some respects this category of recent film romance might appear progressive in that it undertakes social diagnosis, it must not be mistaken for a searching analysis of contemporary culture. Rather, the films offer a conservative cultural escape route in which American women are coupled with European men who will lead them out of the public sphere. The romances resettle their heroines in ways that finally camouflage the problems that catalyzed their identity quests. One of the ways that this is accomplished is through strong pictorial representations of an idealized harmony with nature. The "right" men in such films are often literally and metaphorically grounded—associated with the land. In *French Kiss*, Luc teaches Kate to "read" nature in a scene in which he cues her to identify all of the contributing flavors in a locally produced wine. In *Only You*, Peter speaks of his love for trees and states that he would be happy doing nothing for the rest of his life but growing them, while in *The Matchmaker*, Sean has opted out of urban life in favor of a retreat to the country. In all of the films, the couples take scenic walks together—walks that seem symbolically to cement their relationship to their environment. In *The Matchmaker*, Marcy and Sean take a crucial walk along the sea cliffs in the Aran Islands that seems to clinch their feelings for one another, while in the hit romantic comedy *Notting Hill*, protagonist pair Anna Scott (Julia Roberts) and William Thacker (Hugh Grant) take an evening walk in the eponymous neighborhood that leads them to a garden retreat. Where they are not directly connected to land itself, the European heroes are at least shown to be in a state of harmonious accord with their environment. In *Notting Hill*, William is depicted as fully a creature of his environment—most evidently in a symbolic season-transcending walk through a freshmarket in his neighborhood. Although this is urban space, it is defined by flowers, fruits, and vegetables, and various natural signs of seasonal change.

In this category of film, European men are distinguished by their willingness to take life at a slower pace, and by a strong sense of identity linked to their environment. If the heroines are dispossessed at a crucial level from place-oriented community (they do not know where they are from) the heroes are inevitably living their lives in just the right place. Their settledness in contrast to the heroines' nomadism is related to their status as representatives of a social harmony that is meant to contrast distinctly with the implied social chaos of contemporary American life.

The tourist romance and the promise of community membership

Fantasies of long-term settlement lie at the heart of the tourist romance. As I have indicated, the heroines are inevitably socially isolated—through romance they acquire membership in a literal or symbolic family. In *Four Weddings and a Funeral* American Carrie (Andie MacDowell) is virtually always alone as is Anna in *Notting Hill*, while in both films British Hugh Grant is incessantly surrounded by a close-knit group of friends. In *The Matchmaker* Sean woos Marcy with a song whose lyrics imply the promise of community membership, "Won't you stay, stay a while with your own ones?"

The films' Europeans[3] are depicted as understanding and honoring the rules of community membership in contrast to a US public sphere in which competition has supplanted community. This is vividly conveyed in *The Matchmaker* when Marcy (with the assistance of the residents of the small Irish town of Bally na Gra) stages an obscene tableau of rural Irish life for her American politician employer that satirizes US definitions of Irish community. By now an insider, Marcy is able to author a scene that reflects her newfound knowledge of the distinction between authentic and fabricated community and legitimately reproach her employer for his desire to manufacture Irish roots for US political gain. Marcy's incorporation into the community is possible because she refuses to exploit it.

Humane local authorities are often key accessory figures in the tourist films, and they frequently act to validate the heroine's emotional agenda. In *Only You* Faith's assimilation into European ethnicity is tellingly signaled by the contrasting outcomes of two hasty searches in airports at the beginning and end of the film. Early on, as Faith bolts through an American airport in her wedding dress hoping to intercept the man she believes she's fated to marry before he boards his plane, she is represented as an object of scrutiny, and the subject of bemused gazes throughout the airport. It is clear that her execution of an emotional agenda in public space is bewilderingly inappropriate to those around her. Making it to the gate, she attempts to explain herself to the American Airlines personnel, who call security when Faith asks them to call the plane back to the gate. The moment is paralleled and corrected at the conclusion as Faith runs to stop another plane from leaving in the Rome airport (this one carries the man coded as "right" for Faith). In this cultural context, intense emotional expressiveness is not seen as aberrant. This time Faith is significantly able to communicate her emotional agenda to the sympathetic Alitalia staff who drop everything to assist her when they understand what is at stake. The film concludes as the closed jetway is reopened for Faith, who reunites with the hero aboard the plane.

Just as the films fantasize hospitable natives as accessories to romance, and a social environment that is uniquely accommodating to the needs and desires of the heroine, they also depict a communal interest in and agreement to the burgeoning romance. This communal interest is most clearly expressed in the endings of the films which character-istically assemble a group of the hero's native friends to bring the couple together (this occurs in *The Matchmaker* and *Notting Hill*) or nominate a local representative to do so (Luc's police detective friend plays this role in *French Kiss*). These characters, whether operating collectively or individually, assist the films in bearing witness to the fact that the onset of modernity has not precipitated the dissolution of community cohesiveness. Emphatically insisting upon the authenticity of their locations, the films employ travelogue aesthetics and fetishistic camerawork to produce a deep and resonant vision of place that effectively compensates for a contemporary sense of American placelessness.[4] [. . .]

Recent American emphasis on various forms of a domestic landscape of nostalgia (commercially reconstructed colonial towns, the emergence of the highly ornamental postmodern Victorian as a major model for the high-end American home, and the invention of an entire Disney town, Celebration, Florida) attests to a widespread desire to simulate the physical and social models of the past. In the tourist romance, intensely romanticized public spaces correct for the culture of retreat that prevails in the late twentieth century US. Symbolically reconciled are the desire for privacy and the desire for communal member-ship. In *Notting Hill* (a film whose narrative strategies I discuss more fully in the next section), Anna and William's romance is linked significantly to a communal garden symbolic of the European urban paradise that is the staging ground for coupling. Yet, the communal gardens, the defining feature of the Notting Hill neighborhood, according to one recent article, are (despite their name), limited access only:

> It is the communal gardens that make the houses in these streets so special. London is famous for its garden squares, but the Notting Hill gardens are different. Sandwiched in the gaps between the terraces, many of these communal gardens are only glimpsed from the road with access solely through the houses themselves.
>
> (Masey 1999)

The somatic subtext of the tourist romance: *Notting Hill*

As I have suggested, the contemporary tourist romance is devoted to generating new national contexts that resolve the contradictions and dilemmas of "normative" contemporary American femininity. This mode of redemptive tourism proposes deliverance from the economic and sexual dynamics of US culture. Yet in its search for more stable ground for female identity, this new narrative paradigm focuses continually on the status of the body and the films' criteria for evaluation are consistently tied to conservative, consumer-oriented somatic definitions. Consequently, the films in this category evaluate women's bodies in travel and probe the connection of the body to food, to clothing, to sex, etc. Indeed, a preoccupation runs through the films with somatic versions of national status as the American female body is rendered hysterical (via traces of slapstick comedy in *French Kiss* and *Only You*) or neurotic, or simply problematic (the potentially unruly body of Jeaneane Garofolo serves this function in *The Matchmaker*)[5] in contrast to the European body at ease with itself. Vital to these films' presentation of cultural contrast is their assumption that the European body retains a close bond with the realm of the natural, communing easily with the landscape, with animals, with food, etc., while the American body's relationship with the natural is seem to be disrupted or severed in some way. The establishment of a romance involves the correction of this dysfunctional relation to the natural realm. These preoccupations are developed most fully in *Notting Hill*, in which Julia Roberts' Anna, a major American film star who clearly resembles the actress herself, is defined by her exclusion from the warm modes of community enjoyed by William, a travel bookstore owner whose placement in a warm coterie of friends, and easy, settled relationship to place, are his defining traits. The film deeply fetishizes the pleasures of a geographically defined home, and invests Notting Hill (a suburb of West London) with an enormous amount of narrative power as a source of stability. William experiences no disjuncture between life and work; this is symbolically communicated by the fact that he lives nearly across the street from his workplace. *Notting Hill*'s thematics of refuge work in such a way as also to showcase the communal garden ("they're like little villages," says William) in which there is a wooden bench inscribed by a long-time husband to his deceased wife.

Here, as in many of the other films in this category, the heroine's discovery of homeland involves a reoriented relationship to food. Comfort food is a particularly important element in creating the ground for the fiction. In *Notting Hill*, William is continually associated with comfort foods of various kinds—in the film's first scene he enters his apartment to make toast. He meets Anna briefly in his bookstore and then shortly after they meet again when he inadvertently spills a glass of orange juice on her in the street. On their first date to a dinner party celebrating his sister's birthday (in a scene of remarkable expository efficiency) a final brownie is vied for by the guests who explain in turn why they most deserve the morsel of comfort food. Anna recounts not the stresses and strains of her job, but instead makes a speech whose primary focus is on the status of her body, speaking of her plastic surgeries and telling the group, "I've been on a diet every day since I was nineteen, which basically means I've been hungry for a decade."

We meet Jeff King (Alec Baldwin), Anna's callow American movie star boyfriend in just one scene but it is enough for us to glean understanding of his status as an agent of those industrial and cultural forces that police Anna's food intake. In contrast to the time spent together by Anna and William, who are seen comfortably eating together on several occasions, the dysfunctions of Anna's relationship with Jeff are indicated by his admonishment to her "not to overdo it" on her room service order, because "I don't want people saying there goes that famous actor with the big fat girlfriend." His Americanness is underscored in his room service order for cold water "unless it's illegal here to serve water above room temperature." The distinctive sole appearance by Roberts' American boyfriend consists of a reminder to her not to eat too much, and mistaking William for their room service waiter.

The film's obsessive subtext about bodies and food is brought full circle in the character of Bella, William's close friend and former girlfriend. Bella's body has been damaged (she has suffered paralysis as a result of an accident the film leaves mysterious) yet she is nurtured and cared for by a loving partner. The film gives us to understand that even lacking an ideal body, she retains value. The new national context is thus associated with alternative definitions of femininity that are not simply and exclusively oriented around the idealized body. In this regard, Notting Hill activates an established contrast between the US as a site of body dysfunction and Europe as a place in which women enjoy an easy, settled relationship to food and an untroubled somatic identity.[6] The film's ending, in which a pregnant Anna relaxes with William in the communal garden, implies that Anna has gained somatic control in a way that contrasts with the public ownership of her body (strict regulation of diet in service of the body that is professionally required, bodily exposure through the publication of nude photographs, etc.) and an unreality defined in relation to American celebrity culture (as Anna tells William "Fame isn't real"). In its connections between a vision of British utopianism and food, Notting Hill thus gives evidence of the way that fantasies of the gratified body stand alongside fantasies of environmental integration in the tourist romance.

Romance narratives have long operated as confirmation that our social system is working the way that it should. For recent evidence of this, one need only turn to 1999's Runaway Bride where an hysterically "all is made right" method of closure leads strangers to cheer and couples to embrace on the street at the news that the protagonist pair has finally tied the knot.[7] In this discussion, I have sought to show that, despite its enduring ideological conservatism, the genre of contemporary romance has nevertheless given rise to an interesting permutation that distinctly fails the confidence test. The "expatriate romances" are unified in their commitment to staging coupling outside of US borders altogether, and because of this they gesture at (although perhaps not as fully as one might wish) an indictment of contemporary American social and economic structures that has rarely been seen in the genre.

Notes

1   In Hollywood film, the most emblematic instance of this return is of course Dorothy's discovery in The Wizard of Oz (1939) that there really is "no place like home."

2   That the trope of Europeanization inevitably centralizes female transformation is attributable to more than the fact that the romance conventionally tells the stories of women. For a counter-example, consider The Talented Mr. Ripley (1999), a film that pathologizes male identity transformation in Europe. This did not, however, prevent the film from inspiring travel-related press pieces advising readers on the towns, cities, and beaches to visit to reconstruct Ripley's travels in Italy. See Rebello 2000, 42–45.

3   Such characters are frequently played by a small group of actors whose European identities have become archetypal over the course of their careers (Hugh Grant, Jean Reno, Kristen Scott Thomas, etc.).

4   In this regard, it would be interesting to consider Before Sunrise, another tourist romance, but one quite different in tone from such films as French Kiss and Only You. A somber meditation on the transitory nature of human connection, the film derives its pathos in part from the fact that neither member of the protagonist couple (Celine, a Frenchwoman, and Jesse, an American) can stay on in the location in which they have come together. The film simply charts the conversation and growing intimacy of the couple during one night in Vienna. (Jesse is to fly home in the morning, bringing to an end a failed vacation he had begun to visit his American girlfriend in Madrid; Celine is en route from a visit to her

grandmother in Budapest back to Paris). The film solidifies our tourist sensibility in a closing montage that takes place after the couple's departure. Here, the camera revisits many of the locations through which Celine and Jesse traveled, mourning their absence on one level, but also inscribing the landscape with a powerful, pleasurable nostalgia. Through its deviations from the narrative paradigm of the expatriate romance, *Before Sunrise* underscores the importance of a local figure to the romance formula.

5 A brief scene in *The Matchmaker*, in which Garofalo's Marcy (having hurt her ankle) is carried into a pub by Sean, gives rise to the only overt anxiety expressed about Marcy's body. A pub patron turns to Sean and says, "She looks a heavy carry," to which Sean replies "No, sure no." Garofalo, whose body fails to conform to Hollywood mandates of size and slimness, had been earlier vividly contrasted with Uma Thurman in a romance entirely centered around body anxiety, *The Truth About Cats and Dogs* (1996).

6 In Susan Bordo's useful discussion of the European stereotypes at work in a FibreThin diet pill commercial she details how "a metaphor of European 'difference' reveals itself as a means of representing that enviable and truly foreign 'other': the woman for whom food is merely ordinary, who can take it or leave it" (Bordo 1993: 100).

7 Of course, a more subversive reading of the film's conclusion might stipulate that the excessive celebration is really tied to the fact that the single woman's potential challenge to patriarchy has now been extinguished.

Bibliography

Anderson, Benedict (1983) *Imagined Communities: Reflections on the Origin and Spread of Nationalism*, London: Verso.

Bordo, Susan (1993) *Unbearable Weight: Feminism, Western Culture, and the Body*, Berkeley: University of California Press.

Connor, John and Sylvia Harvey, eds (1991) *Enterprise and Heritage: Crosscurrents of National Culture*, London: Routledge.

Cook, Pam (1998) "No Fixed Address: The Women's Picture from *Outrage* to *Blue Steel*," in Steve Neale and Murray Smith, eds, *Contemporary Hollywood Cinema*, London: Routledge, 229–246.

Culler, Jonathan (1988) "The Semiotics of Tourism," in *Framing the Sign: Criticism and Its Institutions*, Norman: University of Oklahoma Press, 153–167.

Decker, Jeffrey Louis (1997) *Made in America: Self-Styled Success from Horatio Alger to Oprah Winfrey*, Minneapolis: University of Minnesota Press.

Desmond, Jane C. (1999) *Staging Tourism: Bodies on Display from Waikiki to Sea World*, Chicago: University of Chicago Press.

Dickerson, Martha (1996) "Women on the Road: More and More Are Setting Out to Explore the World on Their Own Terms," *Minneapolis Star Tribune*, November 24, 5G.

Dyer, Richard (1997) *White*, London: Routledge.

Gritten, David (1999) "A Familiar Neighborhood," *Newsday*, May 24: B2.

Harney, Alexandra (2000) "American Women Abroad: How Far Would You Go for the Man You Love?" *Marie Claire*, March: 78–86.

Haskell, Molly (1998) "A Touch of the 1940s Woman in the 90s," *The New York Times*, November 15, 1998.

Kaplan, Caren (1998) *Questions of Travel: Postmodern Discourses of Displacement*, Durham, NC: Duke University Press.

Kinnaird, Vivian and Derek Hall (1994) *Tourism: A Gender Analysis*, New York: John Wiley & Sons.

Kirshenblatt-Gimblett, Barbara (1998) *Destination Culture: Tourism, Museums, and Heritage*, Berkeley: University of California Press.

Leach, William (1999) *Country of Exiles: The Destruction of Place in American Life*, New York: Pantheon.

Marshment, Margaret (1997) "Gender Takes a Holiday: Representation in Holiday Brochures," in M. Thea Sinclair, ed., *Gender, Work and Tourism*, London: Routledge, 16–34.

Masey, Anthea (1999) "House & Home: Why Notting Hill is the Star" *London Telegraph*, May 2.

Miringhoff, Marc and Marque-Luisa Miringhoff (1999) *The Social Health of the Nation: How America Is Really Doing*, Oxford: Oxford University Press.

Neuharth, Al (2000) "How New Mags Rate: Oprah's 'O' a Winner," USA *Today* (April 21), 12.

Preston, Catherine L. (2000) "Hanging on a Star: The Resurrection of the Romance Film in the 1990s," in Wheeler Winston Dixon, ed., *Film Genre 2000: New Critical Essays*, Albany: SUNY Press, 227–243.

Rafferty, Jean Bond. (1994) "Notting Hill on the Rise: London's New Bohemia Is a Hip Hotbed of the Cheeky and the Chic," *Town & Country* 148 (October 1), 118.

Rebello, Stephen (2000) "Ripley's Italian Seacoast," *Movieline* 11(7) (April): 42–45.

Riley, Robert B. (1994) "Speculations on the New American Landscapes," in Kenneth E. Foote, Peter J. Hugill, Kent Mathewson, and Jonathan M. Smith, eds, *Re-Reading Cultural Geography*, Austin: University of Texas Press, 139–155.

Ryan, Sarah (1999) "Management by Stress: The Reorganization of Work Hits Home in the 1990s," in Stephanie Coontz, ed., *American Families: A Multicultural Reader*, New York: Routledge, 332–341.

Spano, Susan (1998) "Traveling Romance: Love It or Leave It," *Newsday*, E7.

Urry, John (1990) *The Tourist Gaze: Leisure and Travel in Contemporary Societies*, London: Sage.

Weiler, Betty and Colin Michael Hall, eds (1992) *Special Interest Tourism*, London: Belhaven Press.

Wood, Robin (1998) *Sexual Politics and Narrative Film: Hollywood and Beyond*, New York: Columbia University Press.

Four Forms for Terrorism

Horror, Dystopia, Thriller, and Noir

JOHN S. NELSON

The aftermath of events on September 11, 2001 shows the importance of film, television, and other electronic media in constructing our political realities. Soon the Bush administration was working with Hollywood screenwriters to help anticipate possible targets and scenarios for further terrorist atrocities. Yet the main Hollywood contributions had come earlier, even before September 11, through popular films. These let American audiences experience acts of political terrorism in vicarious, virtual, symbolic, and other modes.[1] Now, in response to the dramatic escalation of terrorist attacks on U.S. institutions, Americans can call on cinematic prefigurations of terrorist strategies, the movements and states that use them, the regimes that support them, and the politics that reply to them.

Hence we do well to consider how Hollywood mythmaking from the 1980s onward has helped us to characterize terrorism, connections between American and Middle-Eastern politics, attacks on the virtue or viability of Western Civilization, and more. Here the emphasis is on the Hollywood aesthetics available to influence American experiences of terrorism and responses to it. What networked figures of sight, sound, story, and concept from popular films contribute to American senses of terrorist acts and world politics in the wake of the September 11 atrocities? What are their principal sources? And what may be said of their political trajectories?

The argument is that, especially through the aesthetic packages that we call popular genres, Hollywood cinema has been prefiguring our experiences of the events of September 11, their aftermath, and other acts of political terrorism. Popular genres occur in myriad media.[2] In the movies, they are families of conventions for cinematography, mise-en-scène, story, dialogue, acting, editing, music, even marketing.[3] This is to say that popular genres are aesthetics. They provide templates for our personal and political experiences. Four of these forms are particularly pertinent for analyzing the looks, sounds, and dramas of political terrorism that we encounter on the silver screen. These popular genres of cinema are horror, dystopia, thriller, and noir.

Events over the last decade shifted American sensibilities and Hollywood movies away from a Cold War conflict that had pitted the Communist Iron Curtain in the East against the Free World of Democracy in the West. As much or more than any administration or foreign-affairs contingent, popular movies have been helping to turn American attention away from villainous Commies out to undo Democracy in America. Hollywood has played a leading role in replacing the outdated villains of the Evil Empire with Ruthless Terrorists ranging from the Middle East to Middle America. Often, but not always, cinematic terrorists have hated Western ways. Often, but not always, they have declared total, albeit asymmetrical, war against America's hegemony as the world's only remaining military, political, and cultural super-power. Often, but not always, they have been pointedly or vaguely Arabic in look and sound. (Many nationalities do surface.)

As widely noted, these figures have become so familiar to Americans – principally from Hollywood films – that the journalistic and popular presumption at first was that terrorists with ties to the Middle East had obliterated the federal building in Oklahoma City. Although the American militia movement had not been ignored altogether by the popular media in America, Timothy McVeigh still came as a special shock to the country. Furthermore his mythic figure has yet to become commonplace in popular films about political terrorism. Hollywood already has filled most roles for terrorists with figures from afar, and its arsenals of terrorist plots twist more toward international machinations.

Fortunately for Americans in the twentieth century, Hollywood supplied more numerous and sometimes more vivid instances of political terrorism than the country's enemies. Neither America's political elites nor its mass publics concentrated sustained attention on political terrorism prior to the atrocities wrought in 2001 by al Qaeda. Not even terrorist bombings in the 1990s of the World Trade Center, the Murrah Federal Building, and American foreign embassies crowded out the sights and sounds of terrorism as genred by movie conventions increasingly global in their ambition and impact. This was due in important part to the enormous commercial success and cultural reach of Hollywood products, distributed to audiences almost everywhere in the world. By September 11, the earlier terrorist acts mainly had become fuel for still more imaginative and graphic films. Consequently the phenom-enal field for experiencing and responding to political terrorism remained wide open to prefiguration by Hollywood films.

Figures and Phenomena

Americans have been making sense of terrorist events and concerting themselves to action with the help of Hollywood aesthetics. This is happening even though these popular styles are being disrupted in various degrees by the emerging politics that they have helped to prefigure. Borrowing from the Santa Cruz meta-historian Hayden White, we might observe that popular movies in the last two or three decades have been contributing to a "prefiguration of the phenomenal field" for political terrorism – as we are coming to know and contest it in the wake of 9/11.[4]

Recent dynamics of terrorism are no exception. Through a Hollywood war movie, we could re-experience Mogadishu in Somalia with a Black Hawk Down (2001) years after the dust had settled from the disastrous moments of an aid mission in 1993. Through a political thriller, we could anticipate the experience of New York City under The Siege (1998) of terrorist attacks, years before the fall of 2001. Through a foreign dystopia, set in Bab El Qued City (1994), we could feel the effects of individual moves to resist or escape the encompassing system of regime terrorism in Algeria. Through the experimental cinema of The Tornado (1996), we could do the same for the anarchical system of civil-war terrorism in Lebanon. And through the blockbuster entertainment of The Sum of All Fears (2002), we could sense the frustrating complications in endeavors to resist the residual system of Cold War suspicions when trying to avert nuclear war spurred by rogue acts of nuclear terrorism.

The phenomenal field is the vague situation of events and experiences that start to take particular shapes and come into our specific awareness as we encounter them. Both existential phenomenologists and social cognitionists have suggested in various ways that, even before we consciously configure (let alone interpret) our experiences of events, we must prefigure them as diffuse and initial kinds of occurrences.[5] For cognitive science, the clear implication can seem paradoxical: before – or at least as – we cognize experience, we must re-cognize its elements. Otherwise cognition as form and dynamic must lack any content on which to work. Cognition depends on – more or less prior – recognition. To "apprehend" something in the firm if mental grasp which is what the word means, we must discern something to grasp. We must (know to) turn toward it. Because form and content cannot yet be distinct, we do this with a turn. Indeed the ancient Greek word for such a "turn" is "trope," which even the Greeks appreciated also as a prospective "figure" of speech, experience, making, perhaps even acting.[6]

Popular genres are families of figures. Genres work as wholes; but they also perform in parts, subject to appropriation outside their usual milieus, as fragments when a familiar genre is in disarray, or as remnants when an earlier genre has been dispersed. The conventional elements of genres, as of aesthetics in general, are figures. Even as fragments and remnants, these figures inform our deeds, our words, our thoughts, even our sensations.

Figures and, thus, genres go together by elective affinity.[7] We connect like with like as we discern and choose them. Prefigurations play a role, sometimes a decisive one. Yet we can make different affinities as we like, individually but even more socially. Popular genres work this way: like cultural myths and cognitive networks, they are dynamic webs of associations. The experiential activation of a node almost literally reminds us of linked nodes to the degrees that they have been associated with the first, spreading the activation throughout the web. Each experience reinforces associations that otherwise atrophy, even as it subtly or significantly alters them.

Popular films play prominent roles in our political cognition. Hollywood gives us figures for even beginning to sense political events. This is always already a beginning for our response. Popular cinema is far from our only source of prefiguration for any phenomenal field, including the events of September 11 in particular or political terrorism in general. Nonetheless movies do help prefigure our political experiences and responses, even when their figures have not cohered into a singular genre. What we bring with us into new experiences, we may say, are less political facts than audiovisual "figures," many from movies.[8]

As aesthetics, popular genres are conventional affinities among figures that help define one another. The resurgent genre of noir does not have to link night and rain, but typically it does, and we know it in part from such figures. Conventionally a noir protagonist encounters some dark night of the soul and needs a purging deluge. The figures of night and rain enact or embellish such desired meanings through the "pathetic strategy" common in popular genres.[9] And this holds even when both the night and the rain might be, well, more figural than literal: *The Matrix* give us green figures that rain down the black screens of computers like the deluge down a window pane at night. The families of defining conventions for popular genres are far more numerous – and sometimes far more complicated – than any two or three figures such as night and rain.[10] The relationship is not one of necessary conditions: there are many noir films with no rain and now at least two with no night.[11] Nor is the logic one of sufficient conditions: there are innumerable movies with night and rain but no noir aesthetics. Nor is the connection one of separate causes to contingent effects, as in behavioral paradigms for the social sciences. Rather than atomistically mechanical, our aesthetics, genres, and figures are interdependently systemic. Rather than specifying any directions or degrees of causation, the correlations worth tracing among figures, styles, themes, or other aspects of a genre can help us to appreciate their patterns of meaning. What figures has Hollywood been generating for the phenomenal field of terrorism? How do figures from popular cinema inform our political sense of what to say and do about terrorism? The political aesthetics of horror, dystopia, thriller, and noir suggest answers.

And we need all four. One remarkable development is that mythic figures of terrorism do not exactly constitute a singular genre or even a distinctive aesthetic. That leaves political terror open to exploration in diverse genres with contrasting aesthetics. As conventional networks of figures, popular genres of cinema have been shaping our senses of terrorist ends and means. Four of these generic aesthetics seem especially relevant for informing how we experience terrorist events such as those on September 11 – and therefore how we respond to them.[12]

Horror and Evil

Apocalyptic reactions to 9/11 might suggest that the generic home for terrorism could, even should, be popular horror. President George W. Bush immediately denounced all terrorism as unqualified "evil;" and the enduring phrase from his next State of the Union Address became the condemnation of Iran, Iraq, and North Korea for pursuing weapons of mass destruction and sponsoring international terrorism as "the Axis of Evil." Horror is *the* popular genre of evils.[13] Yet the aesthetics and other conventions of popular horror have not figured prominently in any Hollywood treatments of political terrorism that come to mind, save for the dynamics of regime terrorism and war that Americans elect to keep categorically separate from both "international terrorism" and "domestic terrorism."[14] The genre for regime terrorism has become dystopia, an outlying form of political horror analyzed in the next section. War has a cinematic form of its own, of course, with war movies arguing generically that war is (not so much terror as) hell.[15] When it comes to terrorism, however, the Hollywood dog that has not barked is horror. Hence it helps to contrast terror with horror, as both a family of feelings and a popular genre of films.

Terror is the fraternal twin of horror. As emotions and conditions, the two share much of their genetic material, yet they present distinct faces to the world. Together terror and horror form a complex of action and feeling that can figure momentarily in almost any kind of drama or film. Yet "horror" names a popular genre of movies, a whole family of conventions, whereas "terror" surfaces only in a few conventions of film. And "terrorism" characterizes a prominent form of politics, while "horrorism" remains a word in waiting, with no referents for politics or otherwise. Perhaps an implication is that the intertwined trajectories of horror and terror can be teased apart in the popular operation of politics and possibly in the generic apparatus of cinema. How does Hollywood handle them?

Terror is the overwhelming dread-and-despair that puts us (or our movie stand-ins) at the categorical center of assault. Or it does much the same by dispersing specific assaults into a continuing condition. Terror radicalizes anxiety. It projects death or degradation as immanent possibilities from almost any angle at any time in any place. Therefore terror disables you from action. It diminishes personal movement into mere behavior. It makes people flee or freeze in blind, frantic, unthinking aversion. Terror overflows fear. It overwhelms the appeal of fear to cognitive calculation of punishments and alternatives. It shoves aside the calm, cool apparatus of rationality. It panics people and destroys their identities as individual, responsible beings. It escalates and coagulates anxiety. Terror preempts escape. It prevents hope.[16]

Horror is the overwhelming dread-and-disgust that initially puts someone or something else at the center of assault. Horror happens at first to us as onlookers. We see atrocities that mock any possibility for goodness, truth, or beauty to remain unmixed with monstrosity. Later in horror, however, we look around to realize that the source of perversion is turning to get us, the circle of corruption is coming to encompass us, the sinister system has swallowed us whole. Horror is revulsion for awful acts; it is repulsion from terrible entities.[17] It stems from natural boundaries eradicated or cultural standards transcended. Hence it springs from the strange territory of the uncanny and the sublime, where awful abominations and awesome absolutes turn into one another with each twist in perspective. We might freeze in horror. Or we might refuse to recognize the horrors we glimpse, and go back to daily routines that pretend nothing major is awry. Yet we also might turn to face horrors, making human sense of their threats and finding good ways to resist them. Horror appalls and revolts; yet horror also can revolutionize, provoking fresh perspectives and effective inventions. For good or ill, horror provokes extreme responses that range from willful oblivion to apocalyptic reckoning. Terror disrupts and stops action by the victims; horror interrupts and radicalizes it.[18]

Terrorism can stem from criminals, from corrupt governments, from political or religious movements. Sometimes it serves strategies of war, sometimes oppression, sometimes protest or resistance or rebellion or liberation, sometimes revenge and redistribution; other times psychosis, sheer destruction, or the emergence of some new kind of civilization. At times, terrorism can operate through big-lie and brainwashing techniques. It can use tactics of random death and disappearance. It can impose iron discipline, work through mass hysteria, propagate paranoia, or rely on surveillance. It can anonymize people beneath notice, let alone contempt. It can debase or humiliate most abjectly. It can concentrate citizens like pigs into pens. It can isolate individuals like pigeons into holes or compartments. It can drive parties, interests, even families underground. It can incarcerate whole populations. Nevertheless terror has stayed surprisingly separate from horror, with episodes of political terrorism as rare as a vampire's reflections in the popular genre of horror.

[. . .]

Dystopia and Totalitarianism

In regime terrorism, the political system targets its own inhabitants almost willy-nilly for atrocities such as arbitrary arrests, tortures, disappearances, poisonings, bombings, or other radical disruptions. The aim, insofar as there is a coherent idea at work, is to subjugate, humiliate, and dehumanize the population.[19] In other words, the anti-political purpose of regime terror soon turns into power and cruelty for their own insanely sadistic sake. Picture, wrote George Orwell, "a boot stamping on a human face – forever."[20] This is the totalitarian nightmare of systematic regime terror that drove the democratic imagination throughout most of the twentieth century.[21] By the start of the twenty-first century, events and Hollywood had begun to supplant totalitarian control and regime terrorism with terrorism by movements and insurgent conspiracies as the western template for political hell on earth.

Regime terrorism virtually defines its own (sub)genre of dystopia.[22] This articulates the horror archetype of the Bad Place into an intricate and far-reaching web of figures that remains even today America's primary epitome of political horror.[23] Hollywood seldom produces films in this mode, in important part because relentless downers do not draw lots of viewers or make much money. As far as Hollywood is concerned, dystopia is less a genre in its own right than a subgenre. It is more a subgenre of science fiction than horror. And it tends to omit specific acts of political terrorism. Two of the best dystopias that focus on terrorist acts are popular Middle-Eastern, rather than Hollywood, films: *Bab el Oued City* and *The Tornado*. Remarkable as well is *The Day After* (1983), one of the more sensational movies made for television. Its terrorizing regime is the international system of nuclear deterrence during the Cold War. When the system of Mutual Assured Destruction breaks down, the resulting nuclear holocaust becomes an act of political terrorism that produces an unremitting nightmare. Yet none of these three films seems important, at least for Americans, in prefiguring political terrorism regarded as specific acts by insurgents or anti-western movements.

When Hollywood does venture a dystopia, it is apt to slide from terrorism that targets bystanders to ruthless regimes of surveillance, torture, and punishment that identify dissidents and do them in. Presumably the judgment is that this makes motivations more comprehensible, plots tighter, and settings more plausible for viewers used to people and practices that calculate interests for efficient means to given ends. *Brazil* (1985) and the 1984 version of *1984* are ready examples. As a result, the political terrorism crucial for the dynamics of totalitarian regimes – and apparent also in the actions of some authoritarian polities – seldom surfaces in Hollywood dystopias. For political theorists, terrorism by totalitarian regimes is arbitrary in many particular instances but endemic to the system. It is, in a word, systemic. For Hollywood movies, political terrorism is occasional and instrumental. It springs from relatively specific grievances even though it targets civilians who lack any direct role in producing the grievances.

Again, though, there is a complication. For reasons of dramatic economy and punch, as well as ideology, Hollywood seldom portrays political or other systems overtly as such, in fully literal terms. Instead movies rely on the trope of conspiracy.[24] Examples are easy. *The Parallax View* (1974) uses an assassination conspiracy to trace symbolically how America's two-party system squelches political dissent. *Conspiracy Theory* (1997) does the same to probe oppressive aspects of the political system of the national-security state. *The Skulls* (2000) evokes Yale's notorious secret society for the Bushes to suggest how political elites systematically extend themselves in democratic times. *From Hell* (2001) also deploys a secret society to indict how Victorian culture systematically exploits and represses middle-class dreams and personal freedoms.[25] In popular cinema, conspiracies abound.

Thrillers and Conspiracies

By convention, nonetheless, conspiracies have their primary Hollywood home in thrillers. Not entirely by coincidence, thrillers are the principal genre for films that feature acts of political terrorism. Thrillers typically give viewers unqualified heroes, heroines, and villains.

Yet thriller settings are more familiar, realistic, and up-to-date than those for the far-larger-than-life figures in action-adventure films, let alone superhero movies. In fact, such settings define subgenres for thrillers. These span international intrigues, criminal connivances, governmental and military contests, foreign wars, political potboilers, police stories, business tales, medical sagas, legal dramas, and others at the edges of neighboring genres like detection or action-adventure. The Hollywood disposition to emplot political terrorism in thrillers has several implications for the figures of terrorism widely available to Americans in experiencing events in the wake of 9/11.

The academy and the press share an unfortunate penchant for literalistic criticisms of the Hollywood fondness for conspiracies. We all know the refrain: how epistemically implausible, how social-scientifically unsophisticated, and how politically irresponsible it is to portray some cabal as running the world from behind the scenes.[26] Political scientists have wondered in print whether such Hollywood scripts are written by political rubes who know little about systems or art – and hence personalize everything simplistically – or by political extremists from the left and right who compulsively demonize a few foes as responsible for all the things that go wrong with their worlds.[27] Almost anywhere we turn, and not just Hollywood, American rhetorics of conspiracy are more sophisticated than these options conceive.[28] Yet the frowning equation of conspiracy with crackpot politics surely creeps into American notions of terrorism when popular films insistently show political terrorism conducted by conspiracy.

This is not to say that popular cinema errs in connecting terrorist acts with conspiratorial politics. Conspiracies in a literal sense can be prominent devices of political struggle, especially in republics. Rome named conspiracies (from the Latin *with-breath*) for reliance on planning in whispers outside the hearing of courts or publics.[29] In popular movies with sustained moments of political terrorism, literal conspiracies must be rife. How could they be missing most of the time, when the ruling regimes in Hollywood films are seldom the sources of terrorism? For a group to conceive and conduct illegal acts without preemption by any regime that enforces its laws, secret communication is crucial: actual conspiracy is a must. Even the peculiar acts of political terrorism that do not primarily target a state or regime tend to attack both secondarily. Such terrorism impugns the legitimacy of states and regimes by demonstrating that they cannot meet their responsibility to provide domestic tranquility – by protecting civilians from violence.

Yet if conspiracies appear in many films with political terrorism, and if conspiracies can be Hollywood figures for political systems, how can I say with confidence that few Hollywood films so far have addressed regime terrorism – even in contrast with the run-of-the-mill devices of political oppression portrayed at least in passing by thousands of popular movies? Might the terrorist conspiracies in Hollywood cinema often turn out to symbolize terrorist systems – and thus regime terrorism? Possibly, but concerted efforts to think through the symbols in the films at issue leaves me without a single clear example. It is not that regime terrorism never surfaces at all in Hollywood films. Rather it appears seldom and mostly as a sideshow, not as the focus.

Conceptually and politically, it helps to distinguish occasional conspiracies within larger plots from plots that are conspiracies overall. Among recent thrillers, some forty stress political terrorism. At least thirty include some sort of conspiracy in their plots, although it often is the merest kind of criminal conspiracy. Yet only four of these films have conspiracy plots overall.[30] The ratios are telling: three-fourths of the plots with acts of political terrorism *have* conspiracies, but only one-tenth *are* conspiracies. *Arlington Road* (1999) sounds an alarm about the American militia movement, and it shows how terrorists can use benign politics within America against the government. *The Package* (1989) offers an assassination conspiracy at the end of the Cold War. *The Siege* warns that terrorism can happen here, might elicit an authoritarian and racist response, and could go so far as to provoke something like regime terrorism.

To emplot terrorism in thrillers is to endow its politics with clear heroes and monstrous villains, both acting from motives more personal than ideological. Thrillers treat terrorism as political violence against bystanders – by contrast with military combatants and public officials. This accords with a classic definition of political terrorism.[31] (And it suggests that we set aside for now the many thrillers about actions against political figures.) In thrillers, this puts terrorists unarguably in the wrong: thrillers seldom explore the complications in how one cause's terrorist can be another's freedom fighter. To do that might take tragedy of a classical kind. This is rare in popular films, but among movies on political terrorism perhaps *The Crying Game* (1992) and *The Boxer* (1997) come close, and it is notable that neither is exactly a Hollywood product.

The notion of terrorism as attacking innocents for political gain does not fit the genres of horror and dystopia. In horror, adults are guilty, secretly if not originally. That is how they can know and combat (but also be) the monsters. Children might begin as innocents, yet they must develop the moral and political sophistication born of facing their own eventual evils if they are to survive monstrous attacks. The systematic, encompassing corruption of dystopias means that the civilians targeted by the regime share responsibility for its terrorism. As theorists have made painfully clear, the subjects of totalitarianism contribute to terrorizing themselves.[32] Hence there is little room in horror or dystopia for the dynamics of political terrorism that turn on victimizing bystanders. In the systems of transgression and guilt that both those genres present, nobody is a bystander. Of course, that argument is congenial to political terrorists who take themselves to attack oppressive regimes where, if you are not part of the solution, you are part of the problem. To date, though, terrorists have not made many popular movies, let alone Hollywood releases.[33] Accordingly the thriller has become the Hollywood genre of choice for facing political terrorism.

But we misestimate the craft of popular movies if we infer that Hollywood merely turns terrors into thrills. Critics and scholars do complain that Hollywood thrillers cheapen the politics and denature the terrors.[34] That happens in some thrillers, but it is not the generic pattern. Part of the misunderstanding arises from the modern inclination to treat politics as exhausted by the operations of government and ideology. Not even thrillers about political terrorism show much interest in political ideologies, although the films do give considerable attention to machinations of government in combating terrorism. Fortunately for us, there are many other kinds of politics, they are amply evident in electronic times, and they play signal roles in thrillers on terrorism.[35] These surface in the political projects attributed to the terrorists as villains. That their politics seldom fit such modern ideologies of politics as liberalism, socialism, and conservatism or even the likes of fascism, nazism, and communism should not surprise us. Most terrorist politics have been postmodern or anti-western, and many terrorist thrillers do engage such politics literally or figurally.[36] Thrillers also attend to the political projects enacted by the heroes who resist assaults by terrorists. Again this becomes easier to recognize when we encompass subtexts and we open our eyes to politics that exceed the forms most familiar to modern scholars.[37]

[. . .]

Noir and Sophistication

It is no wonder, then, that Hollywood has started blending thrillers with noirs in order to tackle political terrorism with even greater flair and sophistication. In some Hollywood quarters, noir films seem little more than thrillers become acutely stylish, self-aware, and sophisticated. In others, the mark of noir is realism, in a strongly stylized sense. This realism encompasses seedy settings, grainy colors, and many shadows. It also means moral malaise, political hardball, and rhetorical savvy in social systems that ensnare people left and right. Noir is a genre ready-made for the complexities of political terrorism along with attempts to preempt, repudiate, or punish it.

As political terrorists began targeting the United States more intensely in the 1990s, film noir was returning to the fore in popular movies. The genre had flourished in the 1940s and '50s. Then noir subsided so much in prominence that some scholars defined it as a delimited period rather than a continuing genre. When you look for them, of course, there turn out to have been more than ten noir films released every decade in the 1960s, '70s, and '80s. Nevertheless the Hollywood proportion of noir films had declined, and a few shining exceptions like *Chinatown* (1974) showed how marginal to the aesthetics of Hollywood in this interregnum generic noir had become. By the second half of the '80s, however, film noir was making a comeback. The '90s viewed some fifty new noirs, and the resurgent genre once more became a prominent Hollywood source of sights, sounds, and stories.[38] If we reckon that the new century began in 2000, we may say that already it has contributed another thirty noir films.[39]

Accordingly noir aesthetics have been amply available to help Americans experience the terrorist atrocities of September 11, 2001; and this Hollywood genre is making an impact on our political sensibilities. When Maureen Dowd, the national weathervane of the *New York Times*, addressed that day's terrorist attacks, she took her title from a famous noir film by Orson Welles. It recently had been re-released in a "director's cut," based on requests that Welles made of the studio, which had edited his footage into a logical mess. His movie still was powerful enough aesthetically to attract popular attention half a century later. "Touch of Evil," Dowd called her take on the world in the wake of September 11. She began a commentary with the look and feel of a genre renowned for painting gray on gray: "I've always loved film noir. The grays, the shadows, the mysterious webs of murder, deception and corruption, the morally ambiguous characters." Nonetheless, she wrote, "I never expected to see a noir shadow fall on the white marble hive of Washington. The film noir hero, as Nicholas Christopher wrote, descends 'into an underworld, on a spiral.' The object of his quest 'is elusive,' and he is beset 'by agents of a larger design of which he is only dimly aware.'"[40]

Like most fans, Dowd seems to have thrilled to the genre's ambiguities, its sophisticated sense of foggy complications making for steamy mysteries and stories of the American dream undone by its own ambitions. Even by October, Dowd could observe how "Sept. 11 was a day of crystalline certainty. Thousands of innocent people were dead. We had to find the murderers and unleash hell." Soon there were complications. "But after that things got weirdly muddied. We would have been prepared for a conventional war outside our borders. But we were not prepared for the terrorists' unconventional war inside our heads. We went from never imagining the damage the barbarians inside our gates could do to imagining little else." Noir contributed to the imagining. Even before the United States became super-serious about political terrorism, noir had started to edge into the field of popular films about it. *Fight Club*, *Spy Game*, and *Swordfish* feature the looks, sounds, and structures of film noir; and they are three of the more provocative treatments of political terrorism to issue from Hollywood.

Fight Club and *Swordfish* pay special attention to spectacle, a shared concern of terrorism and cinema.[41] Gabriel Weimann and Conrad Win maintain that "the essence of terrorism is the actual or threatened use of violence against victims of symbolic importance in such a way as to gain psychological impact for the purpose of achieving political objectives."[42] Spectacle is what terrorists promote for this purpose, and spectacle is the stock-in-trade of popular cinema.[43] As a genre, film noir has developed an acute concern for the engines and dangers of spectacle.[44]

The terrorists who star in *Fight Club* and *Swordfish* both pursue the politics of spectacle. In doing this, these characters claim superior realism, yet neither film is the least inclined toward mundane realism in story or cinematic style. Instead they share the sophisticated realism of noir, and they use the genre to expose the corruption of spectacular societies as systems that invite the politics of terror. Such stylish realism stems from their attunement to the cinematic construction of political realities in America – and the world that its media have been busy globalizing. The movies' cinematic devices of terrorism display this knowledge, though playfully in both cases. This locates them in the family of films such as *Simone* (2002), 15 *Minutes* (2001), *EdTV* (1999), *Pleasantville* (1998), *The Truman Show* (1998), *Mad City* (1997), and *Wag the Dog* (1997) that play reflectively and prophetically with media construction. Most of the films with political acts of terrorism show some awareness of such media dynamics and their postmodern politics. Yet among these, only *Three Kings* (1999) and possibly *Spy Game* also might qualify for the family of films that emphasize dynamics of media construction.

The specific brands of postmodern politics in *Fight Club* and *Swordfish* are exceptionally debatable as to types. *Swordfish* has an anti-terrorist terrorist named Gabriel and played by John Travolta. By the end of *Swordfish*, Gabriel's terrorism is financing his own foreign and military policy of counter-terrorist vengeance. This radical, perhaps satirical adjustment of domestic and international politics seems somewhat anarchical in ideology but even more in style. The later politics of terrorism in *Fight Club* also might be categorized as anarchical – or nihilist, since its movement named Project Mayhem claims to pursue a fanaticism of destruction. The obliteration of civilization by bombing credit records is to plunge the world into a kind of chaos. That should return sophisticated cities from the corrupt "barbarism of reflection" to the noble "barbarism of sense," as the republican theorist Giambattista Vico long ago contrasted those two conditions.[45] Western civilization knows this situation, without government as hierarchical rule, to be anarchy in a sense that traces back to Thomas Hobbes.

Yet the charismatic project of liberation by Tyler Durden, the protagonist in *Fight Club*, is devoted less to eliminating all hierarchical order than to reviving pure, impulsive, perfectionist action by Nietzschean nobles in a setting before the West was won. The movie makes such a masculinist trajectory at least borderline patriarchial, hence incipiently hierarchical, though cultic would be a better category. There is in *Swordfish*, by contrast, no perfectionist celebration of impulsive action or primitive culture.[46] Its violence of terrorism is not a Dionysian rite, as in *Fight Club*, but a hardball device for trumping violent terrorists. Gabriel is a planner who leaves few probabilities uncalculated. His enterprise is eminently sophisticated, if fatally cynical – at least to others. Therefore the politics of *Swordfish* are "anarchical," whereas the politics of *Fight Club* are "perfectionist" and Nietzschean, In neither film, though, is the ideology half so detailed or influential politically as the aesthetics of noir. Neither film offers a sober, respectable take on terrorism; and both mobilize noir in similarly playful ways. Yet both have become cult favorites by featuring noir conventions for configuring and prefiguring our senses of political terrorism.

Spy Game uses the stylish realism of noir to indict terrorist tactics by covert operatives for the United States. It moves good-hearted but hard-boiled protagonists played by Brad Pitt and Robert Redford from CIA assassinations during the Vietnam War, Cold War betrayals in Berlin, and political bombings in Beirut, to ruthless trade struggles with China. The film fully acknowledges that American enemies also terrorize, but it suggests that many of America's hard choices have come mainly from being all too hard-headed and heavy-handed in foreign policies. Noir tropes sophisticate the thriller politics until, by the end, personal ties lead the protagonists to renounce the room that Realpolitick makes for sacrificing bystanders to larger political causes.

Like horror and dystopia, noir suspects that systems entrap us even in the most ordinary of everyday activities. The leading figures in noir films are nothing like innocent. When they try hardest to be bystanders, stepping aside from the fray or pretending that they can stay aloof from the systematic corruption, their ignorance ruins their own efforts and other people's lives. Yet the wake-up calls that rouse noir protagonists to recognize their perils and responsibilities activate their residual virtues. These reconstruct the shadows and mirrors of politics into rights and wrongs that make human sense in fallen worlds far from pure innocence or absolute evil. In some ways, we all participate in the regime, the system, the transgressions, even the terrors. But in other ways, there can be bystanders, civilians, victims outside any proper scope of violence – notwithstanding their real contributions, conscious or not, to acts that outrage others. In noir, we can learn how war and terror and freedom-fighting and all other politics face complications that should induce a sense of limits along with a capacity of self-criticism.

Noir sprang from the literary (sub)genre of hardboiled detection. In the 1920s and '30s, the "roman noir" had turned the upper-crust amateur detective operating in the milieu of the country manor into a sometimes suave but always hard-bitten private eye who scrambles to make a living from the seamy side of the city.[47] Like hardboiled detection, classical film noir situates itself in the gritty night of an endlessly corrupt city under siege in every direction from criminals and political manipulators.[48] As a "lone knight of justice," the noir detective cannot hope to restore order or impose justice on the model of the classical detective. He is in over his head, and his interventions in the ongoing dynamics of crime are more likely to aggravate the harm than heal even a small part of the city. Even when the protagonist of classical noir is not exactly a detective – but more a minor-league Faust who blunders toward personal, moral, social, and political catastrophe – the most he can manage is to leave behind a lesson: his cautionary tale about how things went wrong.

[. . .]

Classical noir always favored Los Angeles as its sin city. As a city, however, L.A. was always already decentered and postmodern: more a ramshackle network of suburbs in search of a city than a gleaming beacon on the hill of western imagination.[49] Film noir establishes L.A. with shots from the hill. These look down on a tangle of freeways, aqueducts, and subdivisions in a valley shading into smog and night. The Hollywood sign of celebrity culture and politics labels a neighboring hill. Hollywood films show Arab terrorists in particular as coming from the dark warrens, bright deserts, and sun-washed cities of the Middle East; and the L.A. of film noir manages all three at once, as well as unreal downpours of rain that never can wash the city clean. When we witness a New York suffocated in ash and smoke and grit, or we look upon the ruined-coliseum made by fallen fragments from the twin towers of the World Trade Center, we see with Dowd a noir city left in the twilight of the idols.

Resurgent noir turns the fatally sophisticated city not only into suburbs but also into the abstracted systems of domination and corruption long excoriated by the existentialists.[50] The targets, dynamics, and consequences of political terrorism find themselves and lend themselves to noirish figures that include rather than excuse ourselves from the picture.

[. . .]

Wallace Stevens said that "Politic man ordained / Imagination as the fateful sin."[51] For a civilization now learning more than it ever wanted to know about the politics of terror, noir is a popular genre that has much to recommend it. The shadowy shapes of twin towers at the World Trade Center collapse into a flash of fire, a rain of ash, a darkness of more than night and rubble. These are powerful figures from noir for the terrorism now emerging in Hollywood's politics – and our own.

Notes

1   See John S. Nelson and G. R. Boynon, *Video Rhetorics*, Urbana, University of Illinois Press, 1997, pp. 195–232; John S. Nelson, "Argument by Mood in War Movies: Postmodern Ethos in Electronic Media," *Argument at Century's End*, Thomas A. Hollihan, ed., Annandale, VA, National Communication Association, 2000, pp. 262–269.

2   See Nelson and Boynton, *Video Rhetorics*, pp. 27–86.

3   See Timothy Corrigan, *A Short Guide to Writing about Film*, New York, St. Martin's Press, third edition, 1998; Rick Altman, *Film/Genre*, London, British Film Institute, 1999.

4   See Hayden White: *Metahistory*, Baltimore, Johns Hopkins University Press, 1973; *Tropics of Discourse*, Baltimore, Johns Hopkins University Press, 1978. Also see John S. Nelson: "Review Essay [on *Metahistory* by Hayden White]," *History and Theory*, 14, 1, 1975, pp. 74–91; "Tropal History and the Social Sciences," *History and Theory*, 19, 4, 1980, pp. 80–101.

5   See Maurice Merleau-Ponty: *Phenomenology of Perception*, Colin Smith, tr., New York, Humanities Press, 1962; *The Primacy of Perception*, James M. Edie, ed., Evanston, IL, Northwestern University Press, 1964; *Sense and Non-Sense*, Hubert L. Dreyfus and Patricia A. Dreyfus, trs., Evanston, IL, Northwestern University Press, 1964. Also see Susan T. Fiske and Shelley E. Taylor, *Social Cognition*, New York, McGraw-Hill, (1984), second edition, 1991.

6   See John S. Nelson, *Tropes of Politics*, Madison, University of Wisconsin Press, 1998, especially pp. xvi and 99–114.

7   See Johann Wolfgang von Goethe, *Elective Affinities*, Elizabeth Mayer and Louise Brogan, tr., Chicago, Henry Regnery, 1963.

8   On such audiovisual icons in environmental politics, see Andrew Szasz, "'Toxic Waste' as Icon: A New Mass Issue Is Born," *Ecopopulism*, Minneapolis, University of Minnesota Press,

1994, pp. 38–68; Nelson and Boynton, *Video Rhetorics*, pp. 154–194; Kevin Michael DeLuca, *Image Politics: The New Rhetoric of Environmental Activism*, New York, Guilford Press, 1999. Also see G. R. Boynton and John S. Nelson, "Orchestrating Politics," *Hot Spots: Multimedia Analysis of Political Ads*, Urbana, University of Illinois Press, 1997, third video.

9   See Nelson, *Tropes of Politics*, p. 142.

10 For twenty conventions of film noir, see John S. Nelson, "Noir and Forever: Politics As If Hollywood Were Everywhere," paper for the annual meeting of the American Political Science Association, 2001.

11 See *Insomnia* (2002), directed by Christopher Nolan, and its inspiriting film.

12 On this kind of information, more full-bodied and active than cybernetic and realist modes of information as mere data, see Nelson, *Tropes of Politics*, pp. 124–126.

13 See John S. Nelson, *Deliver Us From Evils: The Politics of Popular Horror*, unpublished manuscript.

14 For a persuasive exception, see Caleb Carr, *The Lessons of Terror*, New York, Random House, 2002.

15 See Nelson, "Argument by Mood in War Movies." Also see John S. Nelson and G. R. Boynton, "Arguing War: Global Television against American Cinema," *Arguing Communication and Culture*, G. Thomas Goodnight, ed., Washington, DC, National Communication Association, 2002, pp. 571–577.

16 See Hannah Arendt, *The Origins of Totalitarianism*, New York, Harcourt, Brace, Jovanovich, (1951), fourth edition, 1973; John S. Nelson, "Orwell's Political Myths and Ours," *The Orwellian Moment*, Robert L. Savage, James E. Combs, and Dan D. Nimmo, eds., Fayetteville, University of Arkansas Press, 1989, pp. 11–44.

17 See John S. Nelson, "Horror Films Face Political Evils in Everyday Life," *Political Communication*, 21, forthcoming.

18 See Stephen King: *Danse Macabre*, New York, Berkley Books, 1981; *Bare Bones*, Tim Underwood and Chuck Miller, eds., New York, McGraw-Hill, 1988. Also see Ron Rosenbaum, "Gooseflesh: The Strange Turn Toward Horror," *Harper's Magazine*, 259, 1552, September, 1979, pp. 86–92.

19 See Hannah Arendt, "The Aftermath of Nazi Rule: Report from Germany," *Commentary*, 10, 4, October, 1950, pp. 342–353.

20 George Orwell, "1984," *Orwell's Nineteen Eighty-Four*, Irving Howe, ed., New York, Harcourt Brace Jovanovich, (1963), second edition, 1982, pp. 3–205, on pp. 175–178.

21 See Nelson, "Orwell's Political Myths and Ours."

22 See Nelson and Boynton, *Video Rhetorics*, pp. 221–230.

23 See King, *Danse Macabre*, pp. 263–294.

24 See Fredric Jameson, "Totality as Conspiracy," *The Geopolitical Aesthetic: Cinema and Space in the World System*, Bloomington, Indiana University Press, 1992, pp. 7–84; John S. Nelson, "Conspiracy as a Hollywood Trope for System," *Political Communication*, 20, 4, October–December, 2003.

25 For the ambitious graphic novel on Jack the Ripper that inspired this striking movie by the Hughes Brothers, see Alan Moore and Eddie Campbell, *From Hell*, Eddie Campbell Comics, Paddington, Australia, 1999.

26 See Rick Marin and T. Trent Gegax, "Conspiracy Mania Feeds Our Growing National Paranoia," *Newsweek*, 128, 27, December 30, 1996 – January 6, 1997, pp. 64–71.

27 For a better effort, see Dan Nimmo and James E. Combs, "Devils and Demons: The Group

Mediation of Conspiracy," *Mediated Political Realities*, New York, Longman, (1983), second edition, 1990, pp. 203–222.

28 See Ted Remington, *Conspiracy Theories as Socially Constructed Mythic Narratives*, Ph.D. dissertation for the University of Iowa Department of Communication Studies, Iowa City, IA, 2002.

29 See John S. Nelson, "The Republic of Myth," paper for the annual meeting of the American Political Science Association, 2001.

30 See John S. Nelson, "Hollywood Prefigures Politics: Cinematic Anticipations of Terror in America," paper for the annual meeting of the American Political Science Association, 2002.

31 See Carr, *The Lessons of Terror*; Brent L. Smith, *Terrorism in America*, Albany, State University of New York Press, 1994.

32 See Orwell, "1984;" Hannah Arendt, *Eichmann in Jerusalem*, New York, Viking Press, (1963), enlarged edition, 1964.

33 It is not hard, however, to see the martyr videos, recruitment movies, and training films from terrorist organizations as possible steps toward a counter-cinema.

34 See Walter Laquer, *The Age of Terrorism*, Boston, Little, Brown, 1987, p. 202.

35 See Nelson, "Hollywood Prefigures Politics."

36 See Mark Juergensmeyer, *Terror in the Mind of God*, Berkeley, University of California Press, (2000), second edition, 2001; Daniel Levitas, *The Terrorist Next Door*, New York, St. Martin's Press, 2002. Also see John S. Nelson, "Terror from Totalitarianism to Tinsel Town: Making Myths of Anti-Western Movements," paper for the annual meeting of the American Political Science Association, 2002.

37 See Nelson, *Tropes of Politics*, pp. 205–230.

38 On the classical period of noir and its inspirations, see J. P. Telotte, *Voices in the Dark: The Narrative Patterns of Film Noir*, Urbana, University of Illinois Press, 1989; Joan Copjec, ed., *Shades of Noir*, London, Verso, 1993; R. Barton Palmer, *Hollywood's Dark Cinema: The American Film Noir*, New York, Twayne, 1994; Alain Silver and James Ursini, eds., *Film Noir Reader*, New York, Limelight Editions, 1996; Paul Duncan, *Film Noir: Films of Trust and Betrayal*, Harpenden, UK, Pocket Essentials, 2000. On recently resurgent noir, see Foster Hirsch, *Detours and Lost Highways. A Map of Neo-Noir*, New York, Limelight Editions, 1999; Nelson, "Noir and Forever."

39 These are *Boiler Room*, *The Crow: Salvation*, *Memento*, *Panic*, *The Pledge*, *Reindeer Games*, *Shaft*, *Traffic*, and *X-Men* in 2000; in 2001, *The Caveman's Valentine*, *The Deep End*, *From Hell*, *The Glass House*, *The Man Who Wasn't There*, *Mulholland Drive*, *Spy Games*, *Swordfish*, and *Training Day*; in 2002, *Blade II*, *City by the Sea*, *Confessions of a Dangerous Mind*, *Femme Fatale*, *Insomnia*, *Minority Report*, *One Hour Photo*, and *The Salton Sea*; plus early in 2003, *Confidence*, *DareDevil*, *The Matrix Reloaded*, even *T3*.

40 Maureen Dowd, "Touch of Evil," *New York Times*, October 7, 2001, http://www.nytimes.com/2001/10/07/opinion/O7DOWD.html? ex=1003468906&ei=1&en=d7d1a5eda5168771.

41 See Guy Debord, *Society of the Spectacle*, Detroit, Black and Red, (1967), 1977; Murray Edelman, *Constructing the Political Spectacle*, Chicago, University of Chicago Press, 1988.

42 Gabriel Weimann and Conrad Winn, *The Theater of Terror: Mass Media and International Terrorism*, New York, Longman, 1994, p. 4.

43 See Larry Beinhart, *American Hero*, New York, Ballantine Books, 1993; Terrence Rafferty, "Lost at Sea," *New Yorker*, 71, 23, August 7, 1995, pp. 83–85.

44 See Nelson, "Noir and Forever."

45 See Giambattista Vico, *The New Science*, Thomas Goddard Bergin and Max Harold Fisch, trans., Ithaca, NY, Cornell University Press, (abridged from the third edition, 1744; 1948), 1961, 1106, pp. 381–382.

46 See John S. Nelson and Anna Lorien Nelson, "Greening Nietzsche: Perfectionist Politics from *Fight Club* to *Magnolia*," paper for the annual meeting of the American Political Science Association, 2002.

47 See William Marling, *The American Roman Noir: Hammett, Cain, and Chandler*, Athens, University of Georgia Press, 1995.

48 See Nicholas Christopher, *Somewhere in the Night: Film Noir and the American City*, New York, Henry Holt, 1997.

49 See Mike Davis, *City of Quartz: Excavating the Future in Los Angeles*, New York, Random House, 1990.

50 See Nelson, "Noir and Forever."

51 Wallace Stevens, "Academic Discourse at Havanna," *The Collected Poems of Wallace Stevens*, New York, Knopf, 1975, pp. 142–145, on p. 143.

Terror and After . . .[1]

14

HOMI K. BHABHA

In these past, dark days it has been difficult to draw a line between the outrage and anxiety provoked by terrorist attacks, and the urgent need for some more humane and historical reflection on the tragedy itself. After such knowledge, what forgiveness? The appalling images of death, destruction and daring that invaded our homes on September 11th left us with no doubt that these unimaginable scenes belonged to a moral universe alien to ours, acts perpetrated by people foreign to the very fibre of our being. But CNN had a sobering tale to tell. While the headline news staggered from one towering inferno to another, the ticker tape at the bottom of the screen interspersed its roll-call of the brave and the dead, with lists of Hollywood movies – films that had told a similar story many times before, and new, unreleased movies that were about to tell it again. What was only an action movie last week, turned on Tuesday into acts of war. Same *mise-en-scene*, different movie.

I do not want to blast Hollywood, nor to rail against the violence of the mass media. And I am certainly not suggesting, wistfully, that life follows art because that only rarely happens. I have chosen to start with the global *genre* of the terrorist action film in order to question the widely canvassed cultural assumptions that have come to frame the deadly events. Tuesday's terrorism was a manifestation of a much deeper 'clash of civilisations', we were frequently told. One night this week, Benjamin Netanyahu developed this thesis and ended up by placing Israel just off the East Coast of America. The next morning deputy secretary of defence Wolfowitz affirmed wide international support for the US from nations that he described as belonging to the 'civilised world' and the 'uncivilised world'.

Returning to CNN's ticker tape of terrorist movies and special effects, demonstrates the futility of framing the event in such a divided and polarized civilizational narrative. Each of the unimaginable actions we were subjected to on our tv screens on Tuesday, have been repeatedly imagined and applauded in movie houses across the country by law-abiding Americans, and successfully exported to other ordinary film-loving folks across the world. However, the decision to *implement* and administer terror, whether it is done in the name of god or the state, is a *political decision*, not a civilizational or cultural practice. Ironically, the 'clash of civilisations' is an aggressive discourse often used by totalitarians and terrorists to justify their worst deeds, to induce holy terror and create a debilitating psychosis of persecution amongst oppressed, powerless peoples. When *we* use the civilizational argument against *them*, we are, unwittingly perhaps, speaking in the divisive tongue of tyrants. When

American foreign and economic policy is conducted in terms of the civilizational divisions of 'them' and 'us', the nation assumes that hawkish, imperialist aspect that provokes a widespread sense of injustice, indignation and fear. The embattled and embalmed narrative of civilizational clash is often deployed to justify the reckless destruction of civilians who are suspected by virtue of their culture (read second nature), of being terrorists or protecting them.

Once we see terrorism as an organized political action, rather than the expression of cultural or civilizational 'difference', we can both fight it and look towards the future. A future that makes common cause between the American victims of terror, and those peoples around the world who are fated to live in countries governed by regimes or organizations that implement such unlawful and inhuman policies. Only those societies of the North and the South that ensure the widest democratic participation and protection for their citizens are in a position to make the deadly difficult decisions that 'just' wars demand. To confront the politics of terror, out of a sense of democratic solidarity rather than retaliation, gives us some faint hope for the future. Hope, that we might be able to establish a vision of a global society, informed by civil liberties and human rights, that carries with it the shared obligations and responsibilities of common, collaborative citizenship.

Note

1   This text was originally published on September 28, 2001 by *The Chronicle for Higher Education*.

Select Bibliography

Acland, Charles R. (2003) *Screen Traffic: Movies, Multiplexes, and Global Culture*, Durham, NC: Duke University Press.

Agger, Gunhild (2001) "National Cinema and TV Fiction in a Transnational Age" in *The Aesthetic of Television*. Gunhild Agger and Jens F. Jensen (eds), Aalborg, Denmark: Aalborg University Press: 53–88.

Armes, Roy (1987) *Third World Film Making and the West*, Berkeley: University of California Press.

Appadurai, Arjun (1996) *Modernity at Large*. Minneapolis: University of Minnesota Press.

Bakker Gerben (2005) "America's master: the European film industry in the United States, 1907–1920," in *An Economic History of Film*, John Sedgwick and Michael Pokorny (eds), London: Routledge: 24–47.

Bordwell, David (2000) *Planet Hong Kong: Popular Cinema and the Art of Entertainment*, Cambridge: Harvard University Press.

Burton, Julianne (ed) (1986) *Cinema and Social Change in Latin America: Conversations with Filmmakers*, Austin: University of Texas Press.

Cazdyn, Eric (2002) *The Flash of Capital: Film and Geopolitics in Japan*, Durham: Duke University Press.

Chapman, James (2003) *Cinemas of the World: Film and Society from 1895 to the Present*, London: Reaktion Books.

Curtin, Michael (2002) "Hong Kong Meets Hollywood in the Extranational Arena of the Culture Industries," in *Sights of Contestation: Localism, Globalism and Cultural Production in Asia and the Pacific*. Kwok-kan Tam, Wimal Dissanayake and Terry Siu-han Yip (eds), Hong Kong: The Chinese University Press: 79–110.

Dancyger, Ken (2001) *Global Scriptwriting*, Boston: Focal Press.

Desai, Jigna (2004) *Beyond Bollywood: The Cultural Politics of South Asian Diasporic Film*, New York: Routledge.

Diawara, Manthia (1992) *African Cinema: Politics and Culture*, Bloomington: Indiana University Press.

Dissanayake, Wimal (ed) (1994) *Colonialism and Nationalism in Asian Cinema*, Bloomington: Indiana University Press.

D'Lugo, Marvin (1997) "Transnational Film Authors and the State of Latin American Cinema," in *Film and Authorship*. Virginia Wright Wexman (ed), New Brunswick, NJ: Rutgers University Press: 112–130.

Doel, Marcus (1999) "Occult Hollywood: Unfolding the Americanization of World Cinema," in *The American Century: Consensus and Coercion in the Projection of American Power*, David Slater and Peter J. Taylor (eds), Oxford, UK: Blackwell: 243–260.

Donald, Stephanie (2000) *Public Secrets, Public Spaces: Cinema and Civility in China*, Lanham, MD: Rowman and Littlefield.

Downing, John D. H. (1987) *Film and Politics in the Third World*, New York; Praeger.

Ezra, Elizabeth (2003) *European Cinema*, Oxford: Oxford University Press.

Foster, Gwendolyn Audrey (1999) *Captive Bodies: Postcolonial Subjectivity in Cinema*, Albany: State University of New York Press.

Frayling, Christopher (1998, 2nd Ed.) *Spaghetti Westerns: Cowboys and Europeans from Karl May to Sergio Leone*, London: I. B. Tauris Publishers.

Ganley, Gladys D. and Oswald H. Ganley (1987) *Global Political Fallout: The First Decade of the* VCR, 1976–1985, Norwood, NJ: ABLEX Publishing Corporation.

Gemunden, Gerd (2004) "Hollywood in Altona: Minority Cinema and the Transnational Imagination," in *German Pop Culture: How "American" Is It*, Agnes C. Mueller (ed), Ann Arbor: University of Michigan Press: 180–190.

Gokturk, Deniz (2000) "Turkish Women on German Streets: Closure and Exposure in Transnational Cinema," in *Spaces in European Cinema*, Myrto Konstantarakos (ed.), Exeter, England: Intellect Press: 64–73.

Gokturk, Deniz (2003) "Turkish Delight–German Fright: Unsettling Oppositions in Transnational Cinema," in *Mapping the Margins: Identity, Politics, and the Media*, Karen Ross and Deniz Derman (eds), Creskill, NJ: Hampton Press: 177–192.

Gregg, Robert W. (1998) *International Relations on Film*, Boulder: CO: Lynne Rienner Publishers.

Harrow, Kenneth W. (1999) *African Cinema: Postcolonial and Feminist Readings*, Trenton, NJ: Africa World Press.

Hitchcock, Lori D. (2002) "Transnational Film and the Politics of Becoming: Negotiating East Asian Identity," in *Asian Cinema*, (Spring–Summer) 13.1: 67–86.

Hsiao-peng Lu, Sheldon (ed) (1997) "Transnational Chinese Cinemas," in *Identity, Nationhood, Gender*, Honolulu: University of Hawaii Press.

Jäckel, Anne (2003) *European Film Industries*, London: BFI Publishing

Jameson, Fredric (1992) *The Geopolitical Aesthetic: Cinema and Space in the World System*, Bloomington: Indiana University Press.

Jayamanne, Laleen (2001) *Toward Cinema and its Double: Cross-Cultural Mimesis*, Bloomington: Indiana University Press.

Jorholt, Eva (2001) "Africa's Modern Cinematic Griots – Oral Tradition and West African Cinema," in *Same and Other: Negotiating African Identity in Cultural Production*, Mai Palmberg and Maria Erikson Baaz (eds), Uppsala: Nordic Africa Institute: 95–118.

Kaplan, E. Ann (1997) *Looking for the Other: Feminism, Film, and the Imperial Gaze*, New York: Routledge.

Kendrick, James (2004) "A Nasty Situation: Social Panics, Transnationalism, and the Video Nasty," in *Horror Film: Creating and Marketing Fear*, Steffen Hantke (ed), Jackson: University Press of Mississippi: 153–172.

Lardner, James (1987) *Fast Forward: Hollywood, the Japanese and the Onslaught of the* VCR, New York: W. W. Norton.

Lev, Peter (1993) *The Euro-American Cinema*, Austin: University of Texas Press.

Litman, Barry R. (1998) The Motion Picture Mega-Industry, Boston: Allyn and Bacon.

Loshitzky, Yosefa (2000) "Orientalist Representations: Palestinians and Arabs in some Postcolonial Film and Literature," in *Cultural Encounters: Representing Otherness*, Elizabeth Hallam and Brian V. Street (eds), London: Routledge: 51–71.

Malkmus, Lizbeth and Roy Armes (1991) *Arab and African Film Making*, London: Zed Books Ltd.

Marks, Laura U. (2000) *The Skin of the Film: Intercultural Cinema, Embodiment, and the Senses*, Durham: Duke University Press.

Martin, Michael T. (ed) (1995) *Cinemas of the Black Disapora: Diversity, Dependence, and Oppositionality*, Detroit: Wayne State University Press.

Martin, Michael T. (ed) (1997) *New Latin American Cinema: Theory, Practices and Transcontinental Articulations*, Detroit: Wayne State University Press.

Miller, Toby, Nitin Govil, John McMurria, and Richard Maxwell (2001) *Global Hollywood*, London: BFI Publishing.

Moran, Albert (ed) (1996) *Film Policy: International, National, and Regional Perspectives*, London: Routledge.

Naficy, Hamid (1999) 'Between Rocks and Hard Places: The Interstitial Mode of Production in Exilic Cinema', in Hamid Naficy, ed., *Home, Exile, Homeland*. New York and London: Routledge: 125–150.

Noriega, Chon A. (ed) (2000) *Visible Nations: Latin American Cinema and Video*, Minneapolis: University of Minnesota Press.

Norindr, Panivong (2001) "The Postcolonial Cinema of Lam Le: Screens, the Sacred, and the Unhomely in Poussiere d'Empire," in *Of Vietnam: Identities in Dialogue*, Jane Bradley Winston and Leakthina Chau-Pech Ollier eds, New York: Palgrave: 143–158.

Nowell-Smith, Geoffrey and Steven Ricci (eds) (1998) *Hollywood and Europe: Economics, Culture, National Identity: 1945–95*, London: BFI Publishing.

Owen, Harold H. Jr, Ken Macrorie and Fred Marcus (1965) *The Motion Picture and the Teaching of English*, New York: Appleton-Century-Crofts.

Petrie, Graham (2002 rev. ed) *Hollywood Destinies: European Directors in America: 1922–1931*, Detroit: Wayne State University Press.

Pick, Zuzanna M. (1993) *The New Latin American Cinema: A Continental Project*, Austin: University of Texas Press.

Pierson, Michele (2002) "The Transnational Matrix of SF" in *Special Effects: Still in Search of Wonder*, New York: Columbia University Press: 159–168.

Pines, Jim and Jim Willeman (1989) *Questions of Third Cinema*, London: BFI.

Plate, S. Brent (2003) *Representing Religion in World Cinema: Filmmaking, Mythmaking, Culture Making*, New York: Palgrave Macmillan.

Prince, Stephen (1992) *Visions of Empire: Political Imagery in Contemporary American Film*, New York: Praeger.

Quayson, Ato (2000) *Postcolonialism: Theory, Practice or Process*, Cambridge: Polity Press.

Rajan, Gita (2002) "Pliant and Compliant: Colonial Indian Art and Postcolonial Cinema" in *Women: A Cultural Review*, (Spring) 13.1: 48–69.

Robin, Diana and Ira Jaffe (ed) (1999) *Redirecting the Gaze: Gender, Theory, and Cinema in the Third World*, Albany: State University of New York Press.

Rosen, David (1992) "Crossover: Hispanic Specialty Films in the U.S. Movie Marketplace," in *Chicanos and Film: Representation and Resistance*, Minneapolis: University of Minnesota Press.

Rueschmann, Eva (1981) *Moving Pictures, Migrating Identities*, Jackson: University Press of Mississippi.

Russell, Sharon (1998) *Guide to African Cinema*, Westport, CT: Greenwood Press.

Schnitman, Jorge A. (1984) *Film Industries in Latin America: Dependency and Development*, Norwood, NJ: ABLEX Publishing Corporation.

Segrave, Kerry (1997) *American Films Abroad: Hollywood's Domination of the World's Movie Screens*, Jefferson, NC: McFarland and Company, Inc. Publishers.

Sherzer, Dina (1996) *Cinema, Colonialism, Postcolonialism: Perspectives from the French and Francophone World*, Austin: University of Texas Press.

Shohat, Ella and Robert Stam (eds) (2003) *Multiculturalism, Postcoloniality, and Transnational Media*, New Brunswick, NJ: Rutgers University Press.

Shohat, Ella and Robert Stam (1994) *Unthinking Eurocentrism: Multiculturism and the Media*, London: Routledge.

Sieglorh, Ulrike (ed) *Heroines without Heroes: Reconstructing Female and National Identities in European Cinema 1945–51*, London: Cassell.

Sklar, Robert (2002) *A World History of Film*, New York: Harry N. Abrams, Inc., Publishers.

Stock, Ann Marie (ed) (1997) *Framing Latin American Cinema: Contemporary Critical Perspectives*, Minneapolis: University of Minnesota Press.

Stone, Judy (ed) (1997) *Eye on the World: Conversations with International Filmmakers*, Los Angeles: Silman-James Press.

Stoller, Martin (2000) *Alternative Empires: European Modernist Cinemas and Cultures of Imperialism*, Exeter: University of Exeter Press.

Street, Sarah (2002) *Transatlantic Crossings: British Feature Films in the United States*, New York: Continuum.

Sun, Wanning (2002) *Leaving China: Media, Migration, and Transnational Imagination*, Lanhan: Rowman & Littlefield.

Tolentino, Rolando B. (2002) "Subcontracting Imagination and Imageries of Bodies and Nations: The Philippines in Contemporary Transnational Asia Pacific Cinemas," in *Sights of Contestation: Localism, Globalism and Cultural Production in Asia and the Pacific*, Kwok-kan Tam, Wimal Dissanayake and Terry Siu-han Yip (eds), Hong Kong: The Chinese University Press: 257–290.

Ulff-Müller, Jens (2001) *Hollywood's Film Wars with France: Film-Trade Diplomacy and the Emergency of the French Film Quota Policy*, Rochester: University of Rochester Press.

Ukadike, Nwachukwu Frank (1994) *Black African Cinema*, Berkeley: University of California Press.

Van der Heide, William (2002) *Malaysian Cinema, Asian Film: Border Crossings and National Cultures*, Amsterdam: Amsterdam University Press.

Vasey, Ruth. (1997) *The World According to Hollywood, 1918–1939*, Madison: University of Wisconsin Press.

Vernon, Kathleen M. (1997) "Reading Hollywood in/and Spanish Cinema: From Trade Wars to Transculturation" in *Refiguring Spain: Cinema, Media, Representation*, Marsha Kinder (ed), Durham: Duke University Press: 35–64.

Vertovec, Steven and Cohen, Robin (eds) (1999) *Migration; Diasporas and Transnationalism*, Cheltenham and Northampton: Edward Elgar Publishing.

Wasco, Janet (1994) *Hollywood in the Information Age*, Austin: University of Texas Press.

White, Mike (2001) *Political Film: The Dialectics of Third Cinema*, London: Pluto Press.

Wilinsky, Barbara (2001) *Sure Seaters: The Emergence of Art House Cinema*, Minneapolis: University of Minnesota Press.

Wilson, Rob and Wimal Dissanayake, (eds) (1996) *Global/Local: Cultural Production and the Transnational Imaginary*, Durham: Duke University Press.

Yau, Esther C. M. (ed) (2001) *At Full Speed: Hong Kong Cinema in a Borderless World*, Minneapolis: University of Minnesota Press.

Zhang, Yingjin (2002) *Screening China: Critical Interventions, Cinematic Reconfigurations, and the Transnational Imaginary in Contemporary Chinese Cinema*, Ann Arbor: University of Michigan Press.

Index

Related titles from Routledge

Cinema & Nation
Mette Hjort & Scott Mackenzie

Ideas of national identity, nationalism and transnationalism are now a central feature of contemporary film studies, as well as primary concerns for film-makers themselves. Embracing a range of national cinemas including Scotland, Poland, France, Turkey, Indonesia, India, Germany and America, *Cinema and Nation* considers the ways in which film production and reception are shaped by ideas of national belonging and examines the implications of globalisation for the concept of national cinema.

In the first three Parts, contributors explore sociological approaches to nationalism, challenge the established definitions of 'national cinema', and consider the ways in which states – from the old Soviet Union to contemporary Scotland – aim to create a national culture through cinema. The final two Parts address the diverse strategies involved in the production of national cinema and consider how images of the nation are used and understood by audiences both at home and abroad.

Hb: 0-415-20862-9
Pb: 0-415-20863-7

Available at all good bookshops
For ordering and further information please visit:
www.routledge.com

Related titles from Routledge

Movie Acting, the F*ilm* Reader
Edited by Pamela Robertson Wojcik

Movie Acting, the Film Reader explores one of the most central aspects of cinema: film acting. Combining recent scholarship with classic essays, it examines key issues such as: What constitutes film acting? How is film acting different from stage acting? How has film acting changed over time? Articles are grouped into thematic sections, each with an introduction by the editor. These include:

- Ontology of the film actor;
- The creation of the film actor;
- Style and technique – case studies of acting styles in specific films and genres;
- Character and type.

Contributors include: Rudolf Arnheim, Siegfried Kracauer, John O'Thompson, Charles Musser, Roberta Pearson, David Thomson, Pamela Robertson Wojcik.

Hb: 0-415-31024-5
Pb: 0-415-31025-3

Available at all good bookshops
For ordering and further information please visit:
www.routledge.com